# Prayers

from the
# Reformed
Tradition

# Prayers
## from the
## Reformed
## Tradition

### In the Company of
### a Great Cloud of Witnesses

Compiled and Edited by Diane Karay Tripp

Witherspoon Press
Louisville, Kentucky

Translations provided by David H. Tripp, Ph.D. and are used with permission. Occasional irregularities in format and/or presentation are because of requirements from permission grantors.

Every effort has been made to trace copyrights on the materials included in this book. If any copyrighted material has nevertheless been included without permission and due acknowledgment, proper credit will be inserted in future printings after notice has been received.

*Edited by Cassandra D. Williams*

*Book interior and cover design by Jeanne Williams and Linda Ramsey*

*First edition*

Published by Witherspoon Press, a Ministry of the General Assembly Council, Congregational Ministries Publishing, Presbyterian Church (U.S.A.), Louisville, Kentucky

Web site address: http://www.pcusa.org/cmp

PRINTED IN THE UNITED STATES OF AMERICA
01 02 03 04 05 06 07 08 09 10 — 10 9 8 7 6 5 4 3 2 1


Library of Congress Cataloging-in-Publication Data

Prayers from the Reformed tradition: in the company of a great cloud of witnesses / compiled and edited by Diane Karay Tripp.—1st. ed.
    p.  cm.
   Includes bibliographical references and indexes.
   ISBN 1-57153-028-2
   1. Reformed Church—Prayer books and devotions—English. 2. Prayers. I. Tripp, Diane Karay.
BX9427.5.P7 P73  2001
242'.8042—dc21                             00-043888

*For my sisters, Elizabeth, Barbara, and Marie*

# CONTENTS

# PREFACE

From 1988 to 1991 I lived and worked in England. Rose, an elderly Scottish Presbyterian woman, gave my husband and me an artwork dated 1957 (to this day we cannot decipher the artist's signature). In the foreground, a person kneels in just-plowed soil with bowed shoulders, planting seed. The trees and shrubs are leafless. But the grass is green, and the sky, turquoise blue. A farmer walks alongside a weathered white barn. Ducks float on the pond, and birds feed in the meadow.

Sadness and joy intertwine: winter barrenness lingers, but spring has come. Soon flowers will bloom, and crops cover the fields. Psalm verses come to mind.

> Weeping may linger for the night,
> but joy comes with the morning.
> —*Ps. 30:5b*

> Those who go out weeping,
> bearing the seed for sowing,
> shall come home with shouts of joy,
> carrying their sheaves.
> —*Ps. 126:6*

This book is the chief fruit of half my working life. The labor was long and often painful; my joy now, all the sweeter, for trusting God.

During the twelve years of researching, editing, and refining this book, I used the resources of many libraries. I warmly thank the staffs of the following libraries in Great Britain: The Birmingham Reference Library and Birmingham University Library; the Bodleian Library in Oxford, particularly the staff of the Duke Humphrey's Room; the British Library; Cambridge University Library, with special thanks to the Rare Book Room librarians; Hugh Owen Library of the University College of Wales in Cardiff; University of Leicester; the Westminster College

Library in Cambridge; Dr. Williams's Library; Worcester Cathedral Library; and the York Minster Library.

My husband, David, collected some prayers from items in the collection of the John Rylands University Library in Manchester and from the Lambeth Palace Library in London. In the United States, I worked in the following libraries: the Associated Mennonite Biblical Seminary in Elkhart, Indiana; Calvin College and Seminary in Grand Rapids, Michigan; Louisville Presbyterian Theological Seminary in Louisville, Kentucky; the Presbyterian Historical Society in Philadelphia, Pennsylvania, with special thanks to Gerald Gillette, John Haas, Ginnie Moore, Norotha Robinson, and Martha Thomas; Princeton Theological Seminary in Princeton, New Jersey, with thanks to Fran Biddle and Margaret Myers; United Theological Seminary in Dayton, Ohio; and Western Theological Seminary in Holland, Michigan.

I am grateful to Rose Humphries of the Bremen Public Library for interlibrary loans, and warmly thank Harold Daniels, who gave me access to both his personal collection of worship books and the resources of the Theology and Worship Ministry Unit of the Presbyterian Church (U.S.A.). Over the years, I have spent the most time using the rich research resources of the Hesburgh Library at the University of Notre Dame. I am especially grateful to the Microtext Room staff for their kind assistance, particularly Claire McGrath, Barbara Connelly, and Betty Hartzer. I also thank the reference librarians for their help.

Many people have helped, encouraged, and prayed for me during the years of work on this book. While I researched in Philadelphia and Princeton, my classmate in the M.A. in Liturgical Studies program at Notre Dame, Sister Barbara M. Bamberger, welcomed me into Camilla Hall, and made me feel at home among the family of Sisters, Servants of the Immaculate Heart of Mary, in Immaculata, Pennsylvania. Alice McElhinney and Frank Heller III, in conversation with the session and pastor of Harvey Browne Memorial Presbyterian Church in Louisville, Kentucky, arranged for me to have a short term as writer-in-residence, to allow concentrated work on the project. I am grateful for that experience and thank all my Harvey Browne friends for their friendship and interest. In Louisville, Harrison and Eva Bailey extended me hospitality for which I am very grateful.

Stanley R. Hall suggested the basic structure of the book, shared resources, and answered many questions. Gerald W. Gillette, John

Mulder, and others provided valuable criticism. John Mulder also introduced me to Charles Hambrick-Stowe's book *The Practice of Piety* (1982), which opened the door to Puritan prayer sources. Various staff members of the Church of Scotland Board of Ministry and the United Reformed Church History Society, as well as various correspondents, patiently answered queries.

While we were living in England, Frank and Sandra Whitehouse took us to the border "book town" of Hay-on-Wye. Businessman John Knowles's interest in the project did not diminish even as the book was repeatedly rejected during a British publishing recession; this comforted me. Our friends Graham and Carol Knowles treated us to outings near and far, as well as the hospitality of their home—I am grateful for their support and encouragement.

Among those who have shared their interest and suggestions, or assisted in some way, I warmly thank Ruth Anne Boklage, Paul Bradshaw, William B. Bynum, Dame Felicitas Corrigan, Kathryn Keener-Han, Marion Liebert, James M. Phillips, James Smylie, Douglas Strong, Arch Taylor, Bernard Thorogood, Francis Vitéz, Alexander and Sibylle Völker, Ernest Miller White, Yenwith Whitney, R. Milton Winter, Neil Weatherhogg, the late Gordon Wakefield, and all those who made their own prayers, or those of relatives, available and gave permission for their use.

The Hyde Brothers Book Sellers, Joel and Sam, of Fort Wayne, run an Indiana booklover's refuge, and there I found a number of Reformed prayer books. Several United Methodist friends had strangely warmed hearts regarding this book. I am grateful to Gene and Barbara Barnes, Charles Hohenstein, Jane Hulen, and James F. White for their support, and to Charles Hohenstein, in addition, for proofreading assistance. The late Armenia Poock gave us her copy of Ian Maclaren's *Beside the Bonnie Brier Bush*, containing a beautiful prayer (see prayer 273) I would not have found otherwise.

The late Carl Kinnard, William Vamos, and my first *Celebration* editor, William Freburger, all supported my work, though they did not live to see it published.

Virginia Sloyan, my friend and one of my editors at The Liturgical Conference, knew the project would be published someday. Her encouragement—and her deadlines—helped me to focus forward. Tom Schwanda and Willard Swartley listened, and both encouraged me to continue to explore avenues for publication. Janet Freeman's understanding of my work, and her strong interest, sustained me during a time of uncertainty. My mother, Luella Karay, cheered me with examples of perseverance, and my late father, Alexander, was able to celebrate the book's acceptance with me, some months before his death.

One Sunday morning, Jinny Miller listened to me talk about the book, then extracted a promise from me to contact Witherspoon Press. Jon Bohannon scanned the book and entered it into a computer. Later, he sent twelve years' work to my editor in one hundred seconds. I am also grateful to Kay Rans for technical assistance of various kinds. Thank you, friends! I am grateful to the staff of Congregational Ministries Publishing and Witherspoon Press for kindnesses extended to me during my bereavement, and express my warmest thanks to my editor, Cassandra Williams, and every staff member for their patient and expert work in seeing this detailed volume to publication.

My husband, David, supported me in my work on this book, assisted my research in numerous ways, translated prayers, brought several pieces to my attention, and upheld me during bleak years. He affirmed my sense that God was calling me to do this work, despite the appearance that no fruit might ever come of the effort. I thank you with all my heart.

# INTRODUCTION

My sins and mine unbelief shut the door
upon thee; but, O Lord,
yet this day let it be said of thee,
that thou art come in,
when the doors are shut.
By thine infinite power
remove the partition wall,
which is between thee and me;
by thy Holy Spirit,
open the door of my soul.

—*Charles Drelincourt*[1]

During the first months of work on this book, I was allowed to rummage through many boxes of books that had been weeded out of the collection of a venerable institution and to purchase some volumes. I lowered boxes, read title pages, and hoisted boxes back on the shelves. Suddenly, alone in the basement, with dusty hands, I felt a poignant presence—the cloud of witnesses.

I sensed a great richness of faith and life, now neglected and forgotten. Through a closed door, the saints in light silently appealed to me. They wanted to be remembered. I knew that old books, such as those around me, would be crucial in opening that door.

Since childhood I have professed the church's faith in the Apostles' Creed: "I believe . . . in the communion of saints." God allowed me to sense the reality of that communion. Christ's Body embraces all members of the divine household in heaven and on earth. Together we are growing spiritually into a dwelling place for God (Eph. 2:19–22).

Companions on the spiritual journey help us sense how God is working in our lives. We cannot always discern God's hand by ourselves. For many people, these prayers will open a door on the faith of Reformed people; their faith can guide and enrich ours in graceful, challenging ways.

Susanna Anthony teaches us that we need not fear admitting our spiritual ignorance to God (prayer 14). Daniel Defoe reassures us that none who humbly approach the Lord are sent away empty (prayer 24). John Willison encourages us to be bold and persistent before God: "Lord, in I must be. Out I cannot stay" (prayer 75).

The authors of the prayers within this book have known heartache, grief and sickness, harassment, persecution, imprisonment, oppression, and war. They have also felt God's comfort, the Spirit melting into the soul like rain on parched ground, inexplicable glory.

This book also offers a doorway to God. How God may open the door of your soul through the prayers is known only to God.

### Conversation with God

Prayer is conversation with God.[2] At first, our prayer is often like the conversation of a very young child: one-sided, rambling, easily frustrated when desires are not gratified immediately.

As we "grow into salvation" (1 Peter 2:2) we come to understand that prayer is dialogue. Prayer is speaking to God; prayer is keeping silent, listening for the Shepherd's voice. Sometimes prayer is a rich wordless communion of divine love and the human soul.

The pastor and Reformer, Jean Calvin, understood devout attentiveness, or reverence, to be the foundation ("first rule") of prayer. He also knew that thoughts easily disrupt prayer. When attention wanders, God is no longer in focus. Instead we pay attention to a barking dog or traffic noise, problems large and small. Calvin viewed distraction as disrespect of God. But the mind *is* a wanderer, and it is a rare gift to pray rightly.[3] We need help.

Human effort does not secure intimate communion with God, but the first step to deepened prayer is ours. Calvin encourages us to apply ourselves to prayer—to discipline wandering thoughts and to wrestle against distractions.[4] Let us calm and focus ourselves; we are in God's presence. Trust God: the Holy Spirit will help us to pray, and Christ prays for us.[5] By prayer we plant seeds of faith in the depth of God. God will give growth. A joyful harvest is coming. Don't give up! (see Gal. 6:8–9).

### Support and Encouragement

Reformed people have found spiritual encouragement by praying with others, praying at regular times, and using prayer books, if needed.[6] Calvin considered reluctance to pray to be only human. To counter this, he recommended setting aside certain times for prayer: after rising in the morning, and at bedtime; before and after meals, and before beginning work.[7] This book provides prayers for morning and evening, graces, and prayers for use before work (the last prayer in each weekday morning section). Prayers for other times and needs are also included.

Prayer books and other devotional works have long been used by Reformed people as support and encouragement in prayer. Some believe that the devout of other generations did not need written prayers. But prayer books have been written and used by Reformed folks extensively. Of course, extempore prayer was treasured, for many prayed without a book in front of them. Their minds and hearts were steeped in Scripture; they absorbed extempore prayer from an early age through family prayer. Some who prayed this way liked to have prayer books or "forms" available.

The English Congregationalist Hannah Housman (ca. 1697–1735) learned to pray using written prayer. After her conversion at the age of thirteen, she began to leave "forms" aside. But sometimes, she turned back to written prayers. English Puritan Margaret Baxter (1636–1681) asked her husband, Richard, to write a prayer for her. After she died, he found it among her papers, but did not know if she had ever used it, since she had such warmth of feeling and "freedom of expression without it." In nineteenth-century Scotland, minister Thomas Wright commented that there must always be some who are "altogether destitute of the power of performing their private devotions in a satisfactory manner, without the help of some manual," while others found their prayers inspired by encountering the piety of others in books.[8] Strange as it may seem, even many Puritans who valued freedom in public worship often used written prayers in the household for both family and private worship.[9]

## Reformed Prayer Books

Prayer books and other devotional works containing prayer have been used by Reformed people throughout the centuries. This section concentrates on prayer books, while the next looks at various devotional books; there is some overlap.

In the sixteenth century, booklets for family catechism instruction often included prayers. The *Genevan Catechism* (1542), also known as "Calvin's Catechism," is one example. A version of this catechism was appended to the Church of Scotland's 1564 *Book of Common Order*. English Puritans Edward Dering, Stephen Egerton, William Gouge, and Eusebius Paget also published catechism pamphlets with prayers. Such booklets or books have been used into the twentieth century in some churches.[10]

Some Reformed devotional works were based on the psalms. Théodore de Bèze's *Christian Meditations upon Eight Psalms of the Prophet David*, written for popular use, was printed in English in 1582 (see prayers 45 and 114). Philippe Duplessis-Mornay's *Christian Discourses and Meditations* (published 1610–1611) also contained rich prayers based on the psalms (see prayer 269, which is based on Psalm 25).

Other writers, such as the English martyr John Bradford, based their prayers on the Lord's Prayer, the Apostles' Creed, and the Ten Commandments. Huguenot minister Daniel Toussaint wrote prayers and meditations on the Apostles' Creed for *The Exercise of the Faithful Soul* (published in English in 1583).

From the late sixteenth century on, Puritans published many prayer books and devotional books with prayers included. Many of these works were best-sellers, translated into many languages, and widely used by Reformed people. In 1624, Puritan John Brinsley made a list of one hundred and ninety-seven "Protestant helps for Devotion."[11] Among these "helps" were the English prayer book *A Castle for the Soul* (1578) published and perhaps composed by Robert Waldegrave and Thomas Sampson's *Prayers and Meditations Apostolic* (1593). Around the same time, Puritan John Norden published *A Pensive Man's Practice* (1584), one of the most popular devotional works of the period, with over forty impressions printed before 1640.[12] He went on to pen over a dozen other prayer books.

Thomas Sorocold, another English Puritan, wrote an enduring prayer book, *Supplications of Saints*, which first appeared in 1608 and went through forty-five editions by 1754 (see prayers 2, 74, 116, and others). Likewise popular, *Crumbs of Comfort,* compiled and published by Puritan bookseller Michael Sparke. It was first published a little before 1627, and enjoyed a forty-second edition in 1722. Lewis Bayly's *The Practice of Piety*, written around 1610, entered a seventy-fourth English edition in 1821 and is in print as the third millennium dawns. Richard Baxter's *The Poor Man's Family Book* (1674) included a number of prayer "forms," for those who needed them. He invited the rich and well-off to give copies to the poor, and urged landlords to give copies to all their tenants (see prayers 207, 213, 312, and 474).[13]

Among eighteenth-century prayer books in English were Presbyterian Benjamin Bennet's *The Christian Oratory* (published in 1728, with editions available over the next century), two prayer books published by Samuel Bourn, and Matthew Henry's *A Method of Prayer*, first published in 1710 and still in circulation more than one hundred seventy years later (see prayers 60, 98, and others).

In the nineteenth century, prayer books written in English included titles by Charles Brooks, Jeremiah Good, Henry Harbaugh, Robert Lee, John Morison, George Smith, Joseph Stratton, and James W. Weir.[14]

Notable twentieth-century prayer books are John Baillie's popular *A Diary of Private Prayer*, first published in 1936, translated into over a dozen languages, and available in four American editions alone, at the present; John Joseph Stoudt's *Private Devotions for Home and Church* (1956); and George F. MacLeod's *The Whole Earth Shall Cry Glory* (1985). Significant French prayer books that served as sources for this book include Pierre Du Moulin (the Elder), *The Right Way to Heaven* (1630), and a work by his son, Pierre Du Moulin (the Younger), *A Week of Soliloquies and Prayers* (1657). Michel Bouttier's appealing *Prayers for My Village* was first published in 1954, again in 1982, and in English translation in 1994. Dutch author Georg Willem's *Solitary Conversations of a Devout Soul with His God* was published in Amsterdam in 1698, and was still available half a century later; the book was also published in English.[15]

Swiss author Georg J. Zollikofer's *Devotional Exercises and Prayers* was used in the late eighteenth and early nineteenth centuries, with editions available in German and English. German folk in Germany and America used the prayers found in *Core of Old and New Spirit-filled Hymns*, published in 1752 and several later editions.

Hungarian Reformed bishop László Ravasz's book *Homeward Bound . . .* (1925) is still available, in Hungarian, through the Calvin Synod of the United Church of Christ (published in 1984; prayer 274 is an English translation of a prayer from this book).[16]

In short, over the centuries, Reformed people have written and used many prayer books. Those represented in this book skim the surface of what has been published.

## Other Reformed Sources

Prayers can also be found in a variety of other sources: devotional books, missionary accounts, spiritual memoirs, biographical accounts, as well as church service books, and books of prayer for public worship. French author Charles Drelincourt's classic, *The Christian's*

*Defence Against the Fears of Death*, was first published in 1651 and was available in French, Dutch, and English reprints over one hundred and sixty years (see prayers 69, 314, 392, 423, and 433).

English Presbyterian Puritan Joseph Alleine's book *An Alarm to Unconverted Sinners* (also published under the title *A Sure Guide to Heaven*) was first published in 1671, and has been published in numerous editions, in a variety of languages, ever since. This devotional classic is the source of a long "Covenant Prayer" (see prayer 10 for an excerpt), deeply influential in both Reformed and Methodist piety.[17]

Prayers are also sometimes found in the memoirs of missionaries. Experience Mayhew recorded a number of prayers by Puritan Native Americans in *Indian Converts* (1727) (see prayers 169, 458, and 461). The English Congregational missionary John Williams (1796–1839), who worked principally in Tahiti, Samoa, and the Society Islands, preserves the Communion prayer of a gifted layman (see prayer 346). Prayers are more likely to be preserved in early missionary accounts.

Diaries, journals, spiritual memoirs, and biographies often contain prayers. The prayers of Susanna Anthony, Sarah Osborn, Martha Laurens Ramsay, Sarah Davy, and Elisabeth West appear in their spiritual memoirs. Puritan Samuel Clarke's *A Collection of the Lives of Ten Eminent Divines* (1661–1662) is the source of John Cotton's "Thankful Acknowledgement of God's Providence," a prayer in poem form (see prayer 188).

A number of Reformed service books from a variety of countries were also useful prayer sources. *The Church Order of the Electoral Palatinate*, published in 1684, *The Liturgy of the Reformed Church of France* (1963), and the 1993 American *Book of Common Worship* are just three such sources represented here. Sourcebooks of prayer for public worship such as *Flames of the Spirit*, edited by Ruth C. Duck (1985), and Hughes Oliphant Old's *Leading in Prayer: A Workbook for Worship* (1995) contain prayers suitable for private as well as public use.

In some of the genres of books mentioned above, it is not uncommon to find extempore prayer. Such prayer was likely to be remembered and published if the person praying was exceptionally devout or well-known, and had a pastor inclined to write books.

In the mid-eighteenth century, missionary David Brainerd recorded a small portion of extempore prayer by a newly converted anonymous

Native American woman, probably Delaware; some weeks later she
was baptized and received into the Presbyterian church:

> O blessed Lord, do come, do come!
> O do take me away,
> do let me die and go to Jesus Christ!
> I am afraid if I live I shall sin again!
> O do let me die now!
> O dear Jesus, do come!
> I can't stay, I can't stay!
> O how can I live in this world!
> Do take me away from this sinful place!
> O let me never sin any more!
> O what shall I do, what shall I do!
> Dear Jesus, O dear Jesus . . .

She prayed like this, sometimes in English, sometimes in her native
tongue, aloud, for about two hours. Brainerd remarked that he had
never seen a person more "bowed under the conviction of sin." After
her conversion, she "seemed constantly to breathe the spirit and
temper of the new creature."[18]

Examples of extempore prayer in this volume include the prayers
of the native Hawaiian Paul Kanoa, a missionary to Micronesia (see
prayer 130); Native Americans Thomas Waban (see prayer 417);
Abigail Kenump (see prayer 458); and Lydia Ohquanhut (see prayer
467); and the final prayer by Idelette Calvin (see prayer 500).

This book contains five hundred prayers. They are a tiny fraction
of prayers preserved in thousands of Reformed books written over the
centuries.

## Selection and Presentation of Prayers

The prayers were selected and edited for spiritual depth;
intelligibility; universality across generations and national boundaries;
beauty; theological integrity; and inclusiveness with regard to gender.
As far as possible the prayers are left to speak for themselves.
Punctuation, capitalization, and spelling have been updated; and
sometimes, substitutions made for archaic words. Polemical references
have been omitted. Many prayers are excerpts, or a series of excerpts
from much longer prayers. However, omissions are not indicated by

ellipses, since these would be distracting. These prayers are marked in the text as altered. Several prayers, set originally in prose or verse, may have also been altered in the text and are marked accordingly.

Prayers translated into English have been rendered into inclusive language (with regard to people) wherever the original allows, and into contemporary idiom ("you" for "thee," for example). Where there is inclusive language in English prayers, it is original to the text, with the exception of prayers that were altered for inclusivity or additional inclusivity.[19] Significantly, seventeenth-century Puritans were more likely to use inclusive language than writers of fifty years ago. The phrase "sons and daughters" is always original to texts composed in English. This book includes both representative prayers and gems of Reformed piety, with a balanced selection from the five centuries and the various branches of the Reformed family.[20] About sixteen percent of the prayers are by women.

The term *Reformed* is interpreted in the classic sense of those churches that grew out of the Reformation in Switzerland and the south of Germany, then spread to other European and British countries, and from there, by migration and missionary activity, to other places. Congregational, Presbyterian, Reformed, and united churches are represented.[21] A few prayers by people or religious groups not firmly within the tradition are included because of their importance to the Reformed faith—such as Queen Marguerite of Navarre (who never formally left the Roman Catholic church)—or their influence on Reformed worship—such as the Catholic Apostolic Church—or for other reasons.

## Book Structure and Content

This book provides prayers for morning and evening use for four weeks, and a section of prayers for special needs and times. This same structure was employed in some eighteenth- and nineteenth-century Reformed prayer books, such as George Smith's *The Domestic Prayer Book of 1844.*[22]

Each morning and evening section contains five to seven prayers, generally arranged as follows: approach or praise, confession, petition, intercession, and a concluding prayer. Morning prayer sections end with a brief prayer entrusting the day's work to God, while evening prayer sections conclude with prayer expressing trust of God's vigilant care through the night.

Morning and evening prayers sometimes end with words signaling the use of the Lord's Prayer, and less often, the Apostles' Creed. Early Reformed people commonly used both to conclude prayers. While use of the creed declined, the Lord's Prayer continued to be used this way into the twentieth century. "Our Father . . ." indicates that the Lord's Prayer may be used (see prayers 15, 27, and 227, for example). "I believe in God . . ." indicates that the Apostles' Creed may be used (see prayers 37 and 287).

Part 2 provides prayers for occasional use. Reformed people are familiar with "prayers for illumination," often used in public worship before Scripture is read. Such prayers have been used by Reformed folk in private and family worship also, and are still helpful for many people. A selection of these prayers is provided in the section titled "Before Reading the Word." William Gouge's prayer (see prayer 338) "to be used before the reading of Scripture" was included in a catechism booklet for family use. Scottish Presbyterian Elizabeth Cairns (1685–1741) tended sheep during much of her childhood and youth. She carried her Bible with her to the fields and sang psalms, prayed, and read Scripture while she watched the flock. Typically, she asked "God's blessing on the portion of scripture" she intended to read.[23]

The section titled "Communion Prayers" is also based on traditional Reformed practice of prayer before and after Communion, both in church and at home. These prayers also come from diverse places—from a missionary's account, from books for private and family worship, and from public liturgies.

"The Church's Year" contains prayers for use during the various seasons of the church year, beginning with Advent and concluding with the section titled "With All the Company of Heaven." Though not a major or developed section, the prayers give a taste of Reformed appreciation of the communion of saints.

"The Stations of Life's Journey" provides prayers for pregnant women and new parents, for those contemplating marriage, for use when sick, and to give thanks for recovery. Next is an assortment of prayers for the bereaved, a prayer for those adapting to the weakness that age eventually brings to most, and a section of prayers for those near death. The prayers titled "Last Words" are typical of the way Reformed people prayed in their last mortal moments, commending themselves to God's eternal care, just as Christ prayed on the cross (Luke 23:46).

"Prayers for Various Needs" contains material particularly useful during times of uncertainty, crisis, or suffering. "Sentence Prayers" consists of brief prayers to use anytime.

The prayers of "Prayers for Children" have been carefully selected. Some have been adapted into modern language. They are not teaching tools intended to impress lessons on children, but prayers that may help them open their hearts to God.

"Graces" furnishes prayers for use not only before meals, but afterward as well, as was once traditional. Many of the prayers are suitable for use around a family table. Others give a taste of Reformed expressions of gratitude to God that may help shape extempore prayer.

The "Biographical Index" provides brief notes on individuals, as well as on some churches and books. These are intentionally limited in scope, and as likely to disclose private, spiritual dimensions of an author's life, as simple career information.

## Suggestions for Using this Book

Through the ages, when Reformed people knelt for prayer, they recognized that they were in the presence of God. Puritan Mary Rich, in a letter of spiritual counsel to a friend wrote, "You are going to speak [with] God, before whom the angels and cherubim cover their faces in reverence. . . . Therefore prostrate yourself before the Most High with humility."[24]

Some who use this book will pray a section for morning or evening in its entirety, if time allows, perhaps with silence between prayers. While others may choose one or two prayers, guided by the titles. You may wish to use prayers from Part 2 of the book during seasons such as Advent or Lent, or when special concerns arise. Consider the prayers like a trellis provided for a thriving plant—used for support when needed, but left behind when your soul freely rises to God, and God lifts it up.

The prayers may be used as part of a longer devotional time. One suggestion, based on traditional Reformed practice, is to read (or sing) a psalm, read Scripture, meditate on the reading or rest in contemplative silence, and pray. Reformed people have sometimes used specific psalms for morning and evening.[25] Those appropriate for morning include Psalms 51, 63, 95, 100, 148, and 150. Psalms for evening include 4, 91, 134, 139, and 141.

Another Reformed practice is to read psalms "in course," by beginning with the first psalm, and moving to the next at each subsequent prayer time. Some might also read a portion of Scripture "in course," reading from the Old Testament in the morning, and the New Testament at night (traditional Reformed practice), or following a daily lectionary such as that found in the *Book of Common Worship* (1993).[26] British readers might use the lectionary provided by the Joint Liturgical Group in *The Daily Office Revised* (London: SPCK, 1978).

## Abbreviations Used in This Book

alt. = altered from original prayer

b. = born

ca. = "circa" or "about": used to indicate that a person was born or died "about" a certain time

d. = died

fl. = "flourished": used to indicate a period during which a person lived and worked—birth and death years are unknown

n. = "name": insert name of person, group, or country

## Notes

1. Charles Drelincourt, *Prayers and Meditations Before and After Receiving the Sacrament of the Lord's-Supper*, 2nd ed. (London, 1716), p. 34.
2. *Calvin: Institutes of the Christian Religion*, edited by John T. McNeill, vol. 2, Library of Christian Classics (Philadelphia: The Westminster Press, 1960), 3.20.4, p. 853.
3. Ibid., 3.20.4–5, pp. 853–855. This paragraph relies on Calvin. The Reformer is referred to as "Jean," not "John," to honor his French origin.
4. Ibid., 3.20.5, pp. 854–855.
5. For further study, see James B. Torrance, *Worship, Community, and the Triune God of Grace* (Carlisle, UK: Paternoster Press, 1996; American ed: Downers Grove, IL: InterVarsity Press, 1997).
6. Reformed people have prayed together morning and evening in church and in families; spouses often shared joint devotions. See Diane Karay Tripp, *Daily Prayer in the Reformed Tradition: An Initial Survey*, Joint Liturgical Studies 35, The Alcuin Club and the Group for Renewal of Worship (Cambridge, Eng.: Grove Books, Ltd., 1996), pp. 24–40.
7. Calvin: *Institutes*, 3.20.50, pp. 917–918.
8. Richard Pearsall, ed., *The Power and Pleasure of the Divine Life; Exemplify'd in the late Mrs. [Hannah Pearsall] Housman, of Kidderminster.* . . . , 2nd ed. (London printed; Boston, reprinted, 1755), p. ix; Richard Baxter [ed. by anon.], *Memoirs of Mrs. Margaret Baxter.* . . . [1st ed., 1681, titled *A Breviat of the Life of Margaret.* . . .] (London, 1826), p. 49; [Thomas Wright] *The Morning and Evening Sacrifice; or, Prayers for Private Persons and Families*, new ed. (Edinburgh, 1823), pp. 9–10.
9. Patrick Collinson, *The Elizabethan Puritan Movement* (Berkeley and Los Angeles: University of California Press, 1967), p. 360; Charles Hambrick-Stowe, *The Practice*

*of Piety: Puritan Devotional Disciplines in Seventeenth-Century New England* (Chapel Hill: University of North Carolina Press, 1982), pp. 161, 176, 183–184.

10. Books cited in the introduction that have been used as sources of prayers are listed in the bibliography. Foreign-language titles have been translated into English, and language modernized.

   Church Service Society, *The Book of Common Order of the Church of Scotland Commonly Known as John Knox's Liturgy,* with introduction and notes by G. W. Sprott (Edinburgh and London: William Blackwood and Sons, 1901), pp. 173ff.

   Catechetical resources were used extensively and published in many editions. Egerton's *Brief Method of Catechizing,* first published in 1594, for example, entered a forty-third edition in 1638. For further study, see Ian Green, *The Christian's ABC: Catechism and Catechizing in England, c. 1530–1740* (Oxford: Clarendon Press, 1996), and Hughes Oliphant Old, *The Shaping of the Reformed Baptismal Rite in the Sixteenth Century* (Grand Rapids, MI: William B. Eerdmans Publishing Co., 1992), pp. 279–300. For a twentieth-century example, see James I. Good, *Aid to the Heidelberg Catechism* (Cleveland: Central Publishing House, 1904).

11. [John Brinsley] *The Fourth Part of the True Watch: Containing Prayers and Tears for the Churches.* . . . (London, 1624), sig. v.ff.

12. *The English Experience: Books printed in England before 1640: A descriptive catalogue of . . . facsimile editions now available.* . . . (Amsterdam: Theatrum Orbis Terrarum B.V.; Norwood, NJ: Walter J. Johnson, Inc. [1980?], p. 207.

13. Richard Baxter, *The Poor Mans Family Book,* (London, 1674), sig. A3r.

14. More prayer book titles are given in Diane Karay Tripp, "Daily Prayer in the Reformed Tradition: An Initial Survey," *Studia Liturgica* 21 (1991), pp. 76–107 and 190–219, in footnotes throughout, and in the concluding "Select Bibliography of Reformed Prayerbooks," pp. 218–219. (This is a somewhat different version of the same title mentioned in note 6, above.)

15. In the Netherlands, at least two thousand titles of Reformed prayer books and works of spirituality were available in Dutch during the seventeenth century alone. At least one-third of these were translations of Puritan works. Apparently they were very engrossing: eventually preachers began complaining that people were in danger of neglecting the Bible in favor of devotional literature. See Fred A. van Lieburg, "From Pure Church to Pious Culture: The Further Reformation in the Seventeenth-Century Dutch Republic," in *Later Calvinism: International Perspectives,* edited by W. Fred Graham, Charles G. Nauert, Jr., Gen. Ed., Sixteenth-Century Essays and Studies, vol. 22 (Kirksville, MO: Sixteenth-Century Journal Publishers, Inc., 1994), pp. 424–425.

16. The Hungarian title is *Hazafelé.* . . . In the eighteenth and nineteenth centuries, Hungarian Reformed Christians used *Christian Instructions* in their households. See Edit Fél and Tamás Hofer, *Proper Peasants: Traditional Life in a Hungarian Village,* edited by Sol Tax, Viking Fund Publication in Anthropology, No. 46 (Chicago: Aldine Publishing House, 1969), p. 136, n. 27.

   Hungarian popular piety was shaped by Puritan publications, which, along with Hungarian and foreign works, were available and used from the early seventeenth into the twentieth century. Bayly's *Practice of Piety* had great influence in Hungary. See Jěno Szigeti, "Eighteenth-Century Hungarian Protestant Pietist Literature and John Bunyan," in *Bunyan in England and Abroad,* edited by M. van Os and G. J. Schutte, VU-Studies on Protestant History, no. 1 (Amsterdam: VU University Press, 1990), pp. 133–135.

17. The role of the prayer in Methodist tradition is treated by David H. Tripp in *The Renewal of the Covenant in the Methodist Tradition* (London: Epworth Press, 1969). The whole prayer is given in Appendix II, pp. 185–188.

18. David Brainerd, *Mirabilia Dei inter Indicos. Or the Rise and Progress of a Remarkable Work of Grace amongst a Number of Indians in the Provinces of New-Jersey and Pennsylvania.* . . . (Philadelphia: William Bradford, [1746]), p. 124; Brainerd's observations, pp. 126–127.

19. Prayers altered for inclusivity: 8, 12, 34, 50, 56, 57, 60, 68, 91, 116, 131, 132, 136, 144, 145, 149, 160, 170, 174, 189, 208, 210, 214, 218, 234, 248, 249, 262, 265, 276, 297, 298, 299, 304, 309, 314, 332, 392, 395, 402, 407, 409, 423, 430, 432, 446, 447, 448.

20. The figures are rounded off: twentieth century: 28 percent; nineteenth century: 15 percent; eighteenth century: 18 percent; seventeenth century: 25 percent; sixteenth century: 15 percent; prayers by denominational family: Presbyterian—34 percent; Reformed—29 percent; Congregational—16 percent; other (united churches, unspecified Congregationalist or Presbyterian Puritans, etc.)—21 percent.

21. This description relies on Jean-Jacques Bauswein and Lukas Vischer, eds., *The Reformed Family Worldwide* (Grand Rapids, MI/Cambridge, U.K.: William B. Eerdmans Publishing Co., 1999), p. 2. Also see World Alliance of Reformed Churches, "List of Member Churches" [pamphlet] (Geneva, Switzerland: World Alliance of Reformed Churches, 1998).

22. The title continues: *Morning & Evening Prayers, for One Month, with Occasional Prayers and Thanksgivings.*

23. John Brown, *Practical Piety Exemplified, in the Lives of Thirteen Eminent Christians.* . . . (Pittsburgh, 1818), p. 38. Cairns had a Covenanter heritage and joined the Secession church.

24. On Reformed use of postures and gestures in prayer, see Diane Karay Tripp, "The Reformed Tradition of Embodied Prayer: Glorifying God in the Body," *Liturgy 8* (Summer 1990), pp. 90–97; Tripp, *Daily Prayer in the Reformed Tradition*, pp. 13–18; Daniel Dana, *Memoirs of Eminently Pious Women.* . . . , abridged from the Large Work of Dr. Gibbons (Newburyport, 1803), p. 129.

25. Tripp, *Daily Prayer in the Reformed Tradition*, pp. 19–20.

26. The Theology and Worship Ministry Unit, for the Presbyterian Church (U.S.A.) and the Cumberland Presbyterian Church, *Book of Common Worship* (Louisville: Westminster/John Knox Press, 1993). The "Daily Lectionary" is found on pp. 1050–1095.

 Part 1

Prayers for the
Morning and Evening

## Grant Us Communion with Thee

1

Many and great, O God, are Thy things,
Maker of earth and sky;
Thy hands set the heavens with stars,
Thy fingers spread the mountains and plains.
Lo, at Thy word the waters were formed;
Deep seas obey Thy voice.

Grant unto us communion with Thee,
Thou star-abiding One;
Come unto us and dwell with us:
With Thee are found the gifts of life.
Bless us with life that has no end,
Eternal life with Thee.

*Joseph Renville, ca. 1779–1846*

## Approach and Adoration

2

O Lord Christ Jesus, Son of God, thou holy, mighty and wonderful
God and man: with the Wisemen of the East, I come to seek thee in the
stable in Bethlehem, and with all the Jews, I come to see thee in Mount
Calvary: at Bethlehem, Lord, where thy manger was thy bed to be
born; in Mount Calvary, where the cross was thy bed to die; in
Bethlehem, where a handful of straw was the pillow for thy sacred
head, in Mount Calvary, where a crown of thorns and a number of
nails pierced and fastened both head and body; in Bethlehem, where
coarse swaddling-clothes were thy best robes, and in Mount Calvary,

where thou wast stripped of thy clothes, and thy body hung naked in much misery.

I come, Lord, to adore thee, to praise thee, and to pray thee, that as in thy lifetime, thou wast content to be bred, born, and brought up in manifold infirmities, to demonstrate the truth of thy humanity, and then at thy death, thou wast pleased to disarm thyself and to be broken with  many miseries, for discharge of our captivity, and thereby to seal in our hearts the assurance of our access to thy throne of grace; so I pray thee wilt be pleased, as a gracious King, to hold out thy golden scepter of mercy to my fearful conscience, that I may have warrant to come near unto thee, to look into thy wounds, to plea for compassion and pardon, and to taste of thy goodness, I, who am a sinful wretch and a woeful creature, full of corruption and manifold infirmities.

—*Thomas Sorocold, 1561–1617; alt.*


## 3   *Confession*

Make me, I beseech thee, more and more sensible of my need of a Savior, and that thou art just such a Savior as I need. Lord, save or I perish. Lord, have mercy, or I am all undone. I am a vile sinner, deserving nothing at thy hands but condemnation. But thou didst descend from heaven to earth to seek and to save that which was lost. Oh! that thou wouldst receive me, accept me, bless me, take me into the number of thy genuine disciples of thy little flock. Save me, I beseech thee, from the guilt and punishment, and also from the power and dominion of sin. Enable me from henceforth to live to thy praise, to be a Christian not in name only, but in deed and in truth.

Show me thy glory. Fill my mind with joy and peace in believing. Remove my doubts. Quiet my fears, console me in adversity, meet me in thy ordinances, support me at all times. Never leave nor forsake me, and do to me and for me exceedingly abundantly above all else that I can ask or think, and to thy thrice holy name be everlasting praise. Amen.

— *Hannah Sinclair, 1780–1818; alt.*

## To Depend on God Only

## 4

Grant, Almighty God, that we may learn, whether in want or in abundance, so to submit ourselves to thee, that it may be our only and perfect felicity to depend on thee and to rest in that salvation, the experience of which thou hast already given us, until we shall reach that eternal rest, where we shall enjoy it in all its fullness, when made partakers of that glory which has been procured for us by the blood of thine only-begotten Son. Amen.

*— Jean Calvin, 1509–1564*

## Intercession: For Healing within Society

## 5

O God of love,
our peace lies in conversion to your will,
our strength in confident trust;
but we would have none of it.
By the gentle power of the Holy Spirit
quieten the turmoil of our minds
and open our hearts to your presence within us,
that we may be still and know that you are God;
through Jesus Christ our Lord,
who lives and reigns with you and the Holy Spirit,
one God, for ever and ever.
Amen.

*—Uniting Church in Australia, 1988*

## For God's Providential Use of Us

Hold us, O God, throughout this day, in Thy merciful providence; that, although we be unmindful of Thee, Thy Spirit may so fill our lives, and Thy care surround us, that, both within and through us, Thy will may be done, and Thy kingdom advanced; through Jesus Christ our Lord. Amen.

*— John U. Stephens, 1901–1984*

7

## For the Divine Indwelling

My Lord and my God,
in your kindness, dwell unceasingly within my soul,
and by your divine presence,
turn all my thoughts to the wise law of your holy will.
Grant me the grace, O my God,
never to lose the fear of offending you,
that my heart, ever burning with the fire of your love,
all my delight shall be solely to please you;
through Jesus Christ our Lord.
Amen.

—*Georg Willem, 1635–1709; alt.*

8

## For Wisdom to Seek the True Joy

O Lord God Almighty! Now is another day passed, and going to be swallowed and lost in its own night. Now we are another step towards our long home. Yet how careless are our thoughts, how cold our hearts, how lifeless is our devotion! We faint, we blush, we repent at reflections upon our own folly, that so little work is done, that so many, who were once behind us in time and in the Christian race, are now out-stripping us, and leaving us far behind them.

Lord, quicken us in our way, by assisting us to look at the glorious prize above us, the example set before us, the spectators round about us, and to attend to the admonitions and encouragements given us on every side.

How busy we have been, for trifles, like ants crowding and jostling for a few grains, while great and serious things have been neglected by us.

Fill us with holy shame at our false zeal for little things, and our coldness towards things eternal.

Kindle in these hearts a holy fire which shall never die, but grow up into such flames as burn in the breasts of the blessed saints and angels above; that at length we may join in those immortal songs which fill thy spacious temple, and may sing as loud and as long as they, that when the evening of our sorrows and darkness is over, the day of eternal light and joy may begin.

Suffer us not, who profess to see heaven before us, to be eager after the great and high things of the earth, nor to envy those who do obtain them.

Let us not throw ourselves down like sullen children who will not stand; and if thy providence throw us down, let us not be like weak children who cannot stand; but by Christian fortitude and faith, bear and improve all the changes of life, and learn in whatever state we are in, patience and contentment.

Help us daily to examine our accounts, how we have spent our time, what profit we daily make, and what good we are every day doing. Let us no longer weary ourselves in catching shadows, flies, vanities and dust, things hard to catch and worth little when caught. But cause us to see the substantial joys of God's kingdom, and those habits of righteousness and virtue which will qualify us for a place in it, always remembering that eternity is at stake.

Indue all people with principles of righteousness and peace. Lead princes and those in authority into reasonable and religious desires and resolutions, that all who are adorned with thy power may be influenced by thy grace, that those who have power to hurt thy interest may not have the will to do it.

Heal wounded spirits and quiet troubled breasts. Remove from them unprofitable scruples and perplexing fears. Support good Christians under those dejections of spirit which they are not able to prevent or resist, and through which easy things appear difficult, and difficult things impossible. Scatter the clouds wherewith they are covered, and restore them to an easy, active, cheerful spirit, that they may see their comforts and take delight in them, and all their duty to God and humanity become their pleasure.

Grant, Lord, we may never provoke thee to cause us to walk in darkness; nor suffer us, by willful sin, to bar out the light of thy countenance.

We are thankful for our daily mercies. We beg a quiet and safe night, and the restored joy of thy salvation in the morning, and assistance in all future duty.

Now unto the King eternal, immortal, invisible, the only wise God, be honor and glory for ever and ever. Amen.

*—Samuel Bourn, 1689–1754; alt.*

## 9            *For Guidance and Strength on the Way*

O God, our eternal hope:
we thank you for providing us the map that directs us
      in our search for the treasure of your kingdom.
    Help us not to be so fascinated by the map
        that we forget our ultimate goal;
      nor to be so obsessed by the excitement of exploring the
        trails that we go astray or get lost in
        wonderment;
      nor to be so overwhelmed by hardships and obstacles
        that we lose hope and abandon your mission.
    Even in the midst of failure and discouragement,
      increase our faith and confidence in your
      promises.
    Give us a sense of joy and achievement
      in small accomplishments.
    Even in the midst of success and prosperity,
      grant us humility, and restrain us from pride
      and boasting.
    Help us to acknowledge that we are but your
     instruments,
      that it is our duty and delight to serve you and
      your people,
      and to give you all the glory. Amen.

*—Hui-chin Loh, contemporary, and I-to Loh, b. 1936*

## To Christ the Bridegroom

O Blessed Jesus, I come to thee hungry, wretched, blind and naked, a guilty condemned malefactor, unworthy to wash the feet of the servants of my Lord, much more unworthy to be solemnly married to the King of glory. But since such is thine unparalleled love, I do here with all my power accept thee, and do take thee for my Head and Husband, for better, for worse, for richer, for poorer, for all times and conditions, to love, honor, and obey thee before all others, and this, to the death. I renounce mine own wisdom and do here take thee for my only guide. I renounce mine own will and take thy will for my law.

And since thou hast told me that I must suffer if I will reign, I do here covenant with thee to take my lot with thee, and, by thy grace, to run all hazards with thee, trusting that neither life nor death shall part between thee and me.

*— Joseph Alleine, 1634–1668; alt.*

## At the Ending of the Day

O most blessed Lord and Savior;
thou who didst, by thy precious death and burial
take away the sting of death and the darkness of the grave:
grant unto me the precious fruit of this holy triumph of thine,
and be my guide both in life and death.
In thy name will I lay me down in peace and rest,
for thou, O Lord, makest me to dwell in safety.
Enlighten, O Lord, the eyes of my understanding,
that I may not sleep the sleep of death.
Into thy hands I commend my spirit,
for thou hast redeemed me,
O thou covenant-keeping God!
Bless and preserve me, therefore, both now and forever.
Amen!

*—Amos Lawrence, 1786–1852; alt.*

12

## For God's Light

O Light of lights, which hast dispersed the darkness to bring light into the world, and to give us for a mirror the beauty of thy works: as thou now bringest upon the earth the brightness of the day and of the sun, bring also, Lord, upon my soul the brightness of thy Holy Spirit.

And seeing that to lead me to thy mercy thou hast been pleased that the Author of light, eternal Wisdom, came down upon earth and there abode for a time, that he might converse amongst us to light the lamp of our souls by the fire of thy holy word, infuse, Lord, by the same bounty, the clear light which thou hast put therein by the operation of thy Holy Spirit, that in thy wedding day, we, finding ourselves adorned with the wedding garment of thy grace, may be led into the participation of thy celestial glory.

*—Pierre Du Moulin, the Elder, 1568–1658; alt.*

13

## For Perseverance

When we are weary of work, and think it fruitless,
when the light of our life has become dim,
and our duty is hard because it seems unprofitable,
help us, O God, we beseech thee,
to think of thy patience and long-suffering,
that so we may again take up our labor and our burden,
and persevere with them unto the end. Amen.

*—Scotland, Home Prayers, 1879; alt.*

## *Prayer for Wisdom*

Lord,
I am as ignorant as a beast before thee.
I fear whether such ignorance be consistent
with a state of grace.
Can I be born of God,
and yet know no more of the mysteries of thy kingdom?
O, however ignorant I am, in other respects,
let me know thee and Jesus Christ,
whom to know is life eternal.

Blessed be thy Name!
Thou hast chosen the foolish and base things of the world.
O then, let me but be able to comprehend,
with all the saints,
what is the breadth and length,
and depth and height,
and to know the love of Christ,
which passeth knowledge,
and I will never envy the most capacious learned
understanding
in the whole universe, who yet knows not thee.

O unveil thy glories to my soul!
O, take me to thyself,
to the open vision,
and I shall then know more of thee,
than the most learned, experienced saint
ever did know in this world.

—*Susanna Anthony, 1726–1791; alt.*

# *Intercession*

Almighty God, Creator of heaven and earth, we thank you from the bottom of our heart that you have made us, that you have kept, fed and nourished us and our children even to this present day, and that you will still keep and govern us in days to come. Especially, however, do we thank you that you have granted us to know your Son Jesus Christ, whom you promised in paradise, and that you have forgiven our sins through his bitter passion and death. And we ask you that through the preaching of your word and the power of your Holy Spirit you would renew in us the image of your Son Jesus Christ, so that we, both in body and soul, may eternally live with you and praise you, for which we were created, and that you would defend us against Satan, lest he tear your holy word from our hearts, as he did to our first parents, Adam and Eve.

Forasmuch as you choose to govern us in this life by the hand of our rulers, we pray you therefore, you that have their hearts in your hand, that you would grant those in authority grace and unity, so that they may direct their whole administration to the end that our Lord Jesus Christ, to whom you have given all authority in heaven and on earth, may be Lord over them and over those subject to them, so that the poor people, who are creatures of your hand and sheep of your pasture, and for whom also the Lord Jesus shed his blood, may be governed in all holiness and justice, and so that we may render them due honor and loyalty for your sake and may be able to lead under them an honorable, peaceful and Christian life.

Grant also your blessing and benediction to the fruit of the earth, that we may know you thereby as Father and source of all mercy and good gifts. Protect us from war, times of need and the terrible scourge of plague.

We pray to you also, not only for ourselves, but also the people of the entire world, that you would graciously show mercy to each and every one.

But especially for those who are fellow members in the Body of Jesus Christ and suffer persecution for the sake of your truth, that you, Father of all graces, would restrain the raging of enemies who persecute your Son Jesus in his members, and that you would strengthen the persecuted with invincible resolution and the power of your Holy Spirit, so that they may accept such persecution at your hand with thankfulness, and in the midst of their distress experience such joy as passes all understanding.

Comfort and strengthen all the poor, the sick, prisoners, widows and orphans, pregnant women, troubled and tempted hearts, and give them your peace, through our Lord Jesus Christ, who has given us the sure promise, "Truly, truly, I say to you, all that you shall ask of the Father in my name, that he will give you," and has also commanded us thus to pray: Our Father . . .

*—Church of the Electoral Palatinate, 1684; alt.*

## *For the Day's Work* 16

O Most Merciful and Eternal God: bless us, we beseech thee, in our calling wherein thou hast set us. Prosper that which thou hast given unto us, and which in thy fear we set our hands unto. Stir us up to employ ourselves faithfully, religiously, and industriously, in our calling. Give us all things needful for this present life, and grant that we may so pass through things temporal, that our affections may not be withdrawn from things eternal.

*—England, A Garden of Spiritual Flowers, 1687 ed.; alt.*

17

## Penitent's Adoration

Lord Jesus,
when, in great rebellion, I departed from thee
and took up arms against thee
and bore more of the fall in me than any
both before and after the day of thy grace to me—
Thou didst call after me
and didst lead me through the great wilderness to thy cross
and didst there show me thy wounded body
and didst turn out the "strong man" armed
and didst continue to forgive much,
hide and cover all my evils,
turning them to good,
always continuing to save me by thy faithfulness,
never leaving me in the deep waters.
Thou not only lovedst but honoredst me,
for which I here adore thy free and sovereign grace.

*—Howell Harris, 1714–1773; alt.*

18

## *Confession*

Lord, how short do I come of my duty in communicating to or
receiving good from others! My soul is empty and barren, or if there
be any treasure in it, it is but as a treasure locked up in some chest
whose key is lost, when it should be opened for the use of others. Ah
Lord! I have sinned greatly, not only by vain words, but sinful silence.
I have been of little use in the world.

How little have I been in communion with others? Some of my
own size or judgment, or that I am otherwise obliged to, I can delight

to converse with. But O where is that largeness of heart and general delight I should have to and in all thy people?

How many of my old dear acquaintances are now in heaven, whose tongues were as choice silver while they were here. And, blessed souls, how communicative were they of what thou gavest them? O what an improvement would I have made of my talent, had I been diligent?

Lord, pardon my neglect of those sweet and blessed advantages. O let all my delight be in thy saints who are the excellent of the earth. O let me never go out of their company without an heart more warmed, quickened, and enlarged than when I came amongst them.

—*John Flavel, ca. 1630–1691*

## *For Union with God's Will* 19

I ask thy love,
With all the blessings I receive;
Nor are they more,
My blessings, than thy favour goes before.
I ask a heart
To value thee and know thee as thou art.
A will resigned to thee, desires confined
To what's thy will, and thy declared mind.
I ask thy self; what can I more? and less
Will not suffice the heart that I possess;
some glances of thy face, 'tis I implore,
too narrow nature can contain no more:
Then take me to thyself, and heaven display,
Where sin shall cease, and sorrow flee away;
There all thy glory shines, there I shall see
Thee as thou art, and be a God like thee:
There thy full presence ever shall appear,
Heaven were no heaven, if thou wert not there.

—*Daniel Defoe, 1660–1731*

## For Protection

O Lord, your power is greater than all powers.
Under your leadership we cannot fear anything.
It is you who have given us prophetical powers and
      have enabled us to foresee and interpret everything.
We know no other leader but you alone.
We beseech you to protect us in all trials and torments.
We know that you are with us, just as you were with
      our ancient ancestors.
Under your protection there is nothing that we
      cannot overcome.
Peace, praise ye Ngai,* peace, peace, peace be with us.

          —*Watu wa Mngu, Kenya, 1938; alt.*

*God

## Intercession

Lord, receive our supplications for this house, family, and country.
Protect the innocent, restrain the greedy and the treacherous, lead
us out of our tribulation into a quiet land.

    Look down upon ourselves and upon our absent dear ones.
Help us and them; prolong our days in peace and honour. Give us
health, food, bright weather, and light hearts. In what we meditate of
evil, frustrate our will; in what of good, further our endeavours. Cause
injuries to be forgot and benefits to be remembered.

    Let us lie down without fear and awake and arise with
exultation.

          —*Robert Louis Stevenson, 1850–1894*

## To Live My Prayers

O Lord, when I read 'tis not calling upon thee, "Lord, Lord," but the
obeying thee as such by doing of thy will, that will give entrance into
thy kingdom: O Lord, how desirous am I to live my prayers. And as I
every day pray as thou hast taught me that thy will may be done, so
Lord, enable me to do thy will, even when 'tis most cross to my own.

Let thy will commanding be my will obeying. O help me to
resign my will wholly to thine, make me cheerfully to do, and patiently
to suffer thy will.

Lord, let thy holy will be done by me and upon me.

*—Mary Rich, 1625–1678*

## At the Ending of the Day

O Almighty God, who hast preserved us during this day: watch over
us the whole night, and keep us from all those accidents to which we
are exposed in this world, to the end that the rest which we shall enjoy
may put us into a condition to glorify thee, and that we may one day
arrive to the eternal rest which thou hast appointed for us.

*—Church of Geneva, 1712*

24            *Coming to Christ for Pardon*

Teach me Lord to whom,
With wings of speed it is I come.
Jesus! It is to Thee,
Who art their refuge that depend on Thee.
To whom none ever came in vain,
Or ever were sent empty home again.
To whom none ever fled for fear,
And were not kept secure.
Thy Name's the tower to which the righteous fly,
Yea Lord and such as I.
Thy general call has no exception made,
To any but such as are afraid:
And all thy promises so full appear,
There can be no unworthiness but fear.
Had merit been our plea, my early hand
should not petition mercy, but demand.
Thy sacred offering then would useless prove,
And heaven were ours in justice, not in love.
But 'tis thy goodness I depend upon,
For if desert be pleaded I am undone.

None ever were received
For worthiness, though not so base as I.
Nor any soul deceived,
That ever heartily but dared to try.
Thy arms are ever spread,
None ever failed of help, that thither fled.
Then why?
Lord! why should others come, and yet not I?
I come, but ah! the clogs of sin,

That still remain, and too much reign within;
Make this their home,
And without them I can not come,
Yet here I am.
What guilt I can't shake off I'll bring, that Thou
Mayest cure the sins I cannot conquer now.
I'll bring my tainted heart
For Thee to cure;
My false and hypocritic part,
For Thee to make sincere.
Defiled and guilty as I am,
I'll cast myself on Thee,
That I may be
Cleansed of that guilt and filth in which I came.
To tarry here
Is certain death, I know no farther fear,
I can but die.
Lord! I'll adventure then, and try:
I have a thousand promises of thine,
That speak encouragement in every line:
And not one trembling instance that I know
Wherein Thou hast said no.
However, be it as it will,
I'll perish crying to Thee still,
And though an unpassed gulf of sins appear,
Presumption's not so sinful as despair.
With all my guilt,
I'll fly unto the blood that Thou hast spilt,
Though no assurance does appear,
My all I'll hazard there.
And with the latest words I can express,
Thy justice, and thy goodness too, confess.

—*Daniel Defoe, 1660–1731*

# A Prayer against Pride

O Lord God, let not pride surmount and overcome my heart. Neither let mine eyes be fiercely elevated and puffed up. Let me attribute nothing to myself, neither purchase or seek for hid secrets contrary to Jesus Christ our Head.

But O good God, let all my will and desire be to be wise, according to thy holy word and according to the grace which thou shalt give me. And if at anytime thou withdrawest from us the sweet milk of consolation, which proceedeth from the knowledge of thy Son Jesus Christ, yet grant us this grace, that we fall not into despair, O Lord, but let us evermore hope and trust in thee with a quiet and peaceable heart. So be it.

*—Possibly by Robert Waldegrave, ca. 1554–1604*

# For Transformation

Gracious God,
O let me behold thy adorable perfections,
till I am swallowed up in admiration
and transformed into the same image.
O fill me as full as this clay vessel can hold,
and when it can hold no more,
Lord, let it break,
that my soul may wing away
as a bird out of its cage,
awake in thy likeness
and be satisfied.

*—Sarah Osborn, 1714–1796; alt.*

## Intercession

Look, Lord, upon the fatherless, the widow, the oppressed and
distressed. Give them comfort. Fill their hungry bellies. Clothe their
naked backs. Comfort their comfortless souls. Heal the wounded and
sick. Strengthen the weak. Ease the oppressed, and deliver all that be in
danger. Assist them with thy divine providence for the salvation of
their sinful souls, and have mercy upon them all.

Receive us, ours, and all about us, into thy protection, tuition
and government, that we may this day and forever hereafter, walk in
thy laws, study thy statutes, obey thine ordinances, always meditate on
thy precepts, live in thy fear and die in thy favor, and rest in everlasting
happiness in thy kingdom of glory, which hasten, Lord, we beseech
thee, and grant in the prayer thou hast taught us: Our Father . . .

—*Michael Sparke (compiler)*, Crumms of Comfort: The Second Part, *1652; alt.*

## Intercession

Increase, O God, in those who stumble amid chaos, assurance that
Thou rulest over all; and, unto them whom pain and darkness
compass, mercifully reveal that through all things Thy holy will is
wrought; until Thou shalt be found of all, in all; and all shall praise
Thy Name; through Jesus Christ our Lord. Amen.

—*John U. Stephens, 1901–1984*

## For the Day's Work

Lord God, give me light sufficient to instruct me, and strength
sufficient to enable me to put my good resolutions into practice.
O thou Father of all mercy, thou God of all grace, forgive all my sins,
and grant me all that assistance which shall be requisite for me in
every situation.

—*Anonymous, an eighteenth-century Englishwoman; alt.*

### Evening Prayer

30

O Gracious God, whose thoughts are turned to us with such infinite pity and love, help us to draw near to thee with true humility and trust.

At the close of this day we thank thee for thine unwearied care over us when we were all unheeding, or occupied with our daily duties, trials, and pleasures. As the days pass may we realize more and more the blessing that the feeling of thy presence gives, and long to share with thee every toiling, tempted, or joyful hour of our daily lives.

O loving Father, remember that we are dust, and frail as the flowers: touch our hearts with the vastness of thine everlasting mercy, that our lives may be renewed, and we may be strengthened—each to live our common life to thy glory.

O Lord, we know that thy pure eyes have seen much in us to cause thee sorrow. We have turned from what was right, and chosen to follow our own foolish and sinful ways; but we pray thee to forgive us. We beseech thee in thy boundless mercy to remove our sins far from us. O thou great Conqueror and Deliverer, subdue the evil in us, that our lives may show forth more of thine own pure beauty, and bring peace and joy to those around us.

O thou patient and tender Friend, as we gather in thy presence tonight, like children round a mother's knee, we know not how to utter all our hearts' longings for those whom we love; but thou knowest, and we trustfully leave them in thy keeping. Whether in joy or sorrow, may each one find rest this night in thee, and rise refreshed when the new day begins. May thy merciful love brood over all our suffering sinful world, and hasten the coming of thy perfect Kingdom.

—*Presbyterian Church in Canada, 1919; alt.*

## For Serenity in Weakness

O Thou who dost open thine hand and satisfy the wants of every living thing, we come to thank thee that our wants have been so liberally supplied by thee this day. We began life as infants, and we carry with us the infant's weakness to the end. We shall never cease to need thy care.

Help us to see the goodness of God in imposing upon us the pain and anxiety of our wants, since these wants become the channels through which thy goodness, in the relief of them, perpetually flows down to us. Help us to glory in our infirmities, since through these we are made conscious that the power of Christ is resting upon us.

Make us willing to endure the earthly privation which introduces us to the fullness of grace which resides in thee; and through the poverty which forces us to ask all things from thee, may we learn that we are infinitely rich in having thee for our portion.

*—Joseph B. Stratton, 1815–1903; alt.*

## For Trust

May thy blessing, O Lord, be upon our persons, upon our labors, upon our substance, and upon all that belongs to us. In prosperity may we not forget thee, and in adversity may we still trust in thy wisdom, mercy, and love; knowing that whatever seeming evils befall us in this valley of tears, they shall all turn out to our advantage. And, whatever thou dost deny us, O withhold not that grace which bringeth salvation.

*—German Reformed Church in the USA, 1857*

## Intercession: For One's Family

O God, the Creator, Preserver, and final Judge of all flesh, bless every individual composing this family and dwelling in this house. Our situation, our character, our hopes and fears are all known to thee. Supply what every member wants. Help us to cultivate a spirit of affection towards each other. Remove every thing which may prevent our being helpers of each other's joy. May each of us receive the kingdom of God as a little child; may we bear with each other's infirmities, and admonish and comfort one another, and so much the more as we see the day approaching. Soon shall we be taken from each other's society and fellowship, and be removed into the eternal world. Help us to act and speak in reference to that period; and at last may we, who have received and enjoyed so many mercies together, obtain a kingdom which cannot be moved, and spend a blissful eternity together before thy throne.

—*George Smith, 1803–1870; alt.*

## 34   *At the Ending of the Day*

O Lord, we are thy poor and needy children; we are thy helpless little ones; and yet the Lord thinkest upon us. The world is hardly aware of our presence in it, and will not miss us when we are gone. But thou dost not overlook us, and thou hast our name in thy family-book. Though forgotten by others, we are not forgotten by our Father in heaven; and we are sure that he who feeds the fowls of the air and clothes the grass of the field will not and does not exclude us from his notice and care. Thine eye has been upon us and thy hand has upheld us through the day. Now spread thy wing, and grant us thy protection for the night. We entrust all our interests to thee—our home, our property, our bodies, the lives of all beneath our roof. We commit our chiefest treasure, our souls, into thy hands. Let thy covenant of peace be established with us. Let the peace which Christ gave to his disciples be breathed into our hearts. Let the excitements, the vexations, and the provocations which through the day disturbed our peace be all allayed. And in the perfect peace of those whose minds are stayed on thee, may we lie down upon our pillows.

—*Joseph B. Stratton, 1815–1903; alt.*

## Approach

I will not leave thee; bid me not be gone.
Repulse me not, for I will take no nay.
As thou dost live, I will pursue thee still,
Nor e'er let go my hold: I'm fixed on this,
To wrestle with thee till I gain the blessing.
I cannot be denied; thy word is past,
'Tis sealed, 'tis ratified; thou art obliged,
Engaged, confined by thy own clemency,
And spotless truth, to listen to my call.

—*Elizabeth Singer Rowe, 1674–1737*

## Confession

God of mercy and of grace,
you know the secrets of our hearts:
how blind we are to our own faults,
yet harsh in judging others;
how swift we are to take for gain,
yet slow to give for others;
how proud we are of our successes,
yet grudging in our praise of others.

Remember, Lord,
your tender care and love unfailing.
Do not remember our sins and offences,
but remember us in your goodness,
in accordance with your endless mercy;
through Jesus Christ our Lord.

—*Church of Scotland, 1994*

## *Prayer for Pardon*

We have sinned and done amiss, we confess our fault.
As justice is thine justly to correct,
so mercy is thine also to pardon and to help the miserable.
We, persuaded of thy goodness towards us in Jesus Christ,
do know that in love thou dost now chastise us as children.
Correct us, O Lord, but not in thy wrath.
Remember thy loving-kindness, and, in the riches of thy
great mercy, pardon and forgive all our sins through which
we have thus offended thee.
O Lord, blot them out of thy remembrance
by the blood of thy Son Jesus.
And let thy good Spirit now transform us from our old evils,
so that we commit them no more.
Rule us to grow in regeneration,
that this our mortal life may bring forth plentifully
those fruits of the Spirit which do please thee.
Turn thy loving countenance to us.
Pour forth thy grace upon us.
Build us up in Christ, and love us still.
In thy name, O Christ our Captain, we ask these things,
and pray unto thee, O Heavenly Father,
saying, Our Father. . . .
O Lord, increase our faith, whereof we make confession:
I believe in God. . . .

—*Robert Crowley, ca. 1518–1588; alt.*

## *Let Me Live to Serve*

Lord, let me live to serve and make a loan
    Of life and soul in love to my heart's own.
And what if they should never care or know
    How dark sometimes and weary are the ways,

How piercing cold and pitiless the snow,
How desolate and lonely are the days
Which life for me holds sometimes in reserve?
And what if those I love esteem above
Me, others all untried and far less true,
And lightly barter off my wealth of love
For careless, strange, and passing comrades new?
O Lord, those, whom I love, I still would serve.

—*George Marion McClellan, 1860–1934*

## For Readiness to Accept God's Will

O Lord, we would not boast of tomorrow, for we know not what a day may bring forth. We would not be lifted up unduly by external advantages which perish in the using, nor trust in anything beneath the skies. May we stand in an attitude of preparation for all thy will, be fitted for every form of trial through which we may be called to pass and endure as beholding thee who art invisible. If called to suffer may we be patient in tribulation, and rejoice that it is given to us on the behalf of Christ, not only to believe in him, but also to suffer for his sake. May we know him and the fellowship of his sufferings, and have the grace to drink the cup he drank, and to be baptized with the baptism wherewith he was baptized. We would be more than content to suffer in a world which was the scene of his unnumbered woes, nor would we expect to pass to a participation of his glory without sharing his reproach and bearing the cross after him. Imbue us with his spirit, and let the same mind be in us which was in Christ Jesus, so that as we are partakers of his sufferings, we may also share his consolation.

—*George Smith, 1803–1870; alt.*

## Intercession: For the Peace of the Church

O Lord Jesus Christ, you said to your apostles, "Peace I leave you; my peace I give you—not as the world gives do I give you." Therefore, my Lord, do not see my sin but the faith of your holy Christian church (which I believe, though I do not see); and according to your divine will, be pleased to keep it, unite it, and govern it, together with your Father and the Holy Spirit, for you live with them in eternity.

—*Johannes Oecolampadius, 1482–1531*

## *Act of Trust*

Lord, Thou art my fountain,
and I am resolved in thy strength,
that tho' thou grindest me to powder,
I will never leave thee.
I have worldly delights and contents enough,
but, O my Lord,
they will not do.

—*Cotton Mather, 1663–1728; alt.*

## *For the Day's Work*

Faithful God,
even when we fail to keep our promises,
you keep yours.
Give us strength and courage
to keep our commitments,
even when it means inconvenience or loss,
and help us to become faithful stewards
of all that you have entrusted to our care.
Through Jesus Christ. Amen.

—*In Soon Choi, b. 1934; alt.*

## Thanksgiving 43

Lord, whose goodness is infinite, and to whom we owe all the good
things we possess: we praise thee, we bless thee, we give thee thanks
for all the blessings both temporal and spiritual which thou hast
bestowed upon us. Without thee we should be nothing or what is
much worse, we should be most miserable. Thy hand has drawn us
out of nothing, and thy providence does preserve us. Thou nourishest
us with thy fruits; thou watchest for us when we sleep; thou supportest
us in our weaknesses; thou healest us of our sicknesses; and thou
providest liberally for all our wants. But we praise thee above all, O
God, for the inestimable favors which thou hast imparted to us in
thy gospel; for having given us thy Son to perform the work of our
redemption; for having given us the grace to know him and to believe
in him; for having vouchsafed to adopt us for thy children, and for
having reserved for us thy heavenly inheritance. For all these things
we offer to thee the sacrifice of our praises.

*—Church of Geneva, 1712*

## Confession 44

Most merciful and ever-blessed God, I stand in continual need of
mercy to overlook my numerous failings, and to pardon my repeated
offences. I have sometimes sinned through ignorance; I have more
frequently transgressed through carelessness and inattention. If at any
time I have offended through presumption, most gracious God, I
entreat thee, for thy mercy's sake in Jesus Christ, to overlook and
pardon these and all my other iniquities.

*—Anonymous, an eighteenth-century Englishwoman; alt.*

## For Repentance

O God, all-good and all-patient lover of humankind,
  even to the point that for their sake
  you did not spare your only Son,
  equal to you, indeed, one God with yourself:
how can it be
that these creatures
  who despise your goodness that calls them when they
     run away,
   your patience that remains when they rebel,
   your generosity that makes them sharers
    in your eternal joy,
    so great, so far beyond our
     understanding,
    even when they give themselves
    to what is less than nothing,
that these creatures should forget themselves,
even to the point of rejecting your goodness
and making mockery of your patience
and treading such a treasure underfoot?

Alas, yes, Lord, this is only too true;
and what is more,
those most guilty of this offence
are those whom you have most exalted.

But, O my God,
turn back my feet from these wrong paths
into which I wandered all too readily.
Since you have given me this longing for happiness,
show me the way to it,
and give me the will to follow it,
and strength to pursue it
until I attain it, for your honor and glory.

       —*Théodore de Bèze, 1519–1605*

## For Care of Our Neighbors

O God of patience and consolation, be merciful to our infirmities, and make us ever ready to consider the necessities of those around us; and when we are tempted by selfishness or pride, bestow thy grace, that we may with gentleness make allowance for the frailty of others; through Jesus Christ our Lord. Amen.

—*United Free Church of Scotland, 1907*

## Intercession: For the Sick and Those Who Care for Them

God almighty, grant that the remembrance of the sufferings of your Son, our Savior, may fill our hearts with love for all in distress.

Father of mercies, whose Son went from place to place doing good and healing all sorts of diseases, we beg you to continue among us your work of compassion, especially in hospitals, both general and psychiatric, and in all homes afflicted by suffering.

Encourage, heal, and sanctify the sick. Bless the efforts taken to relieve them. Give to physicians, surgeons, and nurses the wisdom, skill, and devotion that they need. We praise you, O God, for those whose thoughts are directed constantly to the good of others. We bless you for the cures you bestow.

O Lord, be mindful of those who suffer without hope of healing: the abnormal, invalids, the infirm, and especially those who are alone and neglected. Help them with your mighty aid, so that they may have the grace not to give in to bitterness or self-pity, not to despair, but to see their affliction transformed into joy through the knowledge of your eternal salvation.

Sanctify your church for which Jesus Christ gave himself up. It is in his name that we bring these prayers before you. Amen.

—*Reformed Church of Berne (Switzerland) 1955; alt.*

## *Commemoration of the Faithful Departed*

Eternal God,
we rejoice to know of all who, through the ages,
have placed their trust in you:
apostles, prophets, saints, and martyrs,
and all the humble believers
whose names are long forgotten.
Give us the assurance
that we belong to that great company
and that we too may find the peace
that passes understanding;
through Jesus Christ our Lord.

—*Uniting Church in Australia, 1988*

## *At the Ending of the Day*

Great peace have they who love thy law, and nothing shall offend
them. O Lord, heavenly King, let thy peace continually dwell in our
hearts, that we may not be afraid for the terror by night; through thee,
Christ, who reignest with the Father in the unity of the Holy Ghost,
world without end. Amen.

—*Scotland,* Daily Offices, *1893*

## *Trust in the All-Knowing God*

Were I the work of chance, did my destiny depend upon a blind necessity or causality, where could I find anchorage for my soul, where a solid, immovable foundation? But no. I am thy work, thy creature, Creator and Father of people, of all beings! The work of thy consummate wisdom and goodness! Even my destiny is ordered and directed by thee, who orderest and directest all things.

Thou knowest what is best and fitting for me and for each of thy creatures, knowest what I, what every one of us all can and should be and become, do and afford, bear and suffer. Thou alone knowest the way and the means which will infallibly lead us all to the perfection and happiness of which we are capable. For thou seest in the present the germ of the future, in the evil the source of the good, in the sowing the harvest.

Here I walk by faith and not by sight. Here I should confide in thee, even when I see nought before me, when I am all surrounded with darkness, and study to obey thee without reluctance.

Thou art father: I am child. Thou the wisest, mightiest, kindest father: I an ignorant, helpless child. Unconditionally and entirely I throw myself upon thee, and exult in the safety and repose I find in thy arms. Nothing however can ravish me from thy guardian care, thy providence, thy parental love! Neither tribulation, nor anguish, neither dangers nor afflictions, neither prosperity nor adversity, neither death nor the grave!

*—Georg J. Zollikofer, 1730–1788; alt.*

# *Confession*

O Gracious God and dear Savior, Jesus Christ: though I say I believe in thee, who wast conceived by the Holy Ghost, yet, alas! I do but babble this. For nothing is in me but unbelief. Of thy power and love, of thine anger and mercy, I have but an opinion, as my insensibleness and unthankfulness declare.

Thou hast suffered much for me: from heaven thou camest into earth to fetch me into heaven; but I, alas, regard it not.

Thou didst bear my sins on thy back, suffering a most bitter death; but I am so far from thankfulness, that I loath thee still more and more.

Thou wouldest enter into communion with me, taking my nature into thee, that I might enter into communion with thee, but I consider it not.

Thou didst die to deliver me from death, but I still more and more give thee cause to die, so ungrateful am I.

Thou didst rise to justify me, but I would still keep thee down, because I would not leave my wickedness.

Thou ascendest to heaven to take possession for me there, to be always in the sight of thy Father for me, to send me down gifts, and to pray for me; but I daily am pulling thee down again, as much as I am able. I am altogether earthly. I hide myself out of thy sight by forgetting thee. I reject and abuse thy gifts. I neglect prayer.

Thou art now in readiness to come to judge both the quick and dead, but I tremble not at this, nor beseech thee before thou comest to be merciful unto me, and not to enter into judgment with me. Yea, I think nothing at all of thy coming.

Save me, for thy great mercy's sake. Give me to believe in thee, in thy death, resurrection, and ascension. Pardon me my sins. Regenerate me daily more and more. Give me faith to ascend into heaven, and to be certain that thou hast already taken possession for me there.

—*John Bradford, 1510–1555; alt.*

## For the Grace to Be Just

Grant, Almighty God, that as thou art pleased to try our patience by requiring mutual justice and the offices of love and benevolence— O grant, that we may not be wolves one to another, but show ourselves to be really thy children, by observing all those duties of justice and kindness which thou commandest, and thus follow what is right and just through the whole course of our life, that we may at length enjoy that blessedness which is laid up for us in heaven, through Christ our Lord. Amen.

*—Jean Calvin, 1509–1564*

## For Freedom from Stubbornness

O God, the only protector and support of all your people, who govern your faithful as the flock of your pasture: hold out your generosity over us and so soften our hearts which by their nature are harder than stone, that we may never be hardened or made obstinate by unbelief against your holy word, that by true and living faith, we may serve you in such a manner that at last we may enter into your rest under the guidance of your dear Son Jesus Christ. Amen.

*—Augustin Marlorat, 1506–1562*

## Intercession: For Liberty

Lord, out of the deep we cry to you. The Tempter is at work to tear us away from you. Lord, help us not to betray our calling. In the confusion of voices of our time, let us not hear unmoved the voice of the Good Shepherd.

Merciful God, we pray to you for our brothers and sisters: free those who are enslaved from their bondage. Let the young people make good use of their powers and gifts. Protect the old from being narrow-minded and bitter. Give to the powerful and wealthy insight and will to serve their neighbors. Let all who earn their daily bread only with great difficulty receive justice. Protect us from all bondage to other people or the forces of history. Keep the church from being unfaithful to your Holy Spirit and from seeking its own ends.

Lord Jesus, you overcame temptation by obedience. In Gethsemane you endured the most severe of all temptations, and obtained the victory for us. We thank you for your powerful aid in the troubled hours of our Christian life. Let us seek the meaning of life in obedience to you and service to our brothers. Amen.

*—The Evangelical Reformed Churches in*
*German-speaking Switzerland, 1972*

55

## *Prayer for Completion*

Lord, deign to complete the work You have
begun in me; deign to bring it to its fullness.
Do not permit me to love You only halfway.
Cut off that which ought to be cut off.
Punish me if necessary, as a father punishes his child.
Correct me, humiliate me in Your love which wants
everything of me, so that I may be without flaw and
without concealment in Your hands,
without murmur or hesitation in my obedience,
whole-hearted and full of joy in my love.
Do not abandon the work of Your hands,
Eternal God.
Do not give up!

*—Michel Bouttier, b. 1921*

## Adoration

O Thou whom my soul desires to love,
where shall I find thee?
If I look to mount Tabor, I see thee in glory
      and I cannot but love thee for that.
If I look to the garden, I see thee lying on the cold ground,
sweating drops of blood for me,
      and I cannot but love thee for that.
If I look to Golgotha,
I see thee nailed to the cross and thy heart pierced,
that I may drink thy blood and live,
      and I cannot but love thee for that.
If I look to mount Olivet,
I see thee ascending far above all the heavens,
      and I cannot but love thee for that also.
In Tabor, thou hadst visible glory, but it soon vanished.
In the garden and Golgotha, thou hadst little visible beauty
      that I should desire thee.
And in Olivet, thou wast quite carried out of my sight.
If then thou liest for me nowhere else,
what hope have I to love thee,
O thou to be loved by all?
Art thou not in the tents of the shepherds?
Dost thou not dwell in the hearts of those of faith?
O let me see thee here below,
in the church, in myself.
Let thy glory go before me,
that I may love thee for ever and ever
and be blessed in thee.

*—John Preston, 1587–1628; alt.*

## Confession

O Lord, we would come to thee with the penitence of the prodigal son, confessing that we have sinned against heaven and in thy sight. Blessed be thy name! Thou givest freely of the bread of life to them that seek thy fullness, and thou bestowest a father's blessing on every returning wanderer.

Alas! We have wandered from thee. We have used the portion of goods which thou gavest us as though it belonged to us, forgetting that our life and breath and all things were given us by thee. Often we have lived as if we had no heavenly Father to thank for his goodness. We joined ourselves to the alien of a far country, but no one gave unto us that which would feed and nourish us. We sought food for our wants in earthly pleasures, but they were only as husks to our souls. And now we come back crying, "Why should we perish with hunger, when there is bread enough in our Father's house to spare?" Oh, we thank thee that we feel our wanderings and have been inclined to come back to thee.

O God, be merciful to all sinners. There is forgiveness with thee that thou mayest be feared. Amen.

*—James W. Weir, 1805–1878; alt.*

## Thanksgiving for Communion

O Blessed Lord, who, when about to suffer for our sins, didst institute the holy sacrament of thy body and blood, and didst command us to observe it for a perpetual memorial of thee until thy coming again; grant, we beseech thee, that neither thy great love nor last command may ever fade from our forgetful hearts; but that in all things following thee, and ever hasting unto thy coming, we may at the last be found of thee in peace; who livest and reignest with the Father and the Holy Ghost, ever one God, world without end. Amen.

*—Scotland,* Daily Offices, *1893*

My God, my Father, my Savior, my almighty Friend:
when shall I see thee in glory?
Thou art the delight of thy own infinite self,
and beholdest thy own infinite perfections
with infinite pleasure.
How then shall thy poor finite worm
be filled, ravished and transported
with the glorious vision!

Could I see no more of thee hereafter than now,
I would be content to struggle and fight
in this field of battle.

But to see God!
A glance of thy infinite perfections
has swallowed up my whole soul in longings
to behold with open face.

I cannot see thy face and live.
O then, let me die
to behold it.

*—Susanna Anthony, 1726–1791; alt.*

## *Intercession: For the Depressed or Doubtful*

60

Lord, enable those that fear thee but walk in darkness and have no
light to trust in the name of the Lord, and to stay themselves upon
their God. And at evening time let it be light.

O strengthen the weak hands, confirm the feeble knees, say to
them that are of a fearful heart, be strong, fear not. Answer them with
good words, and comfortable words, saying unto them "Be of good
cheer, it is I, be not afraid, I am your salvation." And make them to
hear the voice of joy and gladness, that broken bones may rejoice.

O renew a right spirit within them, cast them not away from thy presence, and take not thy Holy Spirit from them, but restore unto them the joy of thy salvation.

O bring them out of this horrible pit and this miry clay, and set their feet upon a rock, establishing their goings, and put a new song in their mouth, even praises to our God. O comfort them again now after the time that thou hast afflicted them. Though for a small moment thou hast forsaken them and hid thy face from them, yet gather them, and have mercy on them with everlasting kindness.

Lord, rebuke the tempter, even the accuser, and let poor tempted souls be as brands plucked out of the burning.

—Matthew Henry, 1662–1714; alt.

## 61      *At the Ending of the Day*

O thou who didst order the blood of a lamb to be sprinkled on the doorposts of the houses of Israel, so that no destruction might come near them, do thou be pleased to see our house this night sprinkled with the blood of Jesus Christ. Make the night to be light about us, so that no evil may oppress us. Send the blessed angels to watch over our dwelling. Give us all peaceful and refreshing sleep, and find us ready, through thy Holy Spirit, for the sudden moment when Jesus Christ shall come for us. Raise us in the morning in renewed health and strength, that we may on the morrow serve thee better than we have done today. We ask these and all our petitions for the merits of the sacrifice of thy Son, Jesus Christ, our Lord and only Savior. Amen.

—William F. Pitcairn, d. 1891; alt.

## *Prayer upon Waking*

62

O Eternal God, gracious from the beginning and merciful to the ending of the world: I give thee humble thanks that, according to thine abundant goodness, thou hast graciously defended me this night from all dangers that might have happened unto me. I beseech thee continue this thy favorable goodness toward me, and so grant me thy grace, that in all my thoughts, words, and actions I may seek thy glory, and evermore so live in thy fear, that I may die in thy favor, for thy Son, my only Savior's sake. Amen.

—*Elizabeth Joscelin, 1596–1622*

## *Drawing Near to Divine Goodness*

63

O Redeemer, shall I fear to draw near to your goodness, seeing that you have deigned to take upon yourself the very flesh that we bear? As God, nothing could touch you, nothing could bring you down to earth from high heaven, if you had not been pleased in love to come down. You have united divinity with our dust. Why? Who can understand it? It was a work which cost you dear. The heart must indeed be iron or rock which cannot be split or melted by love; for without seeming to disturb yourself, you allowed your whole body to be pierced, your feet and hands to be pierced, to accept death on the cross, your holy blood to be shed in streams, in order to mark our foreheads with the sign of the cross. Any that does not love you in return deserves rebuke, and to be deprived of all your benefits.

—*Marguerite of Navarre, 1492–1549*

## For Deliverance from the Adversary

Lord Jesus, redeem me from the power of Satan, for thou only canst, and thou knowest that when I am enabled to be, in any measure serious, I desire to rest on thee for all I want and wish for. What is the fruit of sin but anguish of soul, cuttings of conscience, pain, and grief! Lord, support me under my burden, and put thy precious yoke upon my neck. Defend me against the frailty of my nature and against every temptation. Let me not be torn with Satan's suggestions, but grant me peace of conscience, increase of grace, and perseverance in the way of duty. O King, in the midst of my unworthiness, what reason have I to love and fear and adore thy boundless mercy! Let thy own works praise thee, for I cannot, till renewed by thy power.

—*Frances Cunningham, 1743–1811*

## I Have Chosen the One Thing Needful

O my Savior,
thou hast bid me be of good cheer,
since thou hast overcome the world.
Lord, stand by and strengthen me
and then I will be of good cheer,
for I know with thee all things are possible.
I am weakness, thou art strength.
O let me daily see thee by an eye of faith
and clasp thee in the arms of faith,
and all shall be well.
I will not fear either earth or hell.
O manifest thyself to me,
as thou dost not to the world.
O let me enjoy thee my life, my light, my love.
Let me lie on thy breast or lie at thy feet continually.
O, by thy grace, I have chosen the one thing needful,
that better part.
Let it never be taken from me.

—*Sarah Osborn, 1714–1796; alt.*

O Sovereign God, through Jesus Christ your Son you have humbled yourself in order to exalt us. You became poor to make us rich. You suffered and died, and in so doing you gave us freedom and life. And this eternal mercy and goodness displays your might and majesty as our Creator and Lord, the glory in which we praise you and in the light of which we may live all the days you give to us. For this we thank you.

And in thanking you, we can come to you aright. We are able to spread out before you all that to our understanding seems hard and perplexing and in need of your care. In your mercy remember us all and be merciful to us, now and forever, for without you we can do nothing.

Have mercy on our church on earth in its divisions and dispersion, its weakness and error.

Have mercy on the old and young, on unbelievers far and near, on the godless and the idolators who have not, or have not yet, heard your name in truth. Have mercy on the governments and the peoples of this earth, on their perplexity as they search for peace and righteousness, and also on the confusion in our human endeavors in science, nurture, and education, and on all the difficulties in so many marriages and families.

Have mercy on the countless persons who today suffer starvation, the many who are persecuted and homeless, the sick in body and soul here and in other places, the lonely, prisoners, and all those who suffer punishment at the hands of others.

Have mercy on us all in the hour of trial and the hour of death. Lord, because we believe with certainty that you have overcome, and that with you we too have already overcome, we call upon you now. Show us but the first step of the road to freedom, won at such cost. Amen.

—*Karl Barth, 1886–1968*

## *For the Day's Work*

O Lord,
make me a real servant of thine,
and keep Satan from tempting me to sin;
for thou art my God,
and I am thy servant
solemnly sworn to thee.
O put some work of thine in mine hand
to do for thee in my day and generation.
Lord, help me to perform everything
in the strength of Jesus Christ.
Amen.

> —*Elisabeth West, fl. 1675–1707; alt.*

## Homecoming

O Lord, thou hast called us out of the troublesome disquietness of
the world, into thy quiet rest and peace which the world cannot give,
being a peace as passeth all understanding. Houses are ordained for us,
that we might get away from the injury of weather, from the cruelty of
beasts, from disquietness of people, and from the toils of the world. O
gracious Father, grant that through thy great mercy my body may enter
into this house from outward actions, and may become willing and
obedient to the soul and make no resistance against it; that in soul and
body I may have a godly quietness, and peace to praise thee. Amen.
Peace be to this house, and to all that dwell in the same.

*—John Bradford, 1510–1555; alt.*

## Prayer upon the Passion and Death of Our Lord Jesus Christ

O Merciful Savior, who hast taken our mortal nature that thou
mightest offer it up as a sacrifice to God, vouchsafe me thine
assistance, and an increase of my faith and hope. I embrace thy
cross and passion as mine only relief. I take hold of the horns of this
altar and claim an interest in thy suffering and righteousness. How
grievous were thy torments, O blessed Redeemer, which made thee
sweat drops of blood, required the comfort of angels, and drew from
thee strong crying and tears. Thy death was an atonement for the
sins of the whole world. Thou sufferedst the heavy strokes of God's
wrath, and tookest upon thee the load of our sins. O wonderful
Savior! Thou hast spoiled principalities and powers, showing them
openly, and triumphing over them on the cross.

How marvelous are thy works. Thy violent sufferings are
preventions of my torments. Thy bruises and wounds are my safety
and cure. Thy fears comfort and settle my mind. Thy distressed soul
fills mine full of joy. Thy crying appeases the troubles of my

conscience, and thy drops of blood wash away my tears. Thy bitterness is my sweetness, and thy death my victory, and thy cross my triumph. I shall no longer tremble at the approaches of death since thou hast purchased for me life and immortality, and the kingdom of heaven is thine by a two-fold right, as thou art the Son of God, and heir of all things; and as thou hast paid for it a valuable price, by thine infinite merits.

My hope is in thee, O blessed Lord! By thine own death thou hast conquered death; and by entering into its dark prison, hast given to death its mortal wound. Thy cross, therefore, to me is as Jacob's ladder, where at the bottom I may sleep secure from sin and the fears of the grave, and by it ascend up to the throne of grace, to obtain mercy and help in time of need. It is the source of sweetness, comfort, and joy.

*—Charles Drelincourt, 1595–1669; alt.*

70

## *Thy Will Be Done*

Frame our hearts, good Lord, with such humble obedience to thy holy will, that we may be heartily well content with whatsoever it pleaseth thy goodness to lay upon us, that we may never cease, even in our miseries, to continually call upon thee by hearty prayers. Although we feel no release at all, yet still patiently may we abide and quietly wait for thy good leisure and appointed time of deliverance, when thou knowest it shall be most expedient for us.

*—Edward Dering, ca. 1540–1576*

## Intercession: For the Homeless

Foxes have holes and birds have nests: but you, Lord, did not know
where you would be able to lay your head. You know then the plight
of the homeless. Be their home and their support, and send them
understanding people and just governments, who will enable them
to have food and housing, as justice requires.

*—The Evangelical Reformed Churches
in German-speaking Switzerland, 1972*


## Intercession

O God, who art thyself afflicted in all the afflictions of thy people: hear
the prayers of those who cry to thee in their trouble, and deliver them
out of all their distresses. Heal the sick; comfort the sad, relieve the
needy; and receive the souls of the dying. Let thy strength be given to
all who endure temptation; forgive the sins of those who are penitent;
and in thy great mercy grant us all, when our days on earth are done,
to live with Christ in Paradise.

*—James M. Todd, 1912–1977*


## To See God's Glory

God of life and glory,
you have given us a share
in the inheritance of the saints in light.
They surround our steps as we journey on
towards the splendour of the eternal city.
Open our eyes to see the radiance of your glory;
and bring us to rejoice with them
in your everlasting kingdom,
where there is no dark nor dazzling

but one equal light;
and where in light undimmed, unending,
you are worshipped and adored,
Father, Son, and Holy Spirit,
one God, now and ever.

*—Church of Scotland, 1994*

## *At the Ending of the Day*

O Lord, we beseech thee, let all things work for the best to us that desire truly to love thee. Continue thy favor and goodness unto us this night, that we, taking our natural rest and quietness may through thy protection be defended from all immoderate sleep, fearful dreams, outward violence of our enemies, and all imminent danger. Touch our hearts with a desire and longing after heavenly things, that whensoever it shall please thee to call for us, we may be willing to come unto thee as children to their Father, strangers unto their country, and members of the body unto the head. Grant us, O Lord, these and all other things needful and meet for us, for Jesus Christ's sake, our only Savior and Redeemer. Amen.

*—Thomas Sorocold, 1561–1617*

## Approach 75

Lord, thou hast bid me knock and it shall be opened,
ask, and ye shall receive,
seek, and ye shall find.
Lord, I knock. Open unto me.
Lord, I would be in, I must be in.
Let me but in over the threshold.
Let me in within sight of my Redeemer's face,
within sight of the smiles of his countenance.
Let me within hearing of the songs of the redeemed.
Let me get to the outside of that praising company.
I will be well enough if I get in.
Lord, in I must be.
Out I cannot stay.

*—John Willison, 1680–1750; alt.*

## Adoration 76

O God, when I cease to love and praise thee
  let me cease to breathe and live.
When I forget thee,
  let me forget the name of happiness
  and let every pleasing idea be erased from my memory.
When thou art not my supreme delight,
  let all things else deceive me
  let me grow unacquainted with peace
  and seek repose in vain,
  let delusions mock my gayest hopes
  let my desires find no satisfaction
    till they are terminated all in thee.

When I forget the satisfaction of thy love, O my God!
     let pleasure be a stranger to my soul.
When I prefer not that to my chiefest joy,
     let me be insensible of all delight.
When thy goodness is not dearer to me than life,
     let that life become my burden and my pain.
         —*Elizabeth Singer Rowe, 1674–1737; alt.*

## Confession

I confess this day before thee, my God,
that I have broken all my resolutions,
that I have not been faithful to my vows,
but have transgressed times and ways without number.
I have too often poured my complaint into the creature's ear,
and have not often enough nor conscientiously enough
prayed to my heavenly Father.
I have not listened to the voice of my Redeemer.
Oh, may I hear thy voice saying,
"Turn, thou backsliding daughter, for I am married to you!"
Betroth me to thyself in an everlasting covenant.
Suffer me never again to cherish an evil heart of unbelief
in departing from the living God.

I desire to take a fresh hold of my covenant,
ordered in all things and sure,
for myself, my children, my children's children.
Oh grant that we may all be guided here by thy counsel
and hereafter received to thy glory.

Bless and reward all my friends,
pardon my enemies
and enable me to forgive them
and cherish no bitterness against them;
but may my prayer still be for them in their calamities.

I leave me upon thee.
Do what seemeth to thee good with me,
only take not thy Holy Spirit from me,
but hold me up continually by thy right hand.
To God my Father and Husband, to God my crucified
and risen Savior,
and to God the Holy Spirit,
who comforteth me in all my afflictions,
be glory forever and ever. Amen.

*—Joanna Bethune, 1770–1860; alt.*

## *For Constancy* 78

Grant, Almighty God, that as thou hast once given us such an evidence
of thy infinite power in thy servant Jonah, whose mind, when he was
almost sunk down into hell, thou hadst yet raised up to thyself, and
hadst so supported with firm constancy, that he ceased not to pray and
to call on thee—O grant, that in the trials by which we must be daily
exercised, we may raise upwards our minds to thee, and never cease
to think that thou art near us; and that when the signs of thy wrath
appear, and when our sins thrust themselves before our eyes, to drive
us to despair, may we still constantly struggle, and never surrender the
hope of thy mercy, until, having finished all our contests, we may at
length freely and fully give thanks to thee and praise thy infinite
goodness, such as we daily experience, that being conducted through
continual trials, we may at last come into that blessed rest which is laid
up for us in heaven, through Christ our Lord. Amen.

*—Jean Calvin, 1509–1564*

## Intercession: For the Freedom of the World

Sovereign of worlds! display thy power.
Be this thy Zion's favored hour;
Bid the bright morning star arise,
And point the captive to the skies.

Set up thy throne where Satan reigns,
In western wilds and southern plains;
Far let the gospel's sound be known;
Make thou the universe thy own.

Speak! and the world shall hear thy voice.
Speak! and the desert shall rejoice.
Scatter the gloom of captive night,
Bid every people hail the light.

—*Edwin F. Hatfield, ed.,* Freedom's Lyre, *1840*

## For Trust through the Day

O God, prepare my mind, by holy trust and fortitude, for whatever
night or day may bring forth from all unknown events, yet in the
womb of time. Let them not tempt me to forsake thee, or think ill
of thy service, since they will all be in righteousness, in wisdom, and
in love.

—*Samuel Bourn, 1689–1754; alt.*

## Seeking after an Absent God

81

Why dost thou withdraw thyself and suffer me to pursue thee in vain? If I am surrounded with thy immensity, why am I thus insensible of thee? Why do I not find thee, if thou art everywhere present? I seek thee in the temple where thou hast often met me, there I have seen the traces of thy majesty and beauty, but those sacred visions bless my sight no more. I seek thee in my secret retirements, where I have called upon thy name and have often heard the whispers of thy voice, but I am solaced no more. I listen, but I hear those gentle sounds no more.

Where thou art present, heaven and happiness ensue; hell and damnation fill the breast where thou art absent. While God withdraws, I am encompassed with darkness and despair; the sun and stars shine with an uncomfortable lustre; the faces of my friends grow tiresome; the smile of angels would fail to cheer my languishing spirit. I grow now unacquainted with tranquillity; peace and joy are empty sounds to me, and words without a meaning.

Tell me not of glory and pleasure, there are no such things without my God. While he withdraws, what delight can these trifles afford? All nature cannot repair my loss; heaven and earth would offer their treasures in vain; not all the kingdoms of this world, nor the thrones of archangels, could give me a recompense for an absent God.

O thou who art my boundless treasure, my infinite delight, my all, my ineffable portion, can I part with thee? I may see without light and breathe without air, sooner than be blessed without my God.

I feel an emptiness which nothing but infinite love could fill. I must find thee, or weary myself in an eternal pursuit. Nothing shall divert me in the endless search, no obstacle shall fright me back, no allurement withhold me, nothing shall flatter or relieve my impatience. My bliss, my heaven, my all, depends on the success. Show me where thou art. O my God, conduct me into thy presence, and let thy love confine me there for ever.

—*Elizabeth Singer Rowe, 1674–1737; alt.*

# *Confession*

Merciful Father, at the moment when I come to confess my sins, I wish to remember your most precious gifts. Help me by your Spirit to discover my acts of refusal, so that you may free me from them.

Confronted by the commandments of your holiness, I confess that I have disobeyed your orders, and so have failed my companions in my family, at my work, in the life of my country, and of my church.

Confronted by the prayer which Jesus taught me, I confess that I have not responded with sufficient faith to his demands, and I see how often I have lived in defeat, on the very threshold of your victory.

Confronted by my baptism, I confess that I have not claimed for myself your promises each day and that I have not been a faithful witness.

Confronted by the bread and cup of the Lord's Supper, I confess that I have often remained without love to you, as if it meant nothing to my heart that your Son died and rose again for me.

Confronted by Jesus Christ, I confess that I have often remained distracted or indifferent, full of my own cares and daydreams, neglectful of your service and of the love of my neighbor.

Almighty Father, you that show me my ingratitude, give me the assurance and renewed comfort of forgiveness; cause me to live out more fully all the gifts of your grace. I ask this in the name of Jesus Christ, in whom we have all things abundantly. Amen.

—*Reformed Church in France, 1963*

O Lord, I would have never have loved thee, if thou hadst not loved me first. I would not have desired after thee, if thou hadst not kindled these desires. It cannot be that thy grace itself should be a deceit and misery and intended but to tantalize us, and that thou set thy servants' souls on longing for that which thou wilt never give them. Thou wouldst not have given me the wedding garment when thou didst invite me if thou hadst meant to keep me out. Even the grain of mustard seed which thou sowedst in my heart was a kind of promise of the happiness to which it tendeth. I have loved thee so little that I am ashamed of myself, and confess my cold indifference deserves thy wrath. But that I love thee and desire thee is thy gift. Though I am cold and dull, my eyes are towards thee. It is thee that I mean when I can but groan. O perfect what thou hast begun. And though my life be now hid with thee in God, when thou appearest, let me appear with thee in glory, and in the meantime, let this soul enjoy its part. Give me what thou hast caused me to love, and then I shall more perfectly love thee, when my thirst is satisfied, and the water which thou hast given me shall spring up to everlasting life.

*—Richard Baxter, 1615–1691; alt.*

## Intercession: For the Life of the Spirit in the Church     84

Lord, we thank you for the reality of the church which is your Body, and we bless you for the mysterious calling which has made us members of it.

Grant that we may bear the fruits of the Spirit: joy, peace, love, patience—so that your church, by its holiness, may reveal your presence to the world. Give to it servants who will fulfill your work of salvation.

You that have promised to aid your church by your Spirit, lift it from its sleep, lead it through all dangers, preserve it from all compromise, guard it against all disloyalty.

Make its witness potent like that of the apostles on the day of the first Pentecost. Inspire its preaching. Make it humble and ready to serve, faithful in obedience, unshakable in faith. Throughout the whole earth may your church drive back the power of darkness and cause the light of the gospel to shine forth!

We ask this of you, Lord, for you reign with the Holy Spirit in the glory of God the Father.

Our Father . . .

*—Reformed Church of France, 1963*

85

## *At the Ending of the Day*

In thy merciful protection, O God, we humbly commit ourselves, our dear friends and relations this night. The darkness is no darkness with thee, but the night is as clear as the day. Defend, we beseech thee, our persons, our dwellings, and our possessions. Refresh us with sweet sleep. With the health and strength of our bodies and the vigor of our minds let us serve thee all our days till through the gate of death we enter into that blessed kingdom where is no night, where we all receive the end of our faith, even the salvation of our souls; through Jesus Christ we pray. Amen.

*—Scotland,* A Prayer Book for Families and
other Private Persons, *1850?; alt.*

*Prayers from the Reformed Tradition*

## Praise

O Lord, if our eyes be so tender and weak that they be not able to bear the light of the sun, how can we, alas, behold thee, if thou hadst not declared thyself in thy Son, which is the eternal word and brightness of thy glory?

Thy Son, our Lord, is our life and our resurrection. This is the hope and trust of the afflicted. This is our light in our darkness. This is the dew of our thirsty souls. This is he that doth strengthen us in our weaknesses, and that healeth our wounds. We are sinners, but our sin is not so great and mighty as his mercy. We be wanderers in this world, but he is our Shepherd, and we do wait upon him with a most earnest desire that our bodies may be like unto his glorious body, and that we may, O mighty God, behold thy face.

—*Daniel Toussaint, 1541–1603; alt.*

## Upon Entering Church

O Lord, I have loved the habitation of thy house, and the place where thy honor dwelleth. One thing therefore have I desired of thee that I will require: even that I may dwell in thy house all the days of my life, to behold thy beauty and to visit thy temple. Therefore will I offer in thy tabernacle sacrifices of joy, I will sing and praise the Lord. Hearken unto my voice, O Lord, when I cry; have mercy also upon me and hear me. Doubtless, kindness and mercy shall follow me all the days of my life, and I shall remain a long season in the house of the Lord.

—*Lewis Bayly, 1565–1631*

# *Confession*

Supreme and Sovereign God, we join our prayers to beseech your mercy that we may be cleansed, washed, and purged of our wickedness, misdoings, and crimes. We acknowledge and confess that we have hitherto acted in a depraved manner in your sight, but our sins will never be able to make you act unjustly or to return wrong for wrong. We understand, if we are honest, that we do not deserve your granting the wonderful and most generous things that you have promised. Our need, then, is that your faithfulness and constancy should come quickly to our aid. You see that from the moment of our birth, we came forth into the light corrupt and spoiled, for we had already been conceived in sin. Cleanse our spirits, therefore, and in your goodness adorn them with the beauty that is acceptable to you.

Give us a pure heart, an upright, holy and devoted spirit so that we may not be driven from your presence as ungodly persons, but restored to true joys and lasting happiness. If you free us from the sins which threaten us with the bonds of eternal death, our lips will swiftly be opened to praise you.

Grant, we pray, that we approach you with the only sacrifice in which you take pleasure, that of a broken spirit, of a sorrowful and contrite heart. Cause our present troubles to diminish, and it will be with no ungrateful praises that we shall celebrate you.

Declare your goodness to Zion, that is, the church. You see in the midst of what perils she makes her way. She is oppressed from without and from within. We pray that you would not only keep her from outward foes but would also reform and re-establish her, so that she may no longer be unworthy of you, her bridegroom; through Jesus Christ our Lord. Amen.

—*Peter Martyr Vermigli, 1499–1562*

## Prayer for Pardon

Lord, without thy pardon of our sins we cannot rest satisfied. Without the renovation of our natures by thy grace, our souls can never rest easy. Without the hopes of heaven we can never be at peace, and in these respects will never let thee go till thou bless us. For Zion's sake we will not hold our peace, and for the sake of thy Jerusalem, thy glory, thy church in the world, we will give thee no rest till thou hast made her the joy of the earth.

—*Isaac Watts, 1674–1748*

## For Sabbath Rest

Almighty and everlasting God, Creator of all things, who didst rest from all thy works on the seventh day, grant unto us in the time of this mortal life, the rest and sabbath of the soul, in obeying and following him whose yoke is easy and his burden light; that afterwards, when the works of sin and the labors of vanity are ended, and this transitory world is passed away, we may be made partakers of thy glorious promises and enjoy for ever thy heavenly rest, through Christ our Lord.

—*Robert Lee, 1804–1868*

## Intercession: To Preserve the Fruits of the Earth

O Lord, seeing that thou alone art the Creator and Maker of all things, and hast prepared herbs, seeds, fruits, fish, and flesh to be food for humankind; seeing also that without thy blessing all these thy creatures prosper not but grow out of kind, wither away, perish, die, and come to nought; we most humbly beseech thee to bless us and all the fruits of the earth, with all other creatures which thou hast made for our use and profit.

And forasmuch as neither those that plant nor those that water are anything, but thou, O God, givest the increase, grant, we pray thee, that the earth may give forth her fruit prosperously and plenteously, that we may enjoy the same in due and convenient time, unto our great joy and comfort.

—*Thomas Becon, 1512–1567; alt.*

## *For Strength through the Day*

Great Bunji* God,
you sent your Son Jesus
to be our Saviour, our Guide and our Friend.
At the dawn of this new day
we pray for strength to follow him in his steps,
and to be true witnesses for him
among our people who love the great earth mother,
your gift to them from the dreamtime.
We pray for all people of all countries,
that they may become one great family
with Jesus as Saviour.
As we come to the evening of this day,
may we go to our rest in the quiet hours of the night
knowing that, in spite of our human weaknesses,
we have truly walked with Jesus.
This prayer we offer in the name of Jesus,
our Good Friend. Aralba.**

—*Lazarus Lamilami, 1910–1977*

---

*Bunji* = Aboriginal word for "Father."
**Aralba* = "I have spoken from my heart."

## Adoration

Thou only Good! Eternal All!
What am I when compared with Thee?
A piece of animated clay;
An atom sporting in the ray—
The loss would be but small,
Should I again to non-existence fall.
Nay, if thy glory might but rise,
Cheerful my being I'd resign,
And fall a willing sacrifice
To gain a purpose so divine,
So much more worthy than this little life of mine!

—*Samuel Davies, 1723–1761*

## Confession

O Almighty God, Creator of heaven and earth, in whom and through whom are all things: we confess against ourselves our own sins which are more in number than the hairs of our head. O Lord, we have sinned against heaven and against thee, and are unworthy of the name of thy children. We have rebelled by departing from thy precepts and commandments. We have not hearkened unto thy servants which spoke to us in thy name. We have not obeyed the voice of thee the Lord our God, to walk in thy laws which thou hast set before us. We have done those things that we should not have done. We have left undone those things that we should have done.

Impute not, O Lord, unto us the sins of our youth, neither receive a reckoning of us for the imaginations of our old age, for although, O Lord, that unto us there belong shame and confusion of face, yet to thee, O Lord, belong mercy and forgiveness.

O Lord, hear us. O Lord, forgive us. O Lord, hearken unto our prayers, and avert not thy loving face and countenance from us, for thy favor is better than life.

Fill us, O Lord, with thy mercies, that this day and all the days of our life we may rejoice in thee our God, ever praising thy blessed name. To thee, O Father, Son, and Holy Ghost, be honor, praise, and glory for now and ever. Amen.

—*Peter Howat, ca. 1567–1645; alt.*

95

## *For Strong Faith*

You established the human race, Almighty God, so that you might unite all peoples in the shared praises of your name, and so that this might come to pass, you appointed from of old patriarchs, prophets, and apostles for this task. And now that all things are spoiled by darkness, abuse, and corruptions, you have compelled us into your church for this same work. So that we may be able to carry it out suitably and as fittingly as possible, we pray that our wickednesses may not hinder us, and we beg you that our sins, which we admit to be grave and innumerable, may be done away with by you and forgotten. Now, as you see, we are so hemmed in by dangers, yet not crushed, that in you alone have we sought our only refuge. I ask you therefore to see to it that our faith may be burnished by your Spirit that it may not fail in the midst of these difficulties. Set before our eyes, we pray, your goodness that ever attends the godly, so that, fully and clear-sightedly acknowledging that goodness, we may not doubt that you will, even in our own time, be the church's faithful guardian, through Jesus Christ our Lord. Amen.

—*Peter Martyr Vermigli, 1499–1562*

96

## *For Assurance of God's Favor*

Lord, take this soul that pleads relation to thee. It is the voice of thy child that cryeth to thee. When thou didst call us out of the world unto thee, thou saidst, "I will receive you, and I will be a Father to you, and ye shall be my sons and daughters." O our Father which art in heaven, shut not out thy children, the children of thy love and promise. The compassion that thou hast put into us, engageth us to relieve a neighbor, yea, an enemy, much more to care for a child.

Canst thou exclude thine own and shut them out that cry unto thee? Can that love which washed me and took me home when I lay wallowing in my blood, reject me, when it hath so far recovered me? Can that love now thrust me out of heaven, that lately fetched me from the gates of hell, and placed me among thy saints? Whom thou lovest, thou lovest to the end. Receive me, Lord Jesus, a member of thy body: a weak one indeed, but yet a member who needeth more thy tenderness and compassion.

*—Richard Baxter, 1615–1691; alt.*

## *Intercession: For Families* 97

Holy God, in your wisdom you have created the bond of love between man and woman, between parents and children. In the sacred refuge of the home you have established a safe place for the most intimate personal relations and the well-founded common life. We thank you for this marvelous gift and we ask you for the grace to uphold the dignity and holiness of the marriage bond and of family life.

Grant that married people may guard their love with reverence, so that faithfulness in marriage may be kept irreproachable and holy, Lord we pray.

Grant that young people may grow up with a serious care for moral values and in that personal discipline which assures true liberty, Lord we pray.

That our people may give watchful care to the education of children and to the formation of those who teach them, Lord we pray.

That adults may respect and honor the purity and integrity of young people and adolescents, Lord we pray.

That the members of each household, husband and wife, parents and children, young and old, may never be causes of sin to one another, but, moved by a spirit of mutual help, may be for one another a witness to your power and goodness, Lord we pray.

Bless, Lord, all our homes and establish in them, by your grace, faith, hope, and love, so that their shining example may be a witness to your power and goodness, Lord we pray.

And that we may come at last to our true home with you our Father, through Jesus Christ, your only Son, our Savior. Amen.

—*Reformed Church of Berne (Switzerland) 1955*

## 98 *Thanksgiving for the Communion of Saints*

We bless thee for all those who have been enabled to approve themselves to God in much patience, in afflictions, in distresses, who, when they had been brought before governors and kings for Christ's sake, it has turned to them for a testimony, and God has given them a mouth and wisdom, which all their adversaries were not able to gainsay or resist; that those who for Christ's sake were killed all the day long, and accounted as sheep for the slaughter, yet in all these things we are more than conquerors, through him that loved us; that they overcame "the accuser of the brethren" by the blood of the Lamb, and by the word of the testimony, and not by the loving of their lives unto death.

We bless thee for the cloud of witnesses with which we are encompassed about, for the footsteps of the flock, for the elders that have obtained a good report and are now, through faith and patience, inheriting the promises. Lord, give us to follow them as they followed Christ.

—*Matthew Henry, 1662–1714*

## 99 *At the Ending of the Day*

O Thou Guardian of Israel, who neither slumberest nor sleepest: keep far from this dwelling, and from all who reside in it, all dangers and terrors during the silent and defenseless hours of rest, and cause us all to awake in the morning in health and strength, refreshed with the comfortable repose of this night, and qualified to engage in those duties which may lie before each of us on the ensuing day.

—*Anonymous, an eighteenth-century Englishwoman*

*Prayers from the Reformed Tradition*

## Approach

Most glorious and ever blessed Lord God of hosts, I thine unworthy creature, desire this day to draw near to thee. I desire to give myself up to thee for time and eternity, having no hope of salvation, but only and wholly through the blessed Lord Jesus, my covenanted God and King, God of gods, Lord of lords, God equal with the Father. It is on thee and thee alone I depend for my access to God, my head and surety. Draw me with the cords of thine unbounded love; grant me a token for good. Say unto me, "I have loved thee with an everlasting love; yea, with loving-kindness have I drawn thee."

*—Frances Cunningham, 1743–1811*

## Thanksgiving: I Have Been Drawn by Thee

My God, I have been drawn by thee.
Thou hast known me from my mother's womb
with a merciful and powerful knowledge.
Thou didst call me by name.
Thou didst open mine ear, and I have been attentive.
I have shown forth thy praise in the congregation.
Thy word hath been more sweet in my mouth than honey.
What am I, O Lord! dust and ashes, an earthen vessel,
and yet thou hast been pleased to put into this vessel
an immortal food.
Thou livest, O Lord, and thou quickenest me.
Thou didst choose me before thou gavest me a being.
Thou gavest me to be born of faithful parents.
I am thy servant, O Lord,
thou hast instructed me from my youth;
I have shown forth thy wonders and mercies.

Thy gifts have not been fruitless in me.
Thou dost work by weak instruments.
Thou hast forgiven me; Thou hast strengthened me.
Thou hast accepted the uprightness and sincerity of my heart.
Lord, I give thee my heart;
it is all thou requirest.
Accept this offering.
Receive this gift.

*—André Rivet, ca. 1573–1651; alt.*

## *Confession*

Lord, holy and righteous God, before you we confess that we do not fear or love you above all. We do not find our pleasure in prayer; we spurn your word. We lack joy in your service. We do not have the liberty that belongs to your children. Through our carelessness we fritter away the time that you give us.

We do not truly love our neighbor. We are too interested in ourselves. We are not always in a good temper. We are vain and touchy. We lack a sense of responsibility for our work and a spirit of solidarity. We allow ourselves to benefit from the misfortunes of others. In money matters we are ungenerous. Our hearts are divided and ravaged by guilty doubts and desires.

Before you, O God, we accuse ourselves of this half-heartedness. Come to our help, we beg you. Fill us with the love of Jesus, so that we may forget ourselves and love and serve you whole-heartedly. Amen.

*—Reformed Church of France, 1963*

## To the Holy Spirit, for Grace and Love

True Illuminator of the darkness, Gentle Paraclete: I address this to you. You are the guide of the straying, guard and protector against all dangers, for you deliver our spirit from sorrow and keep it from being oppressed by sin by lifting it out of conflict. For you are the destroyer of vice and the complete restorer of virtues, so much so that you heal even a dead soul if it turns to you. O Life-giver, behold the state my heart is in—parched, dry, without grace or liveliness. Since charity is the mistress of all good gifts, and you the giver, love makes me ask unceasingly for grace and love, and I have no fear that they will be refused.

*—Marguerite of Navarre, 1492–1549*

## For Guidance and Strength

Thy mercies, Lord, are above all thy works; faithful art thou in all thy promises, and just in all thy doings. Be a merciful Father unto us for Christ Jesus thy Son's sake. Govern our ways for we are weak; strengthen us for we are frail; refresh us for we are famished; and plentifully bestow thy good gifts upon us. Defend us from the snares of Satan, our old enemy, that he tempt us not out of the right way, but that we be evermore ready to praise and glorify thy holy Name, through Jesus Christ. So be it.

*—Scottish Psalter, 1595*

## Intercession: For All Who Suffer

Have compassion, we pray thee, upon all those whose hearts are touched with sorrow, whose spirits are troubled or cast down within them. O Lord, remember those to whom the burdens of this life bring dimness or darkness of soul. Send them help from above, and have mercy upon all who suffer in body or mind, from whatever cause. O Lord, have mercy upon them continually.

*—Scotland, Home Prayers, 1879*

## For the Day's Work

Lord, we present ourselves to thee as a living sacrifice. We devote to thee our bodies, our souls, our life, our labor, all that is in us, and all that depends upon us, desiring to employ all to thy glory. O Lord, we submit ourselves to all the events that it shall please thee to bring upon us. Do unto us all that thou shalt think fit to do, and let thy holy will be accomplished in us and by us, for the sake of Jesus Christ our Savior. Amen.

*—Church of Neuchâtel, Switzerland, 1712*

## *Adoration*

O Thou love of all loves:
thou lovedst me before I was,
thou dost love me when I am,
thou dost love me, if I be thine, when I am here no more.
Thou lovest me who deserve less than nothing;
I love not thee who deservest more than all things.
I have hid myself from thee as Adam,
>> yet thou hast pierced through the dark cloud and loved
>> me.
Thou hast opened thyself in the face of my soul,
>> yet in the sight of this Sun I have not loved thee.
How can I be acceptable to thee, my love, my dove, my
>> undefiled?
Thou spreadest out thy hands and art ready for blessing me,
>> but if I open my head, heart, hand,
>> I am apt to receive nothing but anathema from thee.
Can love come to enmity, heaven to hell?
I am hell, my Lord, thou art heaven.
I am hatred, thou art love.
Can I then expect to have the blessing of love
>> or to avoid the curse of not loving?
O show me thy face, for it is comely.
Thou hast often showed me thy riches,
>> and I have loved them,
but, oh, show me thyself, that I may love thee.

*—John Preston, 1587–1628; alt.*

## *Complaint*

Oh, God,
Thou who created us,
we complain to Thee of evil!
Evil continually follows after us;
the feet of the evil things are swift to pursue us.
But we ask Thee, was evil the firstborn
    that he should govern us?
 Good was the firstborn!
 And we beg of Thee who created us
    that Thou will give us good to rule over us!

                —*Ze Tembe, fl. 1915; alt.*

## *To Find One's Life in Grace*

O Lord, who has taught us that to gain the whole world and to lose our souls is great folly, grant us the grace so to lose ourselves that we may truly find ourselves anew in the life of grace, and so to forget ourselves that we may be remembered in your kingdom.

                —*Reinhold Niebuhr, 1892–1971*

## *To Rest in God Alone*

O God, thou fountain of being and blessedness
in whom I live, move, and have my being,
from whom I receive every mercy:
without thy favor I am undone.
Without thy loving-kindness through Christ,
my very being is a burden and terror to me.

I enjoy myself only in the enjoyment of thee
and cannot look on myself or any of my enjoyments
with delight, pleasure, or satisfaction
but in relation to thee.

Lord, may I not appeal to thee who art truth itself
that I have and do abandon all delights and enjoyments
        on earth for thy favor;
that I can and do rest satisfied in thee alone?

Witness my resolute discontent with all things here below.
Witness my entire satisfaction and rest in thy favor through
        Christ.
Lord, let nothing delight me without thee.
I know no other good but thee,
and wilt have no other rest or delight but God in Christ,
        as the centre of my soul.

*—Susanna Anthony, 1726–1791; alt.*

## *Intercession*

God and Father of our Lord Jesus Christ, while with gratitude we remember our distinguished privileges, we anxiously pray that they may be extended to all the children of thy great family, so that all may know thee, the only true God and Jesus Christ, whom thou hast sent.

Be merciful, O Lord, to the whole human race. Known unto thee are all their wants, and thou art able to do exceeding abundantly above what we can ask or think. From thee, who art plenteous in goodness, may they receive those blessings which are expedient for them. May our relations and friends obtain that favor in thy sight which thou bearest to them that love thee, and in everything that concerns them, may they be under the direction of that wisdom which alone can determine what will be most conducive to their present and eternal welfare.

—*Charles Brooks, 1795–1872*

## *At the Ending of the Day*

Almighty God, our heavenly Father, abide with us as the day draws to its close. Grant us the peace of pardoned children, and the security of those who are at home in thy house, fed at thy table, comforted at thy knee, and guarded by thine unsleeping watch: for thy Name's sake. Amen.

—*William Barclay, 1907–1978*

## *Prayer on Rising* 113

In thy name, O Blessed Savior, I arise, who with the Father and the Holy Spirit, created me, and with thine own most precious blood hast redeemed me. I beseech thee this day to govern, keep and bless me. Lead me forth in every good way, therein direct and confirm me, and after this frail and miserable life, bring me to that blessed life which hath no end, for thy great merit and mercy's sake. Amen.

—*Elizabeth Joscelin, 1596–1622*

## *Confession* 114

Lord, in your amazing goodness
you changed and renewed me entirely,
solely by the great grace of your Spirit,
having disposed my understanding to know you,
my judgment to acknowledge your authority,
my will to love you and to take pleasure
in your commandments which are so pure and holy—
in short, you made me a new creature.

But into what darkness have I changed this light!
I have spoiled everything, destroyed and laid waste everything.
Despite this, O God,
begin your work again as if from the beginning.
Be the Creator of this inner man for the second time,
displaying your power
that penetrates even to the foundation of my being,
so as to form within me a new soul
which loathes all sin,
and devotes itself to everything that is good and right.

I know that I am wholly unworthy of your putting your hand
again to this work;
but my God, do not reject me,
and do not entirely deprive me of the sense you had given me
and had not yet wholly taken from me
of knowing that by your grace,
I am numbered with those whom you do not wish to perish,
although I have more than deserved to be totally cut off.

—*Théodore de Bèze, 1519–1605*

115

### *Lord, Teach Us to Love*

It is easy, Lord, to mouth the word,
to say, "I love"
but not practise what it means.

When we see the true love of a lover,
the extent to which such love
is prepared to go for the beloved,
to vault over mountains
and dive under waves,
we know our love is paltry,
self-seeking,
a denial of the word.

When we consider your love,
the love of the cross,
the descent into the depths of hell
in search of us,
your forgiveness which overwhelms
and heals us,
we know our love is cheap,
our forgiveness empty,
judgmental and graceless.

Teach us to love you
with heart, soul and mind,
to love our neighbour
and our enemy.
Teach us to forgive
as you have forgiven us.

—*John W. de Gruchy, b. 1939*

## Intercession 116

O God of glory, because we are all children of one Father and one
mother, God and the church, we pray thee to bless thy holy church
universal, and to comfort all them that mourn in Zion, in conscience
and for conscience. Remember, O Lord, Joseph's afflictions, Paul's
bonds, Mary Magdalene's tears, Job's trials, Lazarus's sickness, and let
Stephen's death be always dear in thy sight. Let our loving affections so
mutually grow one towards another, that we may live together in love,
professing with one heart and mind a true faith, and laboring to keep
a holy and acceptable life, that we may forgive our brethren and sisters
and they us, to pray for them, and they for us, and in the outward
things of this world be helpful unto them, and they to us.

—*Thomas Sorocold, 1561–1617; alt.*

# *For Strength for the Day*

O Gracious God,
since I have left my requests with thee
and all my desires are before thee,
let me, with Hannah, be at rest
and my countenance be no more sad.
Let me not fear always
because of the oppression of the enemy,
but comfort me, my God.
Speak peace, pardon and cleansing to me.
Thou hast mercifully promised
that they who wait on thee
shall renew their strength,
they shall mount up as eagles,
they shall run and not be weary,
they shall walk and not faint.
Lord, strengthen me according to thy word.

*—Sarah Osborn, 1714–1796; alt.*

### Trust and Praise

118

If life is a wager,
O Lord!
On your side I bet.
You are the winner, always.

If life is an offering,
O Lord!
To you I reverently offer my life.
You are the Lord of life.

If life is a testimony,
O Lord!
Watch my thought and deed, I pray,
Lest your name suffer disgrace.

If life is a responsibility,
O Lord!
To do my best I promise.
Will you also give me a hand.

If life is a praise,
O Lord!
To you I lift up my voice of adoration.
And to you be all praise and glory.

> —*Hsu Tien-hsien, contemporary*

### I Beg a Pardon for My Sins

119

Oh Lord Jesus, help me, deliver me,
and save my soul from hell by thine own blood
which thou hast shed for me

when thou didst die for me, and for all my sins.
Help me sincerely to confess all my sins.
Oh pardon all my sins,
I now beg, in the name of Jesus Christ,
a pardon for all my sins,
for thou, O Christ,
art my Redeemer and Deliverer.

*—Piambohu, seventeenth century; alt.*


## 120  *Confession*

I, poor sinner, confess before you, my God and Creator, that I have grievously sinned against you in many serious ways, not only with outward gross sins, but also, and much more, by inborn blindness, unbelief, doubt, fearfulness, impatience, evil ambition, secret jealousy, hatred and ill-will and other wicked failings—as you, my Lord and God well know, and I, grievously, cannot enough confess. My sins are a shame and a sorrow to me; and from my heart I desire your grace, through your dear Son Jesus Christ.

*—Church of the Electoral Palatinate, 1684*


## 121  *Supplication*

Grant us, O Lord,
to know that which is worth knowing,
to love that which is worth loving,
to praise that which pleaseth thee most,
to esteem that highly which to thee is precious,
to abhor that which is displeasing in thy sight,
and above all,
to be ever searching after the good pleasure of thy will;
through Jesus Christ our Lord. Amen.

*—U.S.A. The Pilgrim Hymnal, 1935 rev. ed.; alt.*

## Intercession: For Justice

I pray you, O Lord, listen to my prayer. In your presence our heart, on the one hand, is happy and joyful, but disquieted and restless on the other. Faith and disbelief exist side by side and the distance to the ideal of human rights is still very great. Some of us make the effort to build up, while others are intent on tearing down. Some cherish harmony; others savagely tear apart. How unfortunate this is!

Ah, Sovereign Lord! Let all people come to know you. Let us all know that human rights are precious and dear to you. Let us— monarchs and subjects, rulers and ruled, in the West or in the East— let us all practice your righteousness and carry out your will and desire.

O Lord! Strengthen all those who dedicate themselves to the cause of human rights and grant them your peace. I also pray you, O Lord, to help the unjust as well as the just. Let no one who longs for you fall and let no one become a stumbling block to others for being insolent towards you.

—*Liu Fung-sung, contemporary; alt.*


## At the Ending of the Day

O Lord, which hast made the day and night, and rulest both: now the time is come, which thou hast appointed for rest. Without thee we can neither wake nor sleep, therefore into thy hands we commend our souls and bodies that thou hast bought, that they may serve thee. Restore them, O Lord, to their first image, and keep them to thy service. Resign us not to ourselves again, but finish thy work, that we may every day come nearer and nearer to thy kingdom, till we hate the way to hell as much as hell itself. And let every thought and speech and action be so many steps to heaven. For thy name's sake, for thy promises' sake, for thy Son's sake, O Lord, we lift our hearts, hands and voices unto thee in his name, which suffered for sin and sinned not.

—*Henry Smith, ca. 1550–1591; alt.*

## 124 *Approach*

Great God, incomprehensible, unknown
By sense, we bow at thine exalted throne.
O, while we beg thine excellence to feel,
Thy sacred Spirit to our hearts reveal,
And give us of that mercy to partake,
Which thou hast promised for the Saviour's sake!

—*Phillis Wheatley, ca. 1753–1784*

## 125 *Adoration*

O Lord our God, thou art very great; thou art clothed with glory
and honor. Thou createdst the light and thou formedst the darkness.
Thou didst make all things by the word of thy power, and for thy
pleasure they are and were created. The whole of nature is subject to
thy control, and thy hand is seen in all its operations. Thou causest
thy sun to shine on the evil and the good; thou breathest, and thy
influence is felt in the mildness of spring, in the luxuriance of summer,
and in the maturity of the ripened year. Thou veilest the heavens with
clouds, and it is winter; thou scatterest thy hoarfrost and thy snow like
wool, and thou sealest up the waters. Thou makest thy wind to blow
from the four corners of the heavens, they are dissolved, and the earth
wakens from her slumber. Thou utterest thy voice when it thunders;
thou scatterest thy lightnings over the extensive world; thou makest
the clouds thy chariot, and thou ridest on the wings of the wind.

Keep alive, we pray thee, O Lord, upon our minds, continual
and due impressions of thy being and greatness. May we love thee the
Lord our God, and serve thee as we ought to love thee, with all our
hearts, with all our strength, and with all our mind.

—*William Liston, 1781–1864; alt.*

## For Relief from Sin

God, be merciful to me a sinner. O Lord, I acknowledge that I cannot pray "Pardon me, dear Father, for Jesus Christ's sake, and quicken me with thy Holy Spirit." Give me faith to call upon thee; and I beseech thee graciously to remember thy promise which sayest, "Come unto me, all ye that labor and be heavy laden, and I will ease you." O Lord, I am loaden with my sins, and against all reason they keep me from seeking pardon for them and grace to shun them. Good Father, for Christ's sake, remove my sins far from me, and give me faith in thy Son, which may assure me that thou dost accept me. And although I be most unworthy in myself, yet by thy promises in Christ, which shall never fail, I pray thee accept me.

—*Dorothy Leigh, d. 1616; alt.*

## To See as God Sees

Thou God in Christ, there is no ground anywhere that is not holy ground, for in the cool of the evening thou hast walked upon it and in the heat of the day thou hast died upon it, and at the coming of dawn thou hast returned and art always and everywhere returning to it and to us who walk upon it too, this holy ground, though heedless of its holiness. O make us whole. Set us free.

Thou didst shape us each in the darkness of a womb to give us life and thou knowest us each by name, and not one is forgotten by thee, not one but is precious in thy sight—the ugly with the beautiful, the criminal with the child, the enemy with the friend. Lord, give us eyes to see each other and ourselves more nearly as thou seest us, to see beneath each face we meet, and beneath even our own faces, thy face.

Help us to know that for each thou hast died as though he were the only one. Amen.

—*Frederick Buechner, b. 1926*

## Intercession: For the Rich

Lord, keep those that are rich in the world from being high minded and trusting in uncertain riches and give to them to trust in the living God, who giveth us richly all things to enjoy, that they may do good and be rich in good works, ready to distribute, willing to communicate, that they may lay up in store for themselves a good security for the time to come.

Though it is hard for those who are rich to enter into the kingdom of heaven, yet with thee this is possible.

—*Matthew Henry, 1662–1714*

## For the Day's Work

We commit ourselves to thy care this day, not knowing what a day may bring forth. We desire to set thee, O Lord, always before us, in our business, in our diversions, and in all our conduct, praying that we may be enabled to act agreeably to our increasing obligations and repeated promises.

Suffer us not to forget thee or ourselves, nor by any sinful indulgences to contradict our prayers, and so make bitter work for repentance. Prosper, we pray thee, all our lawful undertakings; provide for our daily wants. Keep us from every evil. Bless us and make us blessings to each other, and to all with whom we have to do.

Lord, hear our prayers and accept our praises, through Jesus Christ our only Mediator and Advocate. Amen.

—*William May, 1706–1756; alt.*

## *Approach*

130

O Jehovah,
the God of Abraham, Isaac, and Jacob:
we have assembled in thy presence to praise thee
and to pray unto thee,
because we are burdened with sin and are distressed.
O rain upon us now,
and let the power of the Highest overshadow us.

—*Paul Kanoa, nineteenth century; alt.*

131

## *Adoration and Confession*

O Good Lord and dear Father, who broughtest thy people of Israel out of Egypt with a mighty hand and a stretched-out power, who gavest thy law upon Mount Sinai in great thundering, lightning, and fire; who spakest by the prophets, and didst send thy dearly beloved Son, Jesus Christ: thou hast brought me from the tyranny and captivity of Satan and this sinful world, whereof the captivity of Egypt under Pharaoh was a figure; and in his blood shed upon the cross thou hast made a covenant with me, which thou wilt never forget, that thou art and wilt be my Lord and my God; that is, thou wilt forgive me my sins and be wholly mine, with all thy power, wisdom, righteousness, truth, glory, and mercy.

In consideration of this, most justly and reasonably thou requirest that, as thou art my Lord God, so I should be thy servant and one of thy people. As thou hast given thyself wholly unto me, to be mine, with all thy power and wisdom, so should I be wholly thine, and give over myself unto thee, to be guided by thy wisdom, defended by thy power, helped, relieved, and comforted by thy mercy.

But alas, dear Father, what shall I say? I have horribly broken this thy law, by trusting in thy creatures, calling upon them, loving, fearing, and obeying many things besides thee and rather than thee, so at this time I am a most miserable wretch.

I am blinded through unbelief and mine own wickedness, so that I see not firmly thy power, wisdom, and goodness, but waver and doubt it. I love thee little or nothing. I fear thee less. I obey thee least of all. Thankfulness and prayer are utterly quenched in me, and therefore I deserve eternal damnation. If thou shalt deal with me only according to thy justice, I am, O Lord, condemned and lost forever. But yet inasmuch as thou hast given thy Son Jesus Christ to be a propitiatory sacrifice slain for the sins of the whole world, so that all which believe in him shall not perish, but be saved, thy truth now requires thee to save me.

O Lord God, because thy mercy is over all thy works, because thou art right good and love itself, because of this thy mercy, gracious God, if thou wilt look thereon, and unite thy truth therewith, then, good Lord, I shall be saved, and praise thy name for evermore.

—*John Bradford, 1510–1555; alt.*


## 132 *For Deliverance*

Thou that art more than most delicious,
Thou that for sweetness, dost all sweets exceed,
Thou whom the angels hold most precious,
Thou upon whom the souls of all do feed,
Thou that most pure and perfect are indeed,
Thou word of truth, by which all things were made,
Thou which shalt stand, when heaven and earth shall fade:

Be thou to me a lantern and a light,
Be thou my rock and castle of defense,
Be thou my sword, against soul-sin to fight,
That I may put the devil from his pretense,
And by thy power expell him quite from hence;
That so myself, poor bird ensnared, may say,
The net is broke, and I escaped away.

—*Thomas Collins, fl. 1610; alt.*

## For Tranquillity of Spirit

Lord God, who are the source of all equity and that know the great assaults that are launched at us from all sides: do not reject our prayers, but make us feel your favor and goodness so that whatever affliction may come upon us, we may never cease to live in peace, joy, and tranquillity of spirit, awaiting that eternal rest which you have promised to your children through your Son Jesus Christ. Amen.

—*Augustin Marlorat, 1506–1562*

## Intercession: For the Sick

Visit, O God, with healing in Thy touch, and peace upon Thy lips, all those who cry in pain for merciful deliverance, whose fever is uncooled, and whose hurt unhealed; that they, being soothed and comforted by Thy presence, may find strength renewed, and health restored; through Jesus Christ our Lord. Amen.

—*John U. Stephens, 1901–1984*

## At the Ending of the Day

Great God, since it is by the wonderful aid of your goodness that we have come to this night, grant that we may pass it happily under your protection. Let your angels encamp about us and let them watch while we sleep, and, you that are the guard of Israel, keep watch yourself.

Protect and defend us against all the devices of Satan and do not allow this sworn enemy of our salvation to triumph over us. Keep us secure by your mighty arm. Let your right hand embrace us and your left hand cover us, so that we, resting happily under your protection, may wake tomorrow more fit to serve you and to honor you.

—*Jean de Gazel de Larambergue, ca. 1684–1749; alt.*

136 ### *For Grace to Worship Gratefully*

Blessed Savior, Rock of our salvation, Desire of the nations, Hope of Israel in time of trouble: thou wast content to be made of no esteem, that thy people might be greatly beloved; to be made a curse, that thy people might become a blessing, content to be made low, that thou mightest exalt them. So thou hast done. Give them an heart to exalt thee, to honor thee, to love thee much, for thou art worthy, Blessed Spirit. Thou hast done great things and marvelous, not by human might nor by power, but by thyself. O Blessed Spirit, take to thyself the glory, even all.

*—Hezekiah Woodward, ca. 1590–1675; alt.*

137 ### *Thanksgiving*

We thank you, Lord God, for your salvation in Jesus Christ.
We thank you, Lord, for all your blessings to us:
>    blessings of rain that make the trees around us, big and
>        small,
>    grass for our cattle,
>    fruit trees and vegetables for our health
and for all our coconuts, cocoa, coffee, kava, and cattle,
>        which bring us prosperity.
We thank you for our daily food,
for manioc, taro, yam, kumala, banana,
breadfruit, and rice,
>        which gives us power.
We thank you, Lord, for our meat,
for beef, pork, goat, chicken,

for fish in the sea,
shellfish on reefs,
coconut crabs that live in the rocks.
We thank you for your gift of love:
for husbands and wives,
for the gift of children,
for homes, for families,
and for friends.

Father of love, you have blessed us with many blessings.
We give you now our love and thanks
for your love for us;
through Jesus Christ our Lord.
—*Presbyterians of the Republic of Vanuatu, 1990; alt.*

## You Know That We Love You                     138

Lord,
we love you
and yet we deny you.

We love you
and yet we have been known
to let denials of you pass
without a murmur.

We love you,
and yet we have resisted,
closed our eyes to,
pretended not to notice,
your love's challenges.

You know that we love you,
and but for that knowledge
we could not be sure we loved you at all.

Forgive our lovelessness,
our faithlessness,
our paltriness,
and let your risen glory shine in us to fill the world.

—*Alan Gaunt, b. 1935*

139

## *For Grace to Serve Humbly*

Lord Jesus, as in the days of old Thou didst gird Thyself to wash Thy
disciples' feet, so may we be girded with humility to serve one another;
and as Thou didst cleanse Thy followers then that they might have full
part with Thee, so cleanse us now from every defilement, that we too,
in fellowship together, may have our part with Thee in quiet service
and in willing sacrifice, for evermore.

—*Charles E. Watson, 1869–1942*

140

## *Lord, Suffer No Rivals*

Lord, help and lay no more on me than thou wilt enable me with grace
and patience to bear, to thy glory. O grant me so much business, so
much sickness, so much health, so much poverty, and so much
prosperity, as will bring me nearest to thyself and most advance thy
glory, and no more of either, Lord, no more of anything than thou wilt
sanctify.

For, except thou sanctify, business will hurry, fatigue, fret, and
carry off my heart; sickness will clog and nothing will be attended to

but an impatient complaining of aches and weakness, an impatient, Jonah-like spirit wishing to die rather than live; health will be wantonly spent in the delights of sense; poverty, unsanctified, will make me murmur and complain, worry, and quarrel with all the dispensations of thy all-wise providence (Oh! Cutting thought!); prosperity will puff me up, pride will rear up its venomous head, and I will be glued to this world and take contentment in it, instead of laying up all my good in thee.

Sanctify, and all these shall work together for good and bring me nearer thyself. Therefore, O my covenant God, sanctify all to me, and do with me what pleaseth thee. Lord, anything, only possess my soul. Suffer no rivals, and it is enough. O keep me from the evil, for I am thine, forever thine.

*—Sarah Osborn, 1714–1796; alt.*

## *Intercession*                                                              141

> Our prayers for those we love,
> for all the sad and all the lonely,
> for the victims of the evil forces of the world and
>      of human disorder,
> for our own people and for all people who seek
>      the city of mutual love,
> for our church and for all churches that call upon your name,
> for those who seek you, for those who ignore you,
> for those who shun you, but for whom you wait,
>      Father, on the doorstep of your house;
> all our prayers, O God, we unite in the prayer
> that Christ gave us:
> Our Father . . .

*—Reformed Church of Berne (Switzerland), 1955*

## For the Day's Work

Father, Son, and Spirit Holy,
we give you thanks and praise,
and dedicate to you
our thoughts, our words,
our gifts, our deeds,
the working of our hands,
the thinking of our minds,
the loving of our hearts.

Shield us this day
for the sake of Christ of the wounds.
Keep us from offence,
and compass us with your love
for ever and for evermore. Amen.

—*Church of Scotland, 1994*

## *For the Gifts of Love and Reverence*     143

Our Heavenly Father, we bless thee that thy love is wisdom. We, finite creatures, ask for finite things, and thou hast given us infinite things. We ask for the petty trivialities of a day. Thou hast given us what money could not buy. We asked for protection and safety for the day. Thou hast given it, and hast assured us of protection and safety for eternity.

We praise thee for thy love which thou dost daily manifest to us, but which thou hast fully shown in its most perfect light in thy dear Son, our Lord and Savior, Jesus Christ. May he dwell in our hearts and in our lives.

Make us charitable, long-suffering, and full of mercy to those who have done us ill, even as thou hast shown thyself merciful. Make us gentle in thought and word, and in our actions. Enable us to bear in mind thy love to us, that we may love our enemies, do good to those who hate us, and use us despitefully.

May we remember thee and may we look to thee not only in troubled times, but may we live in thee and with thee when the voice of joy and safety fills the land. O God, better for us that we should dwell in fear and be with thee, than that we should dwell in safety and forget thee.

These our humble desires we ask thee to grant, knowing that when thou dost give, thou givest above all that we ask or think. We ask it in Christ's name. And to thee, God Almighty, Father, Son, and Holy Spirit, shall be the praise.

*—Helen J. Waddell, 1889–1965; alt.*

## *For Trust in God's Hidden Love*

We rejoice, O Lord our God, to believe that those confusions and
turmoils of life that seem to us strange and mysterious, are before thee
simple; and those things which, to our uninterpreting eye, are evils,
mischiefs, and wastes, to thine eye are messengers of mercy, guiding
and conducting influences; for thou art bringing many sons and
daughters home to glory; and we are not large enough nor wise
enough to understand the footsteps of that way which thou treadest
in dealing with humanity. We forget that thou art the king of time
and the God of all the earth; that thou dwellest in eternity, in light
unapproachable; that all power and wisdom are with thee. Endless
and diversified means are thine, and thou art, through many ways
which seem to us to reverse all good, bringing good to pass, light
out of darkness, good out of evil, and order out of confusion; so that
all the earth doth serve thee, even hates, and wastes, and wars. Thou
dost restrain the wrath of humanity, and cause the remainder thereof
to praise thee.

   We go forward in our journey of life knowing that we are
journeying onwards to sunrise, that the darkness is behind us, and the
light more and more before us. And we desire to be more faithful and
courageous, and enduring unto the end.

—*Henry Ward Beecher, 1813–1887; alt.*

## *That We May Love Our Enemies*

O Lord, thou hast commanded us to love not only our friends, but also
our enemies, to forgive them that offend us, to bless them that curse
us, to do good to them that hate us, to pray for them that do us wrong
and persecute us; yea, if our enemies hunger, to feed them, if they
thirst, to give them drink. But our corrupt nature, which ever striveth
against thy blessed will, seeketh all means possible to be revenged, to
requite tooth for tooth and eye for eye, to render evil for evil, when
vengeance is thine and thou wilt reward. By this means we grievously
offend thee, and break the order of charity and the bond of peace.

O most merciful Lord, through the operation of thy Holy Spirit, may we be content, according to thy blessed commandment, and after the example of thy Son Jesu Christ our Lord, and of that blessed martyr St. Stephen, freely and from the very heart, to forgive our enemies, to speak well of them, to love them, and to do for them whatsoever lieth in our power, and by this means show ourselves to be children of a God which causest the sun to rise on the evil and the good, and sendeth rain on the righteous and on the unrighteous, giving us example, that if we should do likewise and show ourselves kind not only to the good and godly, but also the wicked and ungodly, by this means we may lure even the adversaries of thy truth to speak well of those who profess thy blessed name, and to glorify thee our heavenly Father, which fashionest us according to thy manners, through the mighty working of thy Holy Spirit, to whom, with thee and thy only-begotten Son, be all glory and honor. Amen.

*—Thomas Becon, 1512–1567; alt.*

## *Intercession* 146

Sovereign Monarch of the world, we pray thee to continue to pour out thy blessing upon our state and upon our church. Maintain always therein peace and liberty both temporal and spiritual.

Bless our rulers. Bless the ministers of our church. Bless us all, of what age and condition soever we be. Assist us in our employments. Guide us in our undertakings, and in our occupations, and grant that they may be all directed to thy glory and to our salvation.

Father of mercies, keep the churches that are in being. Raise up new ones, and cast the eyes of thy compassion upon those that suffer. Take care of all the faithful that are exposed to the hatred and to the persecutions of the world because of their adhering to thy pure service. Deliver them from evil, or inspire them with the patience necessary to support them; and grant that we may see thy church in a more peaceful condition upon earth.

O God of comfort, we recommend to thy pity all persons under affliction: widows, orphans, the poor, prisoners, the sick, and in particular, those of our church. Give them all grace to profit by thy chastisements to their sanctification. And if thou takest them out of the world, vouchsafe to retrieve them into thy heavenly kingdom.

We offer up to thee also our prayers for all the people that are without the knowledge of thy pure gospel. Dispel their ignorance by the light of thy truth, and give them grace to enter into the true way of happiness which thou hast revealed in thy word.

*—Church of Geneva, 1712; alt.*

147

## *At the Ending of the Day*

Take me, Jesus, to Thy breast;
Folded close in warmth and rest,
  Keep me near to Thee;
Silenced in the bliss profound
Of the love that wraps me round,
  Every care shall be.
Every breath for Thee alone,
O my heart's beloved One;
  Comfort me in sleep.
Still deep rest art Thou to thine,
Safely in thine arms divine
  Thy beloved keep.

*—Gerhard Tersteegen, 1697–1769*

## *For Singleness of Soul*

O Holy Father, open our minds to understand thy good will to us, that it may not only refresh and quicken our souls, but also stir up in us a desire to meditate on thy word, so that we may do it with profit, that in daily feeding and understanding more and more, our hearts may be stirred up not only to offer thee an acceptable sacrifice of thanksgiving always, but also an earnest care, endeavor and work to live before thee with all singleness of soul in that holiness, O Lord, which thou dost like and love, O Secret Searcher of all thoughts.

—*Thomas Sampson, ca. 1517–1589*

## *Let Not the Devil Be My Master*

Heavenly Father, Thou art my Maker; help me to own thee as my Father. Pity me, relieve me, as one of thy children. Let me and all people glorify thy Name; and let thy Christ be glorious and precious to me, and to all the world.

Teach me thy law, and cause me and all to love love, and keep those lovely laws.

Give me to do heartily all that thou commandest me to do. Give me to bear patiently all that thou orderest me to bear. And let me begin the work of heaven while I am on earth.

Thou knowest what is best for me. Lord, let me lack nothing that shall be good for me.

I have sinned against thee; O pardon all my sins, for the sake of my Savior.

Do good to them that have done evil to me, and do not leave me so much as to wish evil to them. When I am tempted to sin, Oh, let not the temptation be too hard for me; and let not the devil be my master.

O Lord, everything is at thy disposal. Thou canst do everything. Be merciful to me, and all the glory of thy mercy shall be thine forevermore. Amen.

—*Cotton Mather, 1663–1728; written for use by African slaves; alt.*

150

## *From Cross to Crown*

Grant, my Jesus,
that like thee,
I may soon get from the cross to the crown,
from thorns to roses,
from danger to security,
from tribulation to refreshing,
from labor to rest,
from contempt to honor,
from fighting to victory,
from striving to triumphing,
from suffering to glory,
from hope to the thing hoped for,
from believing to enjoying,
from death to life,
and when I get there
I will see what I sought,
have what I longed for.
My Jesus!
I am sick for love, my heart burns after thee.

—*Johann-Jakob Ulrick, 1683–1731; alt.*

Grant, Almighty God, that since thou so kindly invitest us to thyself, and promisest that thy aid should never be wanting to us, provided we do not close the door against thee—O grant, that though many earthly benefits may be granted to us, we may not yet trust in them and depart from thee, but, on the contrary, recumb on thy grace only: and then should it happen to us to be deprived of all helps, that our minds may be awakened, and that we may thus learn to hasten to thee. May nothing impede our course, that we may, with the greatest haste and ardent desire, long to deliver up and devote ourselves wholly to thee, that we may be made safe under the care and protection of thy only-begotten Son, whom thou hast appointed to be the guardian of our safety. Amen.

*—Jean Calvin, 1509–1564; alt.*

### Intercession: For the Unjustly Accused

152

O Lord, strengthen and support, we entreat thee, all persons unjustly accused. Comfort them by the ever present thought that thou knowest the whole truth, and wilt in thine own good time make their righteousness as clear as the light. Give them grace to pray for such as do them wrong, and hear and bless them when they pray. Amen.

*—United Free Church of Scotland, 1907*

# For the Day's Work

Lord, thou must work in us
to will and to do thy good pleasure,
or we never will.
Thou must begin,
Thou must carry on,
and Thou must finish every good work.
All that we can do is to ask Thee
what Thou wouldst have us to do—
make the attempt,
when Thou hast made the path of duty plain,
and plead thy promise to direct our steps.
O Lord, rouse us to the work;
grant us strength according to our day,
and grace according to our need.

—*Joanna Bethune, 1770–1860; alt.*

## For the Gift of Giving Life

154

O Lord!
You are the life of the world.
O Lord!
You are the life of the world.
Enter my heart and fill me
Until I live like you.

O Lord!
Make me a lamp of life.
O Lord!
Make me a lamp of life.
In the places darkest and saddest
Make me shine always.

O Lord!
Make me gush forth water of life.
O Lord!
Make me gush forth water of life.
For the people thirsty and in pain
Make me gush forth life for them.

—*C. M. Kao, contemporary*

## For Integrity and the Treasure of God's Love

155

My Lord and my God, the only good and only worthy to be beloved
with all the heart and soul: I have seen enough of this world to learn
that all is vanity and vexation of spirit. Wealth is a burden. Honors
are golden fetters. Pleasures are follies or crimes. The life of the world
is a tragedy of a few days and a continual pageant. I have been near

enough to that tumultuous noise and lustre without substance to know that it is not a worthy object of my love nor a firm ground for my hopes. And instead of finding there the comfort of the soul and quietness of mind, I have nothing but temptations and sorrows.

Yet, Lord, as it is hard to walk upon the fire and not be burnt, I acknowledge that I have not lived in the world without a taint of its corruption. I have too much loved the world and the things that are in the world. I should have sunk into evil, had not thy Spirit upheld me and thy very rods helped me out.

Lord, where should I begin, either to praise thee for not abandoning me to the temptations of the world, or to crave thy pardon for loving it too much? My God, I will do both together. I will praise thee with my humility and acknowledge that in me abideth no good. I will also acknowledge that it is of thy great mercy that the love of the world hath not quenched the love of the Father in my heart.

O Lord, I have sought my content without thee, and placed my trust and my joy upon other things than thee. But, O my God, as thou lovedest me before I loved thee, now be pleased to love me when I am defective in my love to thee. Blot out my sins by thine eternal love in thy Son Jesus Christ. Renew and increase my love to thee, so that I properly love nothing but thee, and all things else to which my duty obligeth me to love, only for thy sake, and in a degree subordinate to the love which I owe thee. Let me not settle mine affections and mine hopes upon persons and things which it is impossible for me to keep and which must leave me, or I them.

Let me be built upon the rock of thy love to me in Jesus Christ, that when the winds blow and the rains fall and the floods come, I may stand fast while the storm beats to ruin others who are built upon the quicksand of this unstayed and deceitful world. Lord, the fashion of this world passeth away, and I must prepare to remove from this house of clay, my frail body. O give me grace beforehand, to remove my heart from the world, and settle it upon thee, and mine eternal mansion with thee.

Let me not covet those goods which thou givest many times to thine enemies in greater measure, which commonly makes their mind swell with pride and beats it down with fears and cares; that give no satisfaction to the mind and no refuge against thine indignation. But let me be covetous of the true treasures that give a solid content to the soul and follow the soul to heaven when the body dieth. O Lord, enrich my soul with thy love and thy fear. Pour into me the riches of thy grace. Dwell in my heart by faith, for no less than thyself do I ask, and I cannot be satisfied unless thou givest thyself to me. O my God, thou art the portion of my inheritance. Thou art my flock and my rent, mine eternal possession and mine only good. Ease my mind of all earthly cares, which give a torment to no purpose, and give me the grace to seek thy kingdom and thy righteousness, being sure that all things shall be added hereunto. And after all gifts, O my God, again, I beseech thee to give thyself to me. I desire to resign myself wholly to thee, as having nothing in heaven but thee, and there being nothing on earth that I desire besides thee. Lord, thou wilt lead me by thy counsel and afterwards receive me to glory. Amen.

*—Pierre Du Moulin, the Younger, 1601–1684; alt.*

## For Possession by God

156

O Lord, so possess our hearts, that whatsoever benefits we enjoy, we may take it as a spring of the fountain of thy love; and every correction and chastisement, however bitter to the flesh, may be sweetened with this consideration: that all things must turn to the best to them that being loved by thee have grace to love thee again.

*—Peter Howat, ca. 1567–1645*

## Intercession: For Peace

157

Our Father,
let there be peace for all your people!
Through Jesus' Spirit
let there be peace over all the earth
for this faithful flock
whom you see gathering 'round the Good Shepherd
as soon as they hear your voice!

Beneath your gaze, Kind Father!
Keep us safe in peace on the way of light
leading up to heaven!
On that path, give us wisdom to love Jesus
in the sweet joy your Spirit bestows!

—H.A. César Malan, 1787–1864; alt.

## 158 *Thanksgiving for the Faithful Departed*

Most loving Father, how can we render unto thee sufficient thanks for thine inestimable goodness toward thy faithful servants, whom, called out of this wretched world, thou vouchsafest to place in thy heavenly kingdom, among the glorious company of the holy angels and blessed saints. Full precious is the death of the faithful in thy sight! Blessed are the dead that die in thee, O Lord, for they are at rest from their painful travails and labors. The souls of the righteous are in thy hand, O God; and the pain of death shall not touch them. In the sight of the unwise they appear to die, but they are in peace. They glisten as the shining of heaven. They are as stars, world without end. They are as the angels of God. They are clad in white garments and have golden crowns upon their heads. They neither hunger nor thirst anymore, neither doth the sun or any heat fall upon them; for the Lamb which is in the midst of the throne governeth them, and leadeth them unto the living fountain of waters. They have such joys as eye hath not seen, nor ear hath heard, neither is there any heart able to think them. Infinite and unspeakable are the treasures, O Lord, which thou hast laid up for them that depart in faith.

For these thy fatherly benefits towards the souls of the faithful, and that it hath pleased thee to call our brethren and sistern from this vale of misery unto thy heavenly kingdom, we give unto thee most hearty thanks, humbly beseeching thee that thou wilt take like care for us, and so govern us with thy Holy Spirit, both in sickness and in health, that we may live a good and godly life in this present world, and, whensoever it shall be thy good pleasure to call us hence, we may, with strong faith in thee and in thy Son Jesus Christ, commend both our bodies and souls into thy faithful hands, and through thy goodness be placed in thy glorious kingdom among thy faithful chosen people, and so for ever and ever praise and magnify thee our heavenly Father, to whom with thy dearly beloved Son Jesus Christ our Lord and Savior, and the Holy Ghost, that most sweet Comforter, be all glory and honor, world without end. Amen.

*—Thomas Becon, 1512–1567; alt.*

## I Lie Down to Sleep

159

Come,
Lord,
and cover me with the night.
Spread Your grace over us
as you assured us You would do.

Your promises are more
than all the stars in the sky;
Your mercy is deeper than the night.
Lord,
it will be cold.
The night comes with its breath of death.
Night comes,
the end comes,
but Jesus Christ comes also.

Lord,
we wait for Him
day and night.
Amen.

*—D. K. Ofosuapea, contemporary*

160                              *Praise*

Glory to God in the highest,
on earth peace, and good will among people.
I praise thee for this message of peace.
I see, in some measure, its necessity, truth, and beauty.
I trust that it is the sole foundation of my hope.
I renounce every other claim.
I count all things but loss for the excellency
      of the knowledge of Christ Jesus my Lord,
         for whom I have suffered the loss of all things,
         and count them but dung
         that I may win Christ and be found in him.
It grieves me that there is such a backwardness in me
         to give glory to thy name
         and to be indebted to the riches of thy grace.
Subdue my obstinacy and rule by thine own power.
Lord, I believe,
         help thou mine unbelief.

—*John Witherspoon, 1723–1794; alt.*


161                       *For the Grace to Forgive*

O God, since you are love, and since those who do not love you and
do not love their brothers and sisters do not know you, and dwell in
death, keep us from pride, from injustice, from falsehood, from the
spirit of judgment, from envy, from hatred and ill-will. Give us grace
to forgive those who have done us wrong, and to support one another
as you yourself, Lord, support us in your patience and your great
goodness.

—*Eugène Bersier, ed.,* Liturgy, *1874*

## To Leave My Water Pot and My Nets

Lord, when I read that after thou wert pleased to instruct the
Samaritan woman that thou wert the Christ, the Savior of the world,
she presently left her water pot and went into the city to inform
others, that they also might come and be blessed with a sight of him
who is the desire of all nations: O Lord, this doth indeed convince me
that the soul that once findeth thee is presently content to part with
all. For this woman, before thy revealing thyself to her, was busied
about her water pot and her worldly employments, but after she
found the Messiah, she could (as it were for joy) forget her water pot,
and willingly part with it, to inform her neighbors what she had
found, that they also might have a part with her: O Lord, that thou
wouldst enable me also to leave all to follow thee.

May I, like Simon Peter, who when thou calledst him from
fishing, left his nets straightaway and followed thee, leave all my
worldly wealth and follow thee, and count all things dung and dross
to gain thee, and with the man spoken of in the gospel, sell all to
obtain the pearl of great price, that having found Jesus, I may willingly
part with all for thee, and having thee, may I say I have enough.

Lord, I am willing, if thou callest me to it, to leave my water
pot and nets and all for thee.

*—Mary Rich, 1625–1678; alt.*

## Intercession: For Creation

Lord, you love life; we owe our existence to you. Give us reverence
for life and love for every creature. Sharpen our senses so that we shall
recognize the beauty and also the longing of your creation, and, as
befits your children, treat our fellow creatures of the animal and plant
kingdoms with love as our brothers and sisters, in readiness for your
great day, when you will make all things new.

*—The Evangelical Reformed Churches*
*in German-speaking Switzerland, 1972*

# Illumine Me More, Each Day

(based on Ps. 63:1 and Ps. 42:1)

O God, thou art my God;
early will I seek thee.
My soul thirsteth for thee,
my flesh longs for thee in a dry and thirsty land,
where no water is.
As the hart panteth after the water brooks,
so panteth my soul after thee, O God, my God!
I long to behold the light and love of thy face unclouded,
      uninterrupted.
Mercifully deign to illumine me more each day.

             —*William Craig Brownlee, 1783–1860; alt.*

## Approach

Truth, Lord, without thee I can do nothing.
But through Christ strengthening me,
I can do all things.
And hast not thou, my covenant God,
graciously promised
that thou wilt not turn away from doing me good?
In this I trust, O my God:
thou wilt enable me to pour out my whole soul
into thy bosom, while no mortal eye or ear can discern.
Pour out on me a spirit of prayer and supplication,
for Jesus' sake,
in whose name I ask for all my mercies;
whose I am, and by assisting grace,
will be forever.

*—Sarah Osborn, 1714–1796; alt.*

## Thanksgiving

I have taken upon me to speak unto my Lord, that am but dust and ashes. Lead me into thy treasure-house, to behold thy mercies there, which I am no more able to understand than I can the treasures of the snow and hail, nor comprehend no more than I can measure the wind in my fist or heavens with my span.

I look back to thy ancient thoughts towards thy sons and daughters, before the foundation of the world, and behold thy ways there, as undiscernible as the way of an eagle in the air or of a serpent upon the rock, as the path which no soul knoweth.

Blessed be thy name, that even though the soul can find no rest nor feels any bottom, yet in Christ we have a foundation according to the good pleasure of thy will.

For him we bless thee, we praise thee, we adore thee. For thy glorious manifestations, secret inspirations, immediate workings; for all the means whereby heaven is pleased to condescend and have communion with earthly creatures and earthly creatures have fellowship with the Father and the Son. For thy Son's sake for all this therefore, we bless thee for that unspeakable gift.

—*Hezekiah Woodward, ca. 1590–1675; alt.*

## For a Resupply of God's Grace

167

O my Great Redeemer, how many and great are my wants! Lord, I am ruined if thou dost not appear to supply them. There are so many great and constant demands on me for every grace, arising from present circumstances, temptations, corruptions, duties, difficulties, and relations, that I seem to have run all out, and like a broken merchant to have been using sham, sorry, mean, and beggarly methods to keep up my credit. But I can do so no longer. A new supply I must have, or my credit is gone. And thine honor is concerned: I fall not alone. Lord, I have boasted a fountain at hand, a sufficient supply to answer all demands. I have said, "My God shall supply my needs," but my demands are very many, and the tempter sees my weakness and poverty, and grows insolent and threatens ruin. Lord, art thou not surety for thy handmaid? I trust thou art, and I shall not be cast into the prison of hell.

Lord, I have nothing to live upon of my own, and turn which way I will, there is demand upon me for wisdom, for patience, for

meekness, for faith, for love, for humility, or for some grace or other.
O my glorious Head, I pray thee, communicate a supply. What shall
I do if thou dost not? O my blessed Master, bountifully supply my
wants, and I shall be for thee and no other all the days of my life.
And speedily, Lord, for thou knowest the demands of every duty
and temptation are pressing and must be answered from thee.

*—Susanna Anthony, 1726–1791; alt.*

## Intercession: For All Creatures 168

O God who hast crowded the earth, the rocks, the trees, the fields, the
rivers, and the sea with living creatures and dost so care for them all
that not a sparrow falls to the ground without thee; grant that we may
never, through any lack of thought or failure of sympathy, give needless
pain to anything that lives and feels, but may unfailingly defend and
protect those humbler creatures which like ourselves are pensioners on
thy bounty, so that their joy in living may be richer and fuller through
their being in the power of those who are made in thine image to
know and understand and feel.

*—Hugh Cameron, 1855–1934*

## For a Gracious Answer to Prayer 169

O Lord, we beseech thee, that thou wouldest not delay over-long
to give us a gracious answer to our requests. We are poor miserable
creatures, and our faith is exceeding weak. If therefore thou shouldest
long delay to answer us, we should be apt to be stumbled and
discouraged. We therefore entreat thee to answer us speedily.

*—Jonathan Amos, d. 1706; alt.*

## *Commemoration of the Faithful Departed*

Eternal God, in whom do live the spirits of those who depart hence; we remember with quiet and grateful hearts our bretheren and sisters who from the beginning of the world have pleased thee. Mercifully grant that their example and memory may stir us to a better life, that when for us the night cometh when no one can work, we may be counted worthy to join their fellowship in that world where peace and love are perfect and immortal. Amen.

*—John Hunter, 1848–1917; alt.*

## *Evening Blessing*

Thy grace, O Lord Jesus Christ, thy love, O Heavenly Father; thy comfort and consolation, O Holy and blessed Spirit, be with me and dwell in my heart, this night and evermore. Amen.

*—Lewis Bayly, 1565–1631*

# Week III

## *Approach* 172

O Lord God Almighty, the knowledge of whom is life, whom to serve
is to reign, and unto whom to pray is the joy and peace of the soul: we
cannot know thee but in thine own image, Jesus Christ, and that, by
the operation of thy Spirit. Neither can we serve thee, except we follow
thy word, neither can we call upon thee, but in the name of the same
Christ, and according to that form which he himself hath prescribed
for us. Thus every faithful creature sayeth unto thee: Our Father, give
unto us, forgive us. For thy Son, the head of that union which is
among all Christians, hath commanded that our prayers should be
common for all thy people, as being all one body which thou governest
by one Spirit. And forasmuch as our being dependeth upon thee only,
and being in our birth corrupted by sin, thou makest us to be renewed
unto righteousness, through the same eternal Word whereby thou hast
created us, we do rightly call thee, even by a double right, Our Father.
I do believe that I am one of the number of thy children, through thy
mercy, and therefore, O my God, I cannot doubt but that thou dost
lovingly hear me and art inclined to help me and to relieve me in all
my necessities.

Thou art above all this great universal world, in the seat of
thine own glory, from whence thou dost embrace both heaven and
earth, and with thy providence, sustain them. All things depend upon
thee; thou dost by thy subtlety pierce into them, more nearly unto
every creature than it is to itself. In the high heaven doth thy Majesty
shine with open countenance. Thou art with thy gracious presence in
the souls of the righteous, which do harbor thee as a Father in their
hearts.

*—Théodore de Bèze, 1519–1605; alt.*

# *For Deeper Repentance*

O Sweet Jesus!
I adore thee as a God of infinite power,
because thou hast looked such a rebel heart as mine into
      repentance.
O Lord! I abhor myself, because I have sinned against such
      dear love and grace.
It is more than enough that thine enemies dishonor thee,
but that I should do it is intolerable ingratitude!
O dear Jesus! Still look me into deeper repentance.
Look me into faith.
Look me into constant and universal obedience
      to all thy just, holy, good commands.
Do but look, dear Lord,
Satan shall flee before thee.
Every rebel shall quit the field:
unbelief, pride, hypocrisy, self-confidence.
Only look, and every grace shall at once be up and doing,
all upon the wing to execute thy commands and to
      embrace thee.

O Lord, bless thine handmaid
who has enlisted under thy banner.
O make her faithful unto death.
O be with her throughout her warfare
and make her valiant for the truth at all times.
O fill her precious soul with the gifts and graces
      of thy blessed Spirit,
and make her an ornament to her profession all her days.

              —*Sarah Osborn, 1714–1796; alt.*

O my God, my most gracious Father, who hast loved me from all eternity, and wilt yet love me to all eternity, I am too little to comprehend the greatness of thy compassions and the excellency of thy promises to me. O Lord, how excellent is thy loving-kindness! Thou hast not only made me after thy likeness, fed me with thy bounty, and preserved me by thy providence, but thou hast not been sparing of thine own Son, and thy Son hath not been sparing of his own life to redeem me from death and give me the inheritance of thy kingdom. O the depth of the riches both of thy wisdom and mercy! O incomprehensible goodness! O infinite love! What shall I render thee for the inestimable treasure of thy grace? But even this belongs to the infinity of thy love, that thou acceptest the love of thy little creature in exchange of thine infinite love. Come then, let me love thee, let me bless thee, O my God.

O my Savior Jesu, who for my sake hadst thy hands and feet pierced with nails and thy side lanced with a spear, be pleased to make a wholesome wound in my breast with the point of thy love. For as by thy light we see light, so by thy fervent love to us we are inflamed with love to thee.

O thou the first beauty, the first goodness, who only deservest that I make an incense of my affections unto thee with the fire of love; I desire to know thy perfections better, that I may love them better. I desire to love thee with all my heart, and with all mine understanding, and more yet with my heart, because it is more capable to embrace thee than mine understanding to know thee. I will seek thee, O Lord, but I have need that thou seek me and find me and bring me to thyself in love, and put far from me all things and desires that make me go astray from thee.

My God, because I love thee, I desire to please thee, and that I may please thee, I desire to be like unto thee. O great Bridegroom of my soul, when wilt thou make me like unto thee that I may be all handsome and a fit bride for thee? When shall I be clad all about, all over, with the new creature which after God is created in righteousness and true holiness! How ambitious am I to be decked with the precious jewels of faith, charity, zeal, the ornament of a meek and quiet spirit which before thee is of great price. Lord, thou hast adorned me with the imputation of thy perfect righteousness, my glorious wedding gown, whereby I do appear before God, thy Father and mine, all righteous and all perfect.

O Christ who hast already made me fine with the jewels of thy merit, be pleased to add unto them those of thy Spirit, that thy righteousness serve not only to justify me, but much more to sanctify me. For I shall never be a spouse handsome enough for such a perfect Bridegroom till thy virtues pass unto me and into me, and change me into thy likeness by the operation of thy powerful Spirit. O Lord, thy banner over me is love, my wedding livery is love. With that livery I expect to be led by thee into the wedding chamber. O! In that expectation let love produce his best effect in me, which is to change the person loving into the beloved, so that I may truly say, "I am crucified with Christ, nevertheless I live, yet not I, but Christ liveth in me, and the life which I now live in the flesh I live by faith of the Son of God, who loved me and gave himself for me."

I look for an eternal habitation to live with thee and live by thy life. But it is too long for me to expect till thou bring me into that wedding place. I have a wedding room for thee in my heart, not so well furnished as I could wish to receive such a great guest. O Lord, be thou in me and I in thee, as thou Father art in the Son, and thou Son art in the Father, that I also may be one with you by the Holy Ghost, the Spirit and bond of love. And to you, three Persons and one God, be glory for evermore. Amen.

—*Pierre Du Moulin, the Younger, 1601–1684; alt.*

## Intercession: For the Spiritually Homeless

O GOD, who didst hear Peter when he wept, and didst afterwards give to him the keys of the kingdom of heaven, mercifully call home to thy church all careless, sinful, and indifferent folk; that the world may not triumph over them, nor thy church lose them for ever; through Jesus Christ our Lord. Amen.

—*Colin F. Miller, 1911–1988*

---

From *Prayers for Parish Worship* by Colin F. Miller (1948). Reprinted by permission of Oxford University Press.

## Entrusting the Day to God

Great God, we commend and entrust our bodies and our souls into your hands, begging you that whether we live or die, it may be for your glory, for the salvation of our souls, for the edification of our neighbors, and the consolation of our own conscience, for we shall have to give account on the last day. Lord, heed. Lord, forgive. Lord, hear and act for the love of yourself and for the love of Jesus Christ your Son our Lord, in whose precious name we pray to you, saying, Our Father. . . .

—*Jean de Gazel de Larambergue, ca. 1684–1749*

<u>177</u>
## *Thanksgiving for Divine Love*

O Lord, we acknowledge that no creature is able to comprehend the length and breadth, the deepness and height of that thy most excellent love, which moved thee to show mercy where none was deserved, to promise and give life where death had gotten the victory, to receive us into thy grace, when we could do nothing but rebel against thy justice.

O Lord, the blind dullness of our corrupt nature will not suffer us sufficiently to weigh those thy most ample benefits. Yet, nevertheless, we declare and witness before the world that by Jesus Christ alone we have received liberty and life, that by him alone thou dost acknowledge us thy children and heirs, that by him alone we have entrance to the throne of thy grace, that by him alone we are possessed in our spiritual kingdom, to eat and drink at his Table, with whom we have our conversation presently in heaven, and by whom our bodies shall be raised up again from the dust, and shall be placed with him in that endless joy which thou, O Father of mercy, hast prepared for thine elect before the foundation of the world was laid. And these most inestimable benefits we acknowledge and confess to have received of thy free mercy and grace, by thine only beloved Son Jesus Christ, for which therefore we, moved by thy Holy Spirit, render thee all thanks, praise, and glory, for ever and ever. Amen.

—*John Knox, ca. 1514–1572; alt.*

# A Surrender of the Soul to God

Command me what thou wilt, O Lord,
give me but strength to obey thee,
be thy terms ever so severe.
O let us never part.
I resign my will, my liberty, my choice, to thee;
I stand divested of the world,
and ask only thy love as my inheritance.
Give me or deny me what thou wilt,
I leave all the circumstances of my future time
in thy hands.
Here I am.
Do with me what seemeth good in thy sight,
only do not say thou hast no pleasure in me.

Let me not live to dishonor thee,
to bring a reproach on thy name,
to profane the blood of the Son of God,
and grieve the Spirit of grace.
O take not thy loving-kindness from me,
nor suffer thy faithfulness to fail.
Thou hast sworn by thy holiness,
and thou wilt not lie to the seed of thy servants.
Thou hast sworn that the generation of the righteous
shall be blessed; vest me with this character,
O my God, and fulfill this promise
to a worthless creature.

*—Elizabeth Singer Rowe, 1674–1737; alt.*

# For the True Bread

Christ our Lord hath so devised the petitions which we make unto thee, that in seeking first the glory of thy name, he wills that we should have experience of the riches of thy goodness, in all things necessary for this life. Thus wilt thou, O merciful Father, reward with infinite benefits, even our simple thoughts of the brightness of thy glory, and crown thy gifts in us with grace for grace. We do therefore daily crave our bread, and thou dost give it to us, that is to say, even all that is necessary for our maintenance here beneath. Yet dost thou present us with one bread far more excellent and profitable, even the bread of angels and of the blessed spirits. Give me therefore, O Lord, Jesus Christ, God and man, that in him I may live forever, that my understanding may be enlightened with his truth, and my heart kindled with the fire of his love that I perish not.

—*Théodore de Bèze, 1519–1605; alt.*

# "To Pray"

O God, I remember those who can have no joy today!
parents whose children died;
unemployed;
those in prisons, being tortured;
the ill, in pain;
old people, lonely;
peasants, landless;
Indians, living the last days of their people;
those who have nothing to eat.
In some way, may the gentle breath of the Spirit cause hope
    to shine in their hearts, and may they have the courage to
    struggle for a better world,
sacrament of the Kingdom of God.
I remember, also, those who can have no joy because they
    are under the domination of idols,
possessed by evil spirits,

those who think only about their profit, and so exploit the
   poor;
those who can with impunity use arms and violence, and so
   perfume their bodies and mock rights;
those who because they think only about themselves, are
unable to feel the sweet tenderness of solidarity with those
   who suffer.
Help me to rejoice in that sadness from which there springs
   forth nostalgia for the Kingdom of God and to hate the
   sadness of those who have eyes only for themselves.
And may the sad ones of your Kingdom never lack the sweet
   sacrament of the smile of God. Amen.

*—Rubem A. Alves, b. 1933*

Reprinted from I BELIEVE IN THE RESURRECTION OF THE BODY by Rubem Alves,
copyright © 1986 Fortress Press. Used by permission of Augsburg Fortress.

## *At the Ending of the Day* 181

Gracious Lord, under whose protection we rest:
when we wake, give us leave to think of thee,
let us in our dreams draw nearer to thee,
do thou prepare us for thee,
and let us never be taken unprovided, but,
with the wise virgins, ready whensoever thou shalt call us
to go with thee.
And so we recommend ourselves, our souls, and all unto thee,
through Jesus Christ our Lord. Amen.

   *—Michael Sparke (compiler), The Crums of Comfort, 1629 ed.; alt.*

182

## *Approach*

Merciful God, dear Father, from my heart I thank you that you have
not only commanded us to call on you in all times of need, but also
graciously promised that you would hear us and give us what is good
and wholesome for our body and soul. I ask you to pour forth upon
me your Holy Spirit, the Spirit of prayer, so that I may always find joy
and pleasure in praying, may draw near daily to your throne of grace,
consoled and with full confidence in the name of my Lord and Savior
Jesus Christ, and pour out my heart before you, that are the righteous
Father over all your offspring in heaven and on earth. Grant that I may
lift up holy hands to you and may trust firmly and confidently that you
will give heed to my prayer and my beseeching. Set me free from all
burdensome cares and anxious thoughts, so that with all humility and
patience I may wait for the hour of your choice, when you will help
me. By your Holy Spirit, remind me daily of my end and by your grace
prepare me for a blessed departure from this life. Amen.

*—Evangelical Reformed Church of Lippe (Germany), 1925*

183

## *For True Bread*

Ah, Christ,
who had the power to turn stones to bread
and did not,
we tell Thee of our hearts
that they are stone,
and we beg Thee to turn them
to that true bread
which comes down from above!

*—Ze Tembe, fl. 1915; alt.*

## For Grace to Ask a Blessing

Lord, unless thou teachest by thy Holy Spirit, and give us daily supply from thine own self, we can do nothing. O Lord, we are not able to do one good action without thy special grace. But here lies our fault still: we have not the power, no strength, Lord, we have not because we ask not.

O that my soul may abide seeking of thee, that my heart may still more and more be carried out with this sincere love unto thee and thine. O suffer me, dear Lord, once more to say with boldness, through thy grace: I will not let thee go until thou herein will bless me.

*—Sarah Davy, ca. 1638–ca. 1669; alt.*


## Intercession: For All Workers

We pray to you, Lord: guide, protect, and enlighten all who labor to earn their daily bread:

> For all engaged in agriculture,
> For all who work at the production line,
>> We pray to you, Lord!
> For all involved in manufacturing,
> For all active in commerce,
>> We pray to you, Lord!
> For all who live by the strength of their arm
>> or the skill of their hands,
> For employers and managers,
>> We pray to you, Lord!
> For all who enrich our life through art, research,
>> or scholarship,
> For all who form and influence the mind of our age
>> by thought or writing,
> For all who serve in diplomacy and government,
> For physicians and nurses, preachers, and educators,
>> We pray to you, Lord!

For all who must work without joy, recognition, or
satisfaction, or cannot find work,
For all who are forced to work to the point of
exhaustion, without adequate rest or just pay,
For all engaged in dangerous professions,
For prisoners and outcasts,
For those who are victims of other people's desire,
For the sick and the hungry,
We pray to you, Lord!

O God, you that labor untiringly and have given work to
humankind so that we may be your fellow workers, teach us to
recognize your blessing, the rights and nobility of work; and
sanctify all honest and worthwhile work as a pure and well-
pleasing offering to you. Amen.

*—United Evangelical-Protestant Church in Baden (Germany), 1930*

186

## *For the Day's Work*

Be present, good and gracious Father, with me and grant that all things
that I take in hand may begin in knowledge, proceed in fear of thee,
and end in love; that my whole course of life may be blessed with good
effect in all my endeavors; that neither mine enemies rejoice at my
miseries, the godly be offended at my rashness, nor my estate be
hindered by my foolishness. Good Lord, grant this for thy Son's sake.
Amen.

*—John Norden, 1548–1625*

## *For the Gift to Pray Attentively* 187

Grant, we beseech thee, dear Father, that we, being fully persuaded in our hearts of thy fatherly love and affection towards us, may be stirred up to make our petitions with such an affection, ardent desire, love, and reverence to thy Majesty, that our minds be not carried away with distracting thoughts creeping in, but without all wandering, may be fully attentive to the thing we ask, and fully stayed upon thy merciful and just protection.

—*Edward Dering, ca. 1540–1576; alt.*

## *A Thankful Acknowledgement of God's Providence* 188

In mother's womb thy fingers did me make,
And from the womb thou didst me safely take.
From breast thou hast nursed me my life throughout,
That I may say I never wanted aught.

In all my meals my table thou hast spread.
In all my lodgings thou hast made my bed.
Thou hast clad me with changes of array,
And changed my house for better far away.

In youthful wanderings thou didst stay my slide,
In all my journeys thou hast been my guide.
Thou hast saved me from many an unknown danger,
And showed me favor even where I was a stranger.

In both my callings thou hast heard my voice,
In both my matches thou hast made my choice.
Thou gavest me sons, and daughters them to peer.
And givest me hope thou'lt learn them thee to fear.

Oft have I seen thee look with mercy's face,
And through thy Christ have felt thy saving grace.
This is the heaven on earth, if any be;
For this, and all, my soul doth worship thee.

—John Cotton, 1548–1652

## Confession

O Lord God, thou hast given us so many things that we have scarce anything left to pray for. Yet we covet as if we had nothing, and live as though we knew nothing. When we were children we deferred till we were grown. Now we are grown, we defer until we be old. And when we be old, we will defer until death. Thus we steal thy gifts and do nothing for them. Yet we look for as much at thy hands as they which serve thee all their lives.

We are ashamed of many sins in others, and yet we are not ashamed to commit the same sins ourselves, and worse than they. Yea, we have sinned so long almost that we can do nothing else but sin. If we do any evil, we do it cheerfully and quickly and easily. But if we do good, we do it faintly and rudely and slackly. When did we talk without vanity? When did we give without hypocrisy? When did we bargain without deceit? When did we reprove without envy? When did we hear without weariness? When did we pray without tediousness? Such is our corruption, as though we were made to sin in deed, in word, or in thought. We have broken all thy commandments, that we might see what good is in evil.

Some have been won by the word, but we would not suffer it to change us. Some have been reformed by the cross, but we would not suffer it to purge us. Some have been moved by thy benefits, but we would not suffer them to persuade us. Thy blessings make us proud, thy riches covetous, thy peace wanton, thy meats intemperate, thy mercy secure, and all thy benefits are weapons to rebel against thee.

What shall we answer for that which our conscience condemns? Thou might justly forsake us, as we forsake thee, and condemn us, whose conscience condemns ourselves. But who can measure thy goodness, which givest all and forgivest all? Though we are sinful, yet thou lovest us. Though we knock not, yet thou openest. Though we ask not, yet thou givest. Therefore, O Lord, give us a heart to serve thee, and let this be our hour of conversion. Let not evil overcome good, let not thine enemy have his will, but give us strength to resist, patience to endure, and constancy to persevere unto the end.

*—Henry Smith, ca. 1550–1591; alt.*

## For Reconciliation with God 190

Lord Jesus, here I am, a poor captive exile, a lost creature, an enemy to God. Wilt thou, Lord, reconcile me to God and save my soul? Do not, Lord, refuse me; for if thou refuse me, to whom then shall I go? Art not thou he and he alone, whom God the Father hath sealed the Savior of sinners? If I had come in my own name, thou mightest well have put me back; but since I come at the command of the Father, reject me not.

Lord, help me. Lord, save me. I cast myself upon thy grace and mercy; do not refuse me. I have not whither else to go; here I will stay. I will not stir from thy door. On thee will I trust and rest and venture myself. God hath laid my help on thee, and on thee I lay my hope, for pardon, for life, for salvation. If I perish, I perish on thy shoulders. If I sink, I sink in thy vessel. If I die, I die at thy door. Bid me not go away, for I will not go.

*—Richard Alleine, 1611–1681; alt.*

## *Intercession: For All Who Labor*

O Christ, who camest not to be ministered unto but to minister, have mercy on all who labour faithfully to serve the common good. O Christ, who didst feed the hungry multitude with loaves and fishes, have mercy upon all who labour to earn their daily bread. O Christ, who didst call unto Thyself all them that labour and are heavy laden, have mercy upon all whose work is beyond their strength. And to Thee, with the Father and the Holy Spirit, be all the glory and the praise. Amen.

*—John Baillie, 1886–1960*

---

Reprinted with the permission of Scribner, a Division of Simon & Schuster; and by permission of Oxford University Press from A DIARY OF PRIVATE PRAYER by John Baillie. Copyright 1949 by Charles Scribner's Sons; copyright renewed © 1977 by Ian Fowler Baillie. Copyright 1936 Oxford University Press.

## *At the Ending of the Day*

Lord, in as much as thine unsearchable wisdom hath been pleased to divide our whole life into labor and rest, and every one of our days into light and darkness and yet appointest them both to serve thy glory, I lift up my hands unto thee and offer unto thee for an evening sacrifice my heart and my tongue, ruminating in my thoughts that favor wherewith thou hast from morning unto this evening sustained my life, conducted my actions, guided my steps, directed my hands, governed my thoughts, turned away the temptations of this world. I form, in the best manner I am able, a thanksgiving and song of praise to thy infinite goodness.

Grant that my body may take rest in bed, my soul repose in the bosom of thy Son Jesus Christ, and thy Holy Spirit watch over me. Let me awake at a fit hour and exercise myself in holy prayer, thus, all the days of my life sliding on one after another, until it shall please thee to change this temporal into an eternal rest, through the intercession of him that hath purchased us with the price of his blood, our Savior, Jesus Christ. Amen.

*—Pierre Du Moulin, the Elder, 1568–1658; alt.*

## For the Spirit of Prayer                                      193

Lord, O may this place be a Bethel. Here let me, with Jacob, wrestle
with thee for the blessings I want, namely, increase of all the graces of
thy blessed Spirit, knowledge, faith, evangelical repentance, yea, and
humility, that dear and lovely grace; and for a spirit of prayer to be
poured out on me.

      Lord, let me be no longer dumb before thy throne, since prayer
is the very breath and life of the new creature. Lord, all thy works
praise thee and shall I alone be silent, while the angelic hosts and
saints adore thee? O let me, even me, also bear my part.

*—Sarah Osborn, 1714–1796; alt.*

## Confession                                      194

God of all mercy,
we confess before you and each other
that we have been unfaithful to you.
We lack love for our neighbors,
we waste opportunities to do good,
and we look the other way
when you cry out to us in the suffering
of our brothers and sisters in need.
We are sincerely sorry for our sins,
both those we commit deliberately
and those we allow to overtake us.
We ask your forgiveness
and pray for strength
that we may follow in your way
and love all your people
with that perfect love which casts out all fear;
through Jesus Christ our Redeemer. Amen.

*—United Church of Christ, (USA) 1986*

## Prayer for Pardon and Peace

195

O God, have mercy upon us thy penitent children and grant us thy forgiveness through Jesus Christ our Lord. Turn us again unto thyself and suffer us not to fall away from thee, for with thee there is mercy and thou dost redeem thy people from all their iniquities.

O Thou who didst send thy Son Jesus Christ into the world to seek and to save that which was lost, receive us in thy mercy and comfort us with thy salvation.

Create in us a clean heart, O God, and renew a right spirit within us. Cast us not away from thy presence, and take not thy Holy Spirit from us. Amen.

—*Scotland,* Euchologion, *1896; alt.*

## For Perseverance

196

Keep me, O righteous Father, from security or standing at a stay, lest, for not going forward, I go backward in thy justice and run after the evil world. Confirm in me this grace: both carefully and constantly to keep thy watch that I may have boldness, now and ever expect thy coming, crying, "Come, Lord Jesus"; and that in the meantime, though mine adversary should write a book against me, I may wear it as a crown upon my head, and finally, that at thy appearing, I may lift up my head for joy.

—*John Brinsley, fl. 1584–1630; alt.*

## Intercession: For Social Justice

197

Just and Holy God, you suffer in human sin and suffering; lead us into the way of justice and peace.

Bless our church and our country.

Set us free from all corruption and evil. Restrain the power of those who exploit the weakness of their neighbors. Inspire and strengthen the efforts of those who strive to ease the burden of daily suffering weighing on their brothers and sisters. Speed the establishment of a just and charitable order. Grant to each one the will to live for all, and to all, the will to live for each, in Christ our Lord. Give us all good will, honesty, and faithfulness in our task. By the Spirit of your Christ transform relationships between peoples and classes, employers and employees, rich and poor. Let all realize that they are your family, and that they are one in the church of your Son Jesus Christ, through mutual trust and love.

Bless those who work with their hands or with their minds in the service of their neighbors. Keep in your unending protection those whose work is dangerous. Be the light of those called to guide human thought: writers, scholars, specialists, artists.

We entreat you, Father, for men and women anxious for their daily bread, those who have no work and find themselves homeless. Be the help of all the afflicted. Take pity on the rebellious, the desperate, those who are slandered. Come to the aid of the weak who can bear no more, those tempted to take their lives, those who doubt your grace.

Lord, as you have promised us that your reign will come and have taught us to pray for its coming, make us always grateful for the signs of its dawning, and give us the mind to work for that day of joy when we shall see you face to face, and when you shall be all in all, through Jesus Christ our Savior. Amen.

*—Reformed Church of Berne (Switzerland), 1955*

## *For an Answer* 198

O my God, if I do not sincerely desire to glorify thy name, then deny my requests, and let me have no answer of my prayers. But if I do in sincerity desire to serve and glorify thee, then have compassion on me, and deny me not, I pray thee. Upon these terms let me go either with an answer or a denial.

*—Increase Mather, 1639–1723*

# My Family

O mighty and merciful God,
my family
prays to You,
glorifies and praises You,
adores You and pleads with You.
Here stands this small circle
before Your great majesty.
We would not dare pray to You
if Jesus had not said it was all right.

Lord of lords,
we put ourselves
under Your commands.
Most of our family is still in the village.
We are alone here in the city
and do not feel at home yet.
Many temptations and constant danger
surround us.
Lord,
please watch over these little children
when they go to school.
Those trucks and taxis go much too fast.
Lord, in this big city
without friends
we have only You to trust in.
We are afraid to be without a job—
and of death.

Lord,
protect us in this city.
We are at home wherever You are.
Stay with us, we pray.
Amen.

> —A. C. Kumah, contemporary

## Praise

O my sweet Savior, shall I be one with thee,
as thou art one with the Father?
And wilt thou glorify me
with that glory
which thou hadst with the Father
before the world was?
And dost thou so love me,
who am but dust and ashes,
as to make me partaker of glory with thee?

What am I, but a poor wretch,
that thou art so mindful of me?
Oh, how wonderful, how wonderful,
how wonderful is thy love!

Oh, thy love is unspeakable,
who hast dealt so graciously with me!
Oh, I feel thy mercies!
And, oh that my tongue and heart were able
to sound forth thy praises as I ought
and willingly would do!

    —*Katharine Brettargh, 1579–1601; alt.*

O Lord my God and Heavenly Father, I thy most unworthy child
do here in thy sight freely confess that I am a most sinful creature.
I was born and bred in sin, and stained in the womb, so have I
continually brought forth the corrupt and ugly fruits of that infection
and contagion, wherein I was first conceived, in thoughts, words, and
works. If I should go about to reckon up my particular offenses, I
know not where to begin or where to make an end. For they are more
than the hairs of my head; yea, far more than I can possibly feel or
know. Thou only, O Lord, knowest my sins, who knowest my heart;
nothing is hid from thee: thou knowest what I have been and what I
am. In very deed, I am altogether a lump of sin and a mass of misery,
and therefore, I have forfeited thy favor, incurred thy high displeasure
and have given thee just cause to frown upon me.

I have learned from thy mouth that thou art a God full of
mercy, slow to wrath, of great compassion and kindness towards all
such as groan under the burden of their sins. Therefore, extend thy
great mercy towards me, poor sinner, and give me a general pardon for
all mine offenses whatsoever. Seal it in the blood of thy Son, and seal it
to my conscience by thy Spirit, assuring me more and more of thy love
and favor towards me, and that thou art a reconciled Father unto me.
Grant that I may have time to come to love thee much, because much
is given, and of very love, fear thee and obey thee.

*—Arthur Dent, d. 1607; alt.*

## A Monument to God's Goodness

O Lord, thou art merciful and gracious, long-suffering and slow
to anger. This is evident from thy going before me daily with the
blessings of thy goodness. I cannot but admire thy patience, when
I consider how quickly, how easily thou couldst ease thyself of thy
adversary and be avenged of thine enemies. How backward art thou,
O Lord, to whet thy glittering sword and how much space dost thou
give wherein to repent. I adore thee for those illustrations of thy
patience upon record in thy word: thy long-suffering did wait in the

days of Noah upon a world of ungodly sinners for the space of an hundred and twenty years. For the space of forty years didst thou suffer the manners of the Israelites in the wilderness. Yea, so backward art thou to acts of vengeance that thou wouldst not go up in the midst of provoking Israel lest by their iniquities thou shouldst have been provoked to consume them in the way; and afterwards, when thou wast about to give up on Ephraim and to deliver Israel, thy heart was turned within thee and thy repentings were kindled together. But I need not go so far back to find examples of thy patience to mention to thy praise, when I myself am such a monument of thy forbearing goodness.

Thou hast been long-suffering towards me, not willing that I should perish, but that I should come to repentance. O grant that I may not, as I have done, despise the riches of thy goodness, forbearance, and long-suffering, but let thy goodness lead me to repentance. Thou hast waited to be gracious and hast come many years seeking fruit but hast found either none or next to none. O suffer me not [to continue] to abuse thy patience, to provoke thee to cut me down. Grant that henceforth I may have fruit unto holiness and let the end be everlasting life. Hear and answer, for thy Son's sake, to whom with thee and the Holy Ghost, be honor and glory and everlasting praise. Amen.

—*Robert Murrey, fl. 1695–1737; alt.*

## A Prayer of Voyagers

203

Bless our ship.
> May God the Father bless her.

Bless our ship.
> May Jesus Christ bless her.

Bless our ship.
> May the Holy Spirit bless her.

What do ye fear, seeing that God the Father is with you?
> We fear nothing.

What do ye fear, seeing that God the Son is with you?
>We fear nothing.
What do ye fear, seeing that God the Holy Ghost is with you?
>We fear nothing.

May the Almighty God for the sake of his Son Jesus Christ, through the comfort of the Holy Ghost, the one God who brought the children of Israel through the Red Sea miraculously, and brought Jonah to land out of the whale's belly, and brought the apostle Paul and his ship with the crew, out of the great tempest and out of the fierce storm, save us and sanctify and bless us and carry us on with quiet and favoring winds and comfort, over the sea and into the harbor, according to his own good will, which thing we desire from him saying, Our Father . . .

—*Gaelic* Book of Common Order, *1567; alt.*

204

## *Intercession: For Healing within Society*

Almighty God,
through Jesus your Son
you created all things in heaven and on earth;
all nations, authorities and powers
were created through him and for him.
In him all things are held together in unity.
Break down the barriers which separate us from each other,
and bring peace to the troubled affairs of our world.

May divisions (between N and N) be healed.
Instil within our hearts
the desire for true peace, justice, and mercy,
that all people everywhere may live with dignity,
free from the fear of violence;
through Jesus Christ our Lord.
Amen.

—*Uniting Church in Australia, 1988*

## For the Hope of Eternal Life 205

O Lord, the God of the dead and of the living, strengthen our faith in that unseen world over which Christ died to have the dominion, and gather us with all thy saints in the day of his appearing, who liveth and reigneth with thee, one God, world without end. Amen.

—*Possibly by John Cairns, 1818–1892*

## At the Ending of the Day 206

Lord, when my body takes rest and sleep, grant that my mind and imagination may dream of thee and of heavenly joys. And although the dark encompass my body, yet let heavenly light enlighten my soul into eternal bliss and happiness, where is no want of spiritual comfort and eternal joys, which grant, Lord, I beseech thee, and receive my soul and body into thy heavenly protection, now and forever.

—*Michael Sparke (compiler)*, Crums of Comfort:
The Second Part, *1652: alt.*

### 207 *Prayer upon Waking*

Thou, Lord, who art the life of all the world, hast mercifully preserved me in life this night when I could do nothing to keep myself. I thank thee for my health and rest and peace. O now let thy mercies to me be renewed with the day. And let me spend this day in thy protection, by the help of thy Spirit, in love and faithful service to thee, and in watchfulness against my corruptions and temptations; for the sake of Jesus Christ. Amen.

*—Richard Baxter, 1615–1691*

### 208 *Act of Trust*

Why do I address thee, my God, with no more confidence? Can I survey the earth, can I gaze on the structure of the heavens and ask if thou art able to deliver? Can I call in question thy ability to succor me when I consider the general and particular instances of thy goodness and power? One age to another, in long succession, hath conveyed the records of thy glory. My forebears trusted in thee and were delivered. They have encouraged me; my own experience has encouraged me to trust in thee forever.

The sun may fail to rise, but thy truth, thy faithfulness cannot fail. Is anything too hard for God to accomplish? Can the united force of earth and hell resist his will? I apply myself immediately to thee, and renounce all the terror and all the confidence that may rise from heaven or earth besides.

I confess and acknowledge thy providence. Our ways are not at our own disposal, but all our goings are ordered by thee; all events are in thy hands, and thou only canst succeed or disappoint our hopes. If thou blow on our designs, they are for ever blasted; if thou bless them, neither earth nor hell can hinder their success.

At thy command nature and necessity are no more; all things are alike easy to God. Speak but thou the word, and my desires are granted. Thou canst look me into peace when the tumults of thoughts raise a storm within. Bid my soul be still, and all its tempests shall obey thee.

I depend only on thee. Do thou but smile and all the world may frown; do thou succeed my affairs, and I shall fear no obstacle that earth or hell can put in my way. Thou only art the object of my fear and all my desires are directed to thee.

Let no appearance of created things hide thee from my view. With a holy contempt let me survey the ample round of the creation as lying in the hollow of thy hand, and every being in heaven and on earth as immovable by the most potent cause in nature, till commissioned by thee to do good or hurt. O let thy hand be with me to keep me from evil, and let me abide under the shadow of the Almighty. To thee I fly for shelter from all the ills of mortality.

—*Elizabeth Singer Rowe, 1674–1737; alt.*

## *For Trust* 209

Grant us, Heavenly Father, so to come to know Thee in our days of quietude and calm, that, whensoever the storms of life overtake us, we may find our way, undisturbed and unhasting, to Thy sheltering care, sure of our place in Thy love, and of Thy power to protect and save.

—*Charles E. Watson, 1869–1942*

# Intercession: For Peace

O Most High and Glorious God, who art the Author of peace, from whom do proceed holy counsels and righteous desires: give unto us thy servants that peace which the world cannot give, that both our hearts and works may answer thy commandments, and that our days through the protection, may be always quiet from trouble.

Let thy salvation be nigh them that fear thee, that glory may dwell throughout our land. Let mercy and truth meet together; yea, let justice and peace embrace each other.

Bless, Lord, all countries, cities, towns, and places where thy Word doth abide, and increase the number of them in the universal world.

O God of peace, which makest an end of war throughout the world: protect us from war and slaughter. Scatter the kingdoms that delight in war; break and hinder all evil counsels. Let them come to shame and perish.

Give all people a desire of peace, contented minds in their vocation, and a care to advance the welfare of that place they inhabit. Where strife, contention, and discord is present, reconcile hearts and minds that these flames and fires may speedily be put out, for thou canst conclude a truce for us and all people, and make the wolf to dwell with the lamb and the leopard to lie down with the kid.

Make our tabernacles safe and quiet, that about them there may be a rich tranquillity which may abound like the stream running over the banks, and our righteousness as the waves of the sea which is never dry. In thee shall we have our wished for peace, and thy people shall dwell in safe places of comfort.

Hear us, O Lord of peace, and grant that thy peace which passeth all understanding may keep our hearts and minds in the love of our Lord Jesus Christ, who liveth and reigneth with thee in the unity of the Holy Spirit, now and for evermore. Amen.

O Lord increase our faith in peace.

—*John Norden, 1548–1625; alt.*

## To Be at God's Disposal

Make me what thou wilt, Lord,
and set me where thou wilt.
I put myself wholly into thy hands:
put me to what thou wilt;
rank me with whom thou wilt;
put me to doing or put me to suffering;
let me be employed for thee,
or laid aside for thee;
exalted for thee,
or trodden underfoot for thee;
let me be full, or let me be empty;
let me have all things,
or let me have nothing;
I freely and heartily resign all
to thy pleasure and disposal.

                       *—Richard Alleine, 1611–1681; alt.*

## 212 *Humble Approach*

Lord, thou hast bid me come, behold here I am.
I come, Lord, at thy word.
I come for a little water.
I come for thy wine and milk.
I have brought no price in my hand,
but thou hast bid me come
and buy without money and without price.
Though I have no grace,
yet behold at thy word I come for grace.
Though I have no Christ, yet I come for Christ.
Though I cannot call thee Father, yet being called,
I come to thee as fatherless.
Shall earthly orphans find pity
and only spiritual orphans be left orphaned?
If I am not thy child, may I be made thy child?
Hast thou not a child's blessing left yet to bestow on me?

Thou hast bid me come for a blessing; bless me, O Lord.
I come at thy word;
do not say, "Be gone out of my sight."
Lord, I cannot go, I will not go;
for whither shall I go from thee?
Thou hast the words of eternal life.
Since thou wilt have me to speak, Lord, answer.
Though I dare not say, "Be just to me a saint";
yet I do say, "Lord, be merciful to me a sinner."

*—Richard Alleine, 1611–1681; alt.*

Lord, I have an ignorant, a prejudiced, and an unbelieving heart;
it staggereth at thy word. It questioneth the Scriptures. It looketh
strangely upon Christ himself. It looketh doubtingly and amazedly
towards the world to come. I am so captivated in flesh and used to live
by sight and sense, that I can scarce believe or apprehend the things
unseen, though thou hast revealed them with certain evidence. O for
one beam of thy heavenly illumination!

Pity a dark and unbelieving soul! Alas, if unbelief prevail,
Christ will be as no Christ to me, and the promise as no promise, and
heaven as no heaven. O heal this evil heart of unbelief, which hath
neglected Christ, his sacrifice, merits, doctrine, example, his covenant,
and his intercession, and hath departed from the living God. A promise
is left to us of entering into rest. O let me not fall short by unbelief! Let
me be taught by the inward light of thy Spirit to understand the light
of thy holy word, and leave me not in the power of the prince of
darkness.

Is it not thy will that I should pray for grace? Hast thou not
said that thou wilt give thy Holy Spirit to them that ask it? Have mercy
upon me. Sanctify this sinful miserable soul, that I may live in the
faithful and delightful exercise of thy grace unto thy glory here, and
may live in the delights of thy glorious love for evermore, through the
merits and intercession of my blessed Savior, who hath encouraged me
with the Publican, to hand down this ashamed face, and smite upon
this guilty breast, and in hope through his Name, to cry unto thee, God
be merciful to me a sinner! Amen, Amen.

*—Richard Baxter, 1615–1691; alt.*

# Make Me as a Little Child

O my precious Christ,
make me as a little child
every way thou wouldest have me to be so.
O make my heart tender,
as one who is new born.
O may I be easily bowed in spiritual things.
May I be filled with sympathy
when I see others in distress,
weep with those who weep,
and may I ever be easily won
with kindness.

As a little child flies to its parents for help,
so may I fly to Christ.
Make me as a little child,
afraid of the dark when far from home;
so make me sensible of spiritual dangers.
As a little child is afraid of superiors,
apt to dread their anger,
to tremble at their frowns and threatenings,
so let me be with respect to thee.
As a little child approaches superiors with awe,
so may I approach thee with holy awe and reverence.
O God, for Christ's sake,
preserve me from presumptuous boldness.
For I do believe, as Mr. Edwards* says,
"That nothing can be invented that is a greater absurdity,
than a morose, hard, close, high-spirited, spiteful
true Christian."

*—Sarah Osborn, 1714–1796; alt.*

---

*Jonathan Edwards, 1703–1758.

## Intercession: Making Room for God

215

Almighty God, Who hast set us in families so that we may understand Thy fatherhood in the great family of the Church: we pray for all who seek to make place for Thee at the hearths of home.

Open Thy word again in the houses of our people, inspire parents to lead and to teach the young in prayer, that the daily worship of our land may ascend from every Christian home, and Thy sufficiency be known again in things both great and small.

*—George MacLeod, 1895–1991*

## At the Ending of the Day

216

Almighty God, who makest darkness that it may be night, and providest for thy children the gift of rest; mercifully grant, we beseech thee, that while we rest we may rest in thee, and when we wake, we may awake to thy praise, through Jesus Christ our Lord. Amen.

*—John Hunter, 1848–1917*

217　　　　　　　　　*For the Mercy of Christ*

O sweet Jesus, thou hast given me that which thou didst not owe me, and hast forgiven me that which I did owe thee. Thou wast content to be the byword of the people, and the curse of the law for my sake. Blessed be thy Name, blessed be thy life, blessed be thy death. For thy death is my birth. The crown of thorns is my garland. The scars of thy body are the stars of my firmament. Thy bitter myrrh refresheth me. Thine infirmities strengthen me. Thy stripes heal me, and thy blood cleanseth me. Lo, I have nothing but what I have from thee.

O Good Jesus, make good thy name unto me, and let thy passion work compassion for me, that by thy mercy I may obtain remission of my sins and by thy merits obtain everlasting salvation in the kingdom of heaven. Amen.

*—Thomas Sorocold, 1561–1617; alt.*

218　　　　　　　*Whatever I Am, Let Me Be for Thee*

Lord Jesus, I come unto thee as thy clay, thy creature,
towards thee, Fountain of pity:
Behold a spectacle of misery.
Behold my naked soul, not a rag of righteousness to cover it.
Behold my starving soul. Ah! It has fed upon wind and vanity.
Behold my wounded soul bleeding at thy foot,
every part, head and heart, will and affections,
all wounded by sin.
O thou compassionate Samaritan, turn aside,
and pour thy sovereign blood into these bleeding wounds
which, like so many opened mouths, plead for pity.
Behold a returning, submitting rebel,

willing to lay down the weapons of unrighteousness
and to come upon the knee for a pardon.

Oh, I am weary of the service of sin.
I can endure it no longer.
Lord Jesus, thou wast appointed to preach glad tidings to the
       meek,
and to proclaim liberty to the captives
and the opening of the prison to them that are bound.
Come now and knock off those fetters of unbelief.
O set my soul at liberty, that it may praise thee!

Lord, thou wast lifted up to draw people unto thee.
Thou art a drawing Savior, a lovely Jesus.
I have hitherto fled from thee
but it was because I did not know thee.
Mine eyes have been held by unbelief.
I confess, I am not worthy that thou shouldst look upon me.
I expect to be trampled under the feet of justice
rather than to be embraced in thine arms of mercy.

O my Lord, I am willing to submit to any terms,
be they ever so hard and ungrateful to the flesh.
Whatever I shall suffer in thy service
cannot be like what I have suffered or am likely to suffer
by sin.
Henceforth, be thou my Lord and Master.
Be thou my priest and prophet, my wisdom and righteousness.
I resign up myself unto thee:
my poor soul with all its faculties,
my body with all its members to be living instruments
of thy glory.
Let "holiness to the Lord" be now written upon them all:
let my tongue plead for thee,

my hands be lifted up unto thy testimonies,
my feet walk in thy ways.
O let all my affections, as willing servants, wait upon thee
and be active for thee!

Whatever I am, let me be for thee.
Whatever I have, let it be thine.
Whatever I can do, let me do for thee.
Whatever I can suffer, let me suffer for thee.
O that I might say before I go hence,
"My beloved is mine, and I am his!"
O that what I have begged on earth might be ratified
in heaven!
My spirit within sayeth "Amen."
Lord Jesus,
say thou, "Amen."

—*John Flavel, ca. 1630–1691; alt.*


<sub>219</sub>
## For Protection

My God, suffer me not to let go my hold of thy providence. Thou, who didst interpose and by miracle deliver Hagar from her extremity, still interposest for delivery of thy children as effectually as ever, in answer to the prayer of helplessness.

May thy protecting angel extricate me from all my troubles and more especially from all my temptations. Shield me from the influences of an evil world. Suffer me not to be tempted beyond what I am able, but with the temptation, provide a way to escape, that I may be able to bear it. Leave me not, O God, unshielded and alone amid the perils of the dreary wilderness of this world, but cast the mantle of thy protection over me, and give me to experience that though in the world I have trials and troubles on every side, yet in Christ I have safety and peace.

—*Thomas Chalmers, 1780–1847; alt.*

## Prayer on the Jericho Road

Lord, the wounds of the world are too deep for us to heal. We have to bring men and women to you and ask you to look after them—the sick in body and mind, the withered in spirit, the victims of greed and injustice, the prisoners of grief. And yet, Our Father, do not let our prayers excuse us from paying the price of compassion. Make us generous with the resources you have entrusted to us. Let your work of rescue be done in us and through us all.

—*Caryl Micklem, b. 1925, and Roger Tomes, b. 1928*

## Consecration of the Day

Lord, we devote ourselves to thee. We present to thee our bodies and our souls as a living and holy sacrifice. And as we only live by thy bounty, we desire also that we may only live to please thee. Thy will shall be the rule of our behavior, and thy glory the end of it. And if we have been so unfortunate till now as to offend thee, we will labor with all our might to amend our faults, to follow thy commandments.

—*Church of Geneva, 1712*

222

## *Trinity*

I discern You, O Father, leaning over this world whose
horizon and whose light You have created. You enfold it
with such love that, for this world, You prepare the
sacrifice of Your son, Your only begotten.

I see You, O Jesus,
arms outstretched on a cross raised in the village square,
You pour out for this village a particular drop of Your
blood so that Your pardon may take root here.

I watch for You, O Holy Spirit, wind that restores life in the
overpowering heat of summer. As in the first days, as on
Pentecost, You seek here the body which You will make
Your dwelling-place.

*—Michel Bouttier, b. 1921*

223

## *Bridal Song of the Redeemed Soul*

O True, Perfect Husband and Friend, the most loving of all good
lovers: when I was in the most deep place of hell, so far out of the true
way, both in heart and mind, then thou didst call me back, saying,
"Daughter, hark and see and bow thy hearing towards me. Forget the
people with whom thou didst run away from me and also the house
of thine father where thou hast dwelled for so long." But when thou
sawest that this sweet and gracious speaking did me no good then thou
beginnest to cry, "Come unto me all ye which are weary with labor, I
shall receive you and feed you with my bread."

Thy sweet look hath penetrated my heart, wounding it even to
death, giving me remorse for my sins. With both thine arms and with a

sweet and manly heart, thou didst meet with me by the way, and, not reproaching me for my faults, embraced me. Beholding thy countenance, I could not see that ever thou didst perceive mine offense. Thou hast done as much for me as though I had been good and honest and didst hide my fault from everybody, showing that the multitude of my sins are so hidden and overcome by thy great victory, that thou wilt never remember them. Thou seest nothing in me but the graces, gifts and virtues which it pleaseth thy goodness to give me.

Now I have, through thy good grace, recovered the place of thy wife, O happy and desired place: gracious bed, throne right-honorable, seat of peace, rest of all war, high step of honor separate from the earth. Dost thou receive this unworthy creature, giving her the sceptre and crown of thine empire and glorious realm? Who did ever speak of such a thing, as to raise up one so high which of herself was nothing, and maketh of great value this which of itself was naught? Casting mine eyes on high, I see in thee goodness unknown, grace and love so incomprehensible that my sight is left not seeing. How good thou art unto me.

—*Marguerite of Navarre, 1492–1549, translated by Princess (later Queen) Elizabeth, age eleven; alt.*

## *For Spiritual Progress* 224

Carry me forward, O Heavenly Father, in the paths of righteousness, by all the methods of thy providence and grace, till I become fit to be transplanted into the higher world of spirits, where I shall live in everlasting security from all dangers; where I shall no more bewail the darkness of my understanding and the disorder of my heart, but where I shall see thee, my Maker unveiled, where I shall love thee entirely, rejoice in thee triumphantly, and celebrate thy praises to all eternity!

—*William Leechman, 1706–1785; alt.*

## For Steadfast Hope

O Thou who didst bear the burden of the cross, be pleased to lighten our load by strengthening our spirit. Thy ways are a great deep and not to be searched out. O teach us to submit to thy will in all things. Teach us to be content in all changes, to read our duty in thy providence, and in adversity to be steadfast, patient, hopeful. Give us grace to say from the heart, "Thy will, not mine, be done." Grant that the yoke of Christ may become easy to us, and his burden light.

—*Free Church of Scotland, 1898*

## Intercession: For Our Enemies

Lord, give us to love our enemies, to bless them that curse us, and to pray for those that despitefully use us and persecute us. Father, forgive them, for they know not what they do; and lay not their malice against us to their charge. Work in us a disposition to forbear and forgive in love, as thou requirest when we pray. And grant that our ways may so please the Lord, that even our enemies may be at peace with us. Let the wolf and the lamb lie down together, and let there be none to hurt or destroy in all thy holy mountain.

—*Matthew Henry, 1662–1714; alt.*

Lord God, it pleased you to create the night for our rest, just as you appointed the day for our work. In your grace, grant our bodies such rest this night that our souls may ever be awake to you, and our hearts, lifted up in your love. Grant that we may put aside all earthly cares, to find the relief which our weakness requires, so that we may never forget you. Let the support of your goodness and grace remain imprinted within our memory. Grant by this gift that our conscience may find its spiritual rest even as our body takes its own.

Do not let our sleep be excessive, to indulge the laziness of our flesh without restraint; let it simply meet the need of our fragile nature. Order us in our bodies as well as our spirits, and protect us from all dangers. Let even our sleeping be to the glory of your Name.

Since this day has not passed without our offending you in various ways, poor sinners that we are, be pleased to bury all our faults in your mercy, just as everything now is hidden by the darkness that you send upon the earth, that our sins may not keep us from the vision of your face.

Hear us, our God, our Father and Savior, through our Lord Jesus Christ, in whose name we pray to you, saying: Our Father . . .

*—Jean Calvin, 1509–1564; alt.*

## *Praise*

Eternal God,
in silence you behold
the suffering and affliction of your children.
As we shoulder the cross of your Son
in the hardship that is ours,
you feed our souls with hidden food
and reward endurance and quiet faith
with unearthly treasure.
Grant that we may so value your love
above all else,
that in adversity or comfort,
we may lift our hearts in praise,
for you show mercy to all disciples
of your crucified and Risen Son,
Christ our Lord, who reigns with you
and the Holy Spirit, one God,
for ever and ever. Amen.

—*Diane Karay Tripp, b. 1954*

## *Confession*

Eternal God, Almighty and most merciful: we thy unworthy servants, prostrate before thy throne of grace, do yield ourselves, body and soul, unto thee for all thy benefits which thou from our birth hast heaped upon us, as though we had always done thy will, although we, occupied about vain things, never loved, never served, never thanked thee so heartily for them, as we esteem a friend for the least courtesy. Therefore, we come with shame and sorrow to confess our sins which are not small but grievous, not few, but infinite, not past, but present, not secret, but presumptuous, against thy express word and will; against our own conscience, knowledge, and liking.

What shall we do then, but appeal unto thy mercy and humbly desire thy fatherly goodness to extend that compassion towards us, which thy beloved Son our loving Savior hath purchased so mightily, so graciously and so dearly for us? We believe and know that one drop of his blood is sufficient to heal our infirmities, pardon our iniquities, and supply our necessities.

But without thy grace—our light, our strength, our guide— we are unable to do nothing but sin, as woeful experience hath taught us too long. Therefore, good Father, as thou in special favor hast appointed us to serve thee, as thou hast ordained all other creatures to serve us, so may it please thee to send down thy heavenly Spirit into our hearts, change our affections, subdue our reason, regenerate our wills and purify our nature to this duty, so shall not thy benefits nor thy chastisements nor thy word return void, but accomplish that for which they were sent, until we be renewed to the image of thy Son.

—*Henry Smith, ca. 1560–1591; alt.*

## *Treasure Laid Up in Heaven* 230

O my God, suffer me never to live in the neglect of proper means, but use all diligence, casting my care on thee. Grant me prudence in everything. Suffer me never to act the part of a miser or covetous person, nor suffer me needlessly to squander, but thankfully and cheerfully to use what thou, in thy providence, hast provided and trust thee for future supplies. O let us not ungratefully hide thy talent in a napkin, murmur, and complain of poverty, but cheerfully rely on the stores of thy providence, without coveting stores of our own. Thou didst never fail us when we were poor, nor were we ever more happy than when we had nothing laid by, and why must there now be a reserve, why a treasure laid up on earth, where rust may corrupt and thieves break through and steal. O may my heart be set on my treasure that is laid up in heaven—that is worth loving. Could that be exhausted, I should be poor indeed!

—*Sarah Osborn, 1714–1796; alt.*

231

## *For Grace to Walk in the Light*

Grant, Almighty God, whatever revolutions happen daily in the
world, that we may always be intent on the sight of thy glory,
once manifested to us in thy Son. May the splendor of thy majesty
illuminate our hearts, and may we pass beyond the visible heavens,
the sun, the moon, and every shining thing; and may we behold the
blessedness of thy kingdom, which thou proposest to us in the light
of thy gospel. May we walk through the midst of the darkness and
afflictions of the world, content with that light by which thou invitest
us to the hope of the eternal inheritance which thou hast promised to
us, and acquired for us by the blood of thine only begotten Son.
Amen.

*—Jean Calvin, 1509–1564*

232

## *Intercession: For Christ's Church*

O Lord and God, we ask you that you would be pleased to pour out
your unbounded mercy upon your people, for whom your Son Jesus
did not refuse to be handed over to malicious hands and so to suffer
the death of the cross. With him you reign in eternity.

*—Johannes Oecolampadius, 1482–1531*

233

## *For the Day's Work*

Enable us, O God, to do all things as unto Thee; that small things
may be filled with greatness, and great things may be crowned with
humility; through Jesus Christ our Lord. Amen.

*—John U. Stephens, 1901–1984*

## My Soul Follows Hard after God

234

O my God, what can I say but this, that my heart admires thee and adores thee and loves thee? My little vessel is as full as it can hold. Thou art my hope and my help, my glory, and the lifter up of my head. My heart rejoiceth in thy salvation.

I bless thee, O God, for this soul of mine, which thou hast created, which thou hast taught to say "Where is God, my Maker?" I bless thee for the knowledge with which thou hast adorned it. I bless thee for the body which thou hast given me. I bless thee for that ease and freedom with which these limbs of mine move themselves and obey the dictates of my spirit, I hope, as guided by thine.

I praise thee for that royal bounty with which thou providest for the daily support of humankind in general, and for mine in particular; for the table which thou spreadest before me and for the overflowing cup which thou puttest into my hands. I bless thee that I eat not my morsel alone, but share it with so many agreeable friends. I thank thee for so many dear relatives at home.

Nor would I forget to acknowledge thy favor in rendering me capable of serving others and giving me to know how much more "blessed it is to give than to receive." I thank thee for a heart which feels sorrows and a mind which can contrive for their relief.

And surely, O Lord, I adore thee for the streams that water Paradise and maintain it in ever-flourishing, ever-growing delight. I praise thee for the rest, the joy thou art giving to many that were once dear to me on earth, whose sorrows it was my labor to soothe, and whose joys it was the delight of my heart to promote. I praise thee for the blessedness of every saint and every angel that surrounds thy throne above. And now, O my God, what shall I say unto thee? What, but that I love thee above all the powers of language to express. My soul follows hard after God, because his right hand upholds me. Let it still bear me up, and I shall press on towards thee, till all my desires be accomplished in the eternal enjoyment of thee! Amen.

—*Philip Doddridge, 1702–1751; alt.*

## *For True Devotion to Christ the Savior*

O Gracious Lord, Almighty and Everlasting God, the Father of my Lord and Savior Jesus Christ, who was born at Bethlehem in great poverty: grant me, I beseech thee, a room amongst the wisemen of the east, to offer the poor talent of my weak devotion unto him all the days of my life: true faith for pure gold, the perfume of devout prayer for sweet frankincense, and hearty sorrow with bitter tears of repentance for dripping myrrh.

And because he came into this world in such humility, with such a measure of love that he was content without constraint, to be laden with the heavy burden of all our infirmities, and to carry our woeful sorrows, vouchsafe me grace that I may pick up some crumbs under thy table and gather up some fruits at the foot of his cross, that when I shall have seen what Judas sold, and I have gained, I may bathe my soul in the purple stream of his most precious blood, and then entomb Jesus, and lay him up in a believing heart, until his glorious appearance.

O Lord, since he did vouchsafe to undergo a world of injuries and miseries for my sake, and at the last in a shameful death offered up himself in sacrifice for my redemption, strengthen my weakness and cleanse my filthiness, that all the days of my life, I, being washed, being sanctified, and being justified in the Name of the Lord Jesus and by the Spirit of my God, may never be without sorrow for my sins, thankfulness for thy benefits, fear of thy judgments, love of thy mercies, nor remembrance of thy presence. Amen.

*—Thomas Sorocold, 1561–1617; alt.*

## *Prayer for Pardon*

Lord, let my sins be forgiven: for the sake of that love which thou bearest thine own Son, for the sake of that love which thy Son beareth to thee, for the sake of his humble state, when he took flesh upon him that he might look like a sinner and be made a sacrifice, though himself was free from sin; for the sake of his perfect and painful obedience which has given complete honor to thy law; for the sake of the curse which he bore and the death which he suffered, which hath glorified thine authority and honored thy justice more than it was possible for my sins to have affronted it. Remember his dying agonies when the hour of darkness was upon him, and let not the powers of darkness prevail over me. Remember the day when thou stoodest afar from thine own Son and he cried out as one forsaken of God, and let me have thine everlasting presence. Let me never be forsaken, since thy Son hath born that punishment.

—*Isaac Watts, 1674–1748*

### *Take Away the Veil* 237

Lord Jesus, take away the veil from our eyes, that we may contemplate the beauty of thy ideals. Grant to us thy power, to the end that we may be faithful partakers of the joys and sufferings of thy Kingdom.

—*Epaminondas M. do Amaral, 1893–1961*

### *Prayer for Grace* 238

Lord Jesus, whereas I daily fall and am ready to sin, vouchsafe me grace, as oft as I shall, to rise again. Let me never presume, but always most meekly and humbly acknowledge my wretchedness and frailty, and repent with a firm purpose to amend. And let me not despair because of my great frailty, but ever trust in thy most loving mercy and readiness to forgive.

—*Robert Leighton, 1611–1684*

# Intercession: For Social Repentance

Eternal God, Father of all people: we glorify your name for drawing us into the household of faith as one family. Your love is gracious, self-giving and far-reaching, and thus, the most potent force in the world for judgment when rejected.

In our souls we feel the darkness that covers the world, the same darkness which covered the world when your Son was crucified. We see Him crucified in the social relations of our day, and the earth shaken by our inhumanity to those of different race or sex, class, or nation. Father, forgive us.

Hope for justice is so bleak that we cannot believe a morning of change will ever dawn. The light of moral discernment, compassion, and justice, seems to be extinguished. The lives of women, minorities, and the poor seem to count for nothing. The stars have fallen from the sky to the earth, like a fig tree sheds its fruit when shaken in the gale.

Lord of the poor and oppressed, we still have hope, for we know that heaven is silent to listen to your Easter people. The tomb is empty, Christ is alive; so we will pray for those who oppress us. They do not know what they are doing. They reject the love of the One seated on the throne, the Lamb who was slain, yet lives.

Send forth your love in all its power. Help the oppressor to learn the love of the Lamb, and deliver us all from judgment. We pray in the name of the Lamb, who saves us. Amen.

—*Lawrence W. Bottoms, 1908–1994*

## At the Ending of the Day

O come, sweet Savior,
take up thy rest here
in my poor naked soul,
and let my resting place be
under the shadow of thy wings,
then shall I fear no evil,
for thou art my support
and comfort forever.

—*Sarah Davy, ca. 1638–ca. 1669; alt.*

## *Approach* 241

O Love of the Godhead,
Comforter Spirit, Holy Spirit,
ineffable communion of the eternal Father
and of his well-beloved Son,
Sweet Comforter of the afflicted:
come down into my heart by your power,
and by the splendor and overwhelming strength
of your light.
Scatter all darkness and shadows of my heart
that it may be fit to receive you.

*—Georg Willem, 1635–1709; alt.*

## *Recall a Wandering Sheep* 242

Dear, kind Shepherd, for thine own name and for thine honor's sake,
recall a wandering sheep, and bring me to feed again in the sweet
pastures of thy love. O magnify thy grace in me, a poor creature, and
be thou glorified by my consolation. I thank thee and adore thee,
sweet Jesus, for any small streams of comfort, any glimpse of relief,
to my distressed mind. Show me again the reviving light of thy
countenance. Let me once more enjoy sweet communion with thee,
and my trembling soul find refuge in thy bleeding wounds. Help me
to walk more circumspectly, and never to spend another day in so
foolish, vain, and worldly a manner, seeing its dreadful consequences
are the wounding of my own soul, offending my dear Lord, grieving
the Holy Spirit, and filling me full of sorrow, darkness, and indevotion.
O give me strength from above to walk more closely with my God.

*—Martha Laurens Ramsay, 1759–1811*

# *Prayer for Faith*

We are taught by thy holy apostle, O most loving Savior, that whatever is not of faith is sin, and that it is impossible to please thee without faith, and therefore they that come unto thee must believe that thou art God and wilt abundantly reward all them that with true faith seek thee.

Seeing that faith is so precious a jewel in thy sight, and we of our own nature cannot have this most singular treasure except thou givest it unto us from above, we most heartily beseech thee to take away from us all infidelity and unfaithfulness, which we received of old Adam, and to plant in us true faith and undoubted belief, that we may be thoroughly persuaded that thou art the Son of the living God, our only Mediator, Advocate, and Intercessor, our only wisdom, righteousness, sanctification, and redemption.

O Lord God, suffer us not to lean on our own wisdom nor to seek salvation where superstition dreameth, but let our faith be grounded on thy word. Give us grace truly to believe in thee, with all our hearts to put our trust in thee, to look for all good things from thee, to call upon thy blessed name in adversity, and with joyful voices and merry hearts to praise and magnify it in prosperity.

—*Thomas Becon, 1512–1567; alt.*

# *Let Me Love Thee Much*

Lord, I have the one thing needful
and it shall never be taken from me.
There is, then, no occasion of my being careful
    about many things.
Let me sit at thy feet
and hear thy precious words;
let me wash thy feet with my tears
and wipe them with the hairs of my head.
Thou hast forgiven much,
O let me love thee much!

—*Sarah Osborn, 1714–1796; alt.*

## Intercession

Our Heavenly Father, hear, we beseech thee, the prayers of brothers for sisters, of sisters for brothers, of parents for their children, and children for their parents, of friends for friends.

We pray for the sick, for those over whom the rod of weariness hangs heavily. O Lord, have mercy upon them. Be thou their refuge and their strength, a very present help in this their time of trouble. Bring them back again to health and strength if it be thy will. Be present with the dying. Come to them as their everlasting Father, receive them in thine arms. Soothe them, O Father, as a mother doth her child. May they depart fearing no evil, so may they be for ever with thee.

And our God, we would remember those who are in mourning this day for some loved one, those whose wounds the angel of death has opened afresh. Be with them in their sorrow, in their distress. Fill their hearts with thy love. May it be but as a cloud over the sun, making them to gaze up into the heavens hid with thy glory.

We pray for those who give their lives that the knowledge of thy truth may be enlarged. Be with thy servants in every land who seek to bring the glad tidings of thy gospel of peace.

Be with thy church everywhere. May she walk warily in times of peace and quietness, and boldly in times of trouble. Do thou remove all harshness and bitterness from amongst us towards those who walk not in all things with us but who worship our Lord in sincerity and truth. And all this we ask for the sake of thy dear Son. Amen.

—*Helen J. Waddell, 1889–1965; alt.*

## Dedication

Lord, I adore the grace that has saved me. It is by thy grace that I am what I am. I owe thee myself. Help me to devote myself to thee, that as thou hast given me the possession and enjoyment of myself, all I have and am may henceforth be sacred unto thee, be thine entirely and for ever.

—*Benjamin Bennet, 1674–1726*

247 *Approach*

Dear Jesus we now turn to Thee,
    Salvation to obtain;
Our Hearts and Souls do meet again,
    To magnify thy Name.
Come Holy Spirit, Heavenly Dove,
    The Object of our Care;
Salvation doth increase our Love;
    Our hearts hath felt thy fear.
Now Glory be to God on High,
    Salvation high and low;
And thus the Soul on Christ rely,
    To heaven surely go.
Come Blessed Jesus, Heavenly Dove,
    Accept Repentance here;
Salvation give, with tender Love;
    Let us with Angels share.
—*Jupiter Hammon, ca. 1711–ca. 1806*

248 *Affirmation of the Baptismal Covenant*

O Eternal God, thou hast been my God from my mother's womb. Thou didst put me into the waters of regeneration at the porch and entrance of the temple of thy church. Thou didst put upon me the white robe of righteousness, and didst enroll my name with them that are written among the living in Jerusalem. My parents and friends did present me to the Lord in the great congregation, where I was solemnly devoted to thee, O my God, and received the seal of thy holy covenant, the badge and livery of thy soldiers, even baptism. Thereby I was sacramentally engrafted into Christ and there was that day a solemnization of an heavenly marriage between Christ and my soul. That day there was a mutual covenant between God the Father, Son, and Holy Ghost and my poor soul, a deed of gift sealed on both parties, wherein God gave himself to me and my soul was given up to God. I took God the Father and he took me for his adopted child.

But alas, how have I owned this covenant-relation? How sadly did I violate my baptismal vow! I have lived many years since I was marked as God's sheep, but, Lord, what a wretch am I that have been wandering upon the mountains of sin and error the most part of my days. Lord, what shall I do, what amends can I now make? I am a perjured wretch, a sacrilegious villain, a woeful apostate.

But, Lord, the covenant sealed in baptism is a covenant of grace. My soul takes encouragement from my baptism to plead for pardon and acceptance. Didst thou adopt me as thy child and seal up my inheritance, and wilt thou now disinherit me? God, forbid. Thou knowest I am thine.

I come therefore once again, renewing my repentance and vows, acting in faith upon my sweet Savior, whose soldier and servant I am, that thou, sweet Jesus, not suffer me to depart from thee.

I am a Christian. Fortify my spirit against all temptations. Lord, I am enlisted under thy colors, appointed to fight thy battles against flesh, world, and the devil. Wilt thou forsake me in the open field? I am baptized into one body with thy faithful members; oh let me be assimilated to them and have communion with them in spirit. Lord, let the strength of that ordinance be upon my heart, that as Christ was raised up from the dead by the glory of the Father, my soul might henceforth walk in newness of life!

Here I am, Lord. I am wholly thine. The desire of my soul is wholly to follow the Lord and the Lamb through all conditions. Command strength for me. Lead me by thy hand. Act in me by thy Spirit, and bring me to thy kingdom to which I am newborn.

—*Oliver Heywood, 1630–1702; alt.*

# Thanksgiving and Intercession

O Omnipotent Lord God, Heavenly Father, we offer up unto thee our humble praises and thanksgivings for all thy benefits which from the foundation of the world, yea, from all eternity, thou hast been pleased to bestow upon us, in our election, in our creation, in our redemption; for our health and wealth, and all other gracious blessings that we have received from thee for the sustenance both of soul and body, from the days of our infancy until this present hour.

But especially we thank thee that this day, this past week, and all the time past of our lives, thou hast been pleased with thy gracious providence and fatherly care, to bless, preserve, and keep us. Vouchsafe us thy grace, O Lord, that we may keep all these thy great mercies and favors in continual remembrance all the days of our lives; never forgetting to render unto thee our perpetual praises and hearty thanksgivings for the same.

And in a special sense we recommend unto thy gracious care and watchful providence and protection, our souls and bodies, our health and wealth, our children and our children's children, our houses and estates, our city and country, our churches and schools, and all that we are and that we have, that in all these we may be blessed and preserved from henceforth and for evermore.

Moreover, bless, O Lord, our cornfields and vineyards with good and seasonable weather. Preserve the seed in the ground and the fruits on the trees from hail and frost, from thunder and lightning, from mildew and blasting, and from all other harm. Keep our herds and flocks from all hurt, both in the pastures and stables. Prevent our houses and barns from the rage of fire and water, from sudden surprising inroads of our enemies, from theft and robbery, and from all other evil.

Watch thou for us when we are asleep, and while our bodies are taking their natural rest, let our souls, minds, and hearts watch unto thee and increase in love of thee.

O God of all mercies, preserve and increase in us true faith, and when on the ensuing holy day and at any other time, we meet together in thy house, open thou then our ears and hearts, that we may hear the preaching of thy word with devotion and receive and obey it with faith, and grant that thereby, both our lives may be truly reformed and our salvation advanced.

Finally, forasmuch as thou hast commanded us to pray for all people, we beseech thee therefore, for all states and degrees of those whom thou hast ordained: for all governors, presidents, and judges. Rule thou thyself every one of them to the end that they may preside over us with justice and equity, and that we may dutifully obey them in everything that is good and lawful.

We beseech thee for the whole estate of the catholic church; for all faithful laborers in thy word and doctrine. Preserve amongst us, as necessity requireth, a suitable church discipline. Cause thy word which they preach, to make deep and powerful impressions upon the hearers, and let not their labor in the Lord be for us in vain.

We beseech thee for the state of the Christian economy, that thou wouldst bless all godly families and grant that their children may be educated in modesty and good discipline; and that every youth may be brought up in dutiful obedience, and in subjectivity unto their respective superiors, and for us all, parents and children, bless thou the work of our hands.

We commend unto thy fatherly care and trust all poor and needy, all sick and dying persons, all such as are afflicted, tempted, distracted, or in any trouble of mind, all widows and orphans, all such as go astray in any erroneous way, all such as are entangled in any inextricable labyrinth. We beseech thee for all those in the faith, wheresoever oppressed and persecuted, for all thy secret disciples that know thee, and for all those that any way stand in need of thy help, grace, and comfort. Vouchsafe to every one of them suitable supplies, and deliver them from all their several griefs and miseries, and finally, O Lord, be merciful and gracious unto us all, through our dear Lord and Savior Jesus Christ, who hath taught us to pray thus: Our Father . . .

—*Church of Zurich, 1693; alt.*

## *At the Ending of the Day*

My God, who in unity of being
and in Trinity of persons
live and reign eternally:
cover me with the shadow of your wings.
Preserve both my body and soul
through all my earthly pilgrimage
until you bring my whole being home
into your Paradise,
there to enjoy eternally
the delights you have kept for me.

*—Georg Willem, 1635–1709; alt.*

## *Thank God* 251

Almighty! and all wise God our heavenly father!
'tis once more and again that a few of your beloved children
       are gathered together to call upon your holy name.
We bow at your footstool of mercy, Master,
       to thank you for our spared lives.
We thank you that we are able to get up this morning
       clothed in our right mind, for Master,
since we met here, many have been snatched
       out of the land of the living
       and hurled into eternity.

But through your goodness and mercy
we have been spared to assemble ourselves here once more
to call upon a Captain who has never lost a battle.
Oh, throw round us your strong arms of protection.
Bind us together in love and union.
Build us up where we are torn down and
       strengthen us where we are weak.
Oh, Lord! Oh, Lord! take the lead of our minds,
place them on heaven and heavenly divine things.
Oh, God, our Captain and King!
Search our hearts, Master,
as far as the east is from the west.
Now, Lord, you know our hearts, you know our heart's desire.
You know our down-setting and our up-rising.
Lord, you know all about us 'cause you made us.

Lord! Lord! One more kind favor I ask you.
Remember the man that is to stand in the gateway
        and proclaim your Holy Word.
Oh, stand by him.
Strengthen him where he is weak and build him up
where he is torn down.
Oh, let him down into the deep treasures of your word.

And now oh, Lord, when this humble servant is done
        down here in this low land of sorrow:
done sitting down and getting up:
done being called everything but a child of God;
oh, when I am done, done, done,
and this old world can afford me no longer,
right soon in the morning, Lord, right soon in the morning,
meet me down at the river of Jordan,
bid the water to be still,
tuck my little soul away in that low swinging chariot,
and bear it away over yonder in the third heaven
        where every day will be Sunday
        and my sorrows of this old world will have an end,
        is my prayer for Christ my Redeemer's sake and
amen and thank God.

*—African American folk prayer recollected by Melva Wilson Costen,*
   *who heard it in the black Presbyterian church of her youth; alt.*

## For Closeness to God

My God, my God,
thou knowest I love thee above all things.
Let me not despise the bounties of thy providence,
but take me nearer to thyself.
Dost thou not know my desire is after thee?
O does not every wish center in thee?
Dost thou not fill all my thoughts?
Is not the whole bent of my thoughts,
from my first waking to my last, after thee?
Do I not pursue thee all the day?
O let nothing turn me aside,
till I find thee.
O let neither riches, pleasures, nor honors,
nor all the best enjoyments of earth
stay my pursuit or amuse my soul
for a moment.

—*Susanna Anthony, 1726–1791; alt.*

## For Transformation

O my God,
I would be transformed into thine image.
I would be thy temple.
I would have thee live in me, walk in me, make me
   one with thee.
I would be delivered from self-will, self-wisdom, self-seeking.

Lord, enable me continually to receive,
then shall I cease to wander,
then shall I run and not be weary, walk and not faint.
Then shall I run in the way of thy commandments
and no longer turn aside to crooked ways.

Then shall I eat and drink, work and recreate myself
all to thy glory.
Lord, send thy Spirit into my heart
that I may grow and be no longer a babe,
but arrive at the fullness of stature in Christ Jesus,
and more steadily, more purely, more zealously,
    and more humbly,
live to thee and glorify thee in the world. Amen.

*—Isabella Graham, 1742–1814; alt.*

254

## *Intercession: For All God's Children*

O Lord our God, we pray not for ourselves only, but for all thy dear
children, fellow heirs with us, of everlasting happiness, in whatever
part of the world they be. Lord, we pray thee to be continually present
with them with all thy comforts and mercies. Let thy good Spirit lead
them into all truth. Let the wings of thy providence and protection
stretch over them all.

Hasten the conversion of those who as yet lie in profaneness
and under the shadow of death. Reveal unto them the glorious
comforts of grace, and let the powers of darkness hold them no longer.

*—Robert Bolton, 1572–1631; alt.*

255

## *Awaiting God's Commands*

Lord! Here I am waiting thy commands,
persuaded that thou wilt never call me to any duty
which thou wilt not enable me to perform,
nor put me upon any trial,
which thou wilt not give me strength to endure.

*—Petrus Immens, 1664–1720*

## For a Vision of Jesus
256

Give me grace, O sweet Jesus, to rest in thee
above all things in the world.
O Christ, my sweet Spouse and Savior,
O most faithful Lover,
Lord of the whole world:
O that I had wings of true liberty
that I might fly unto thee.
O when shall I behold how sweet thou art,
my Lord, my God?
O when shall I come wholly unto thee,
that I may not know myself,
but thee alone?

—*Henry Smith, ca. 1550–1591; alt.*

## Prayer on Psalm 23
257

O Lord my Shepherd, feed me, your lamb; then I shall lack nothing.
Make me rest in the rich pastures of your delightful word, beside
the pleasant and gracious streams of your Holy Spirit, that my soul
may regain strength and that I may rest upon your holy providence.
Convert my soul to you and refresh it, soothing it from the heat of this
sadness. Lead me in the path of your righteousness for the love of your
name. If I must journey through the midst of shadows and through the
dark valley of death, be pleased to come to my aid so that I may not
fear any distress. Let the rod of your word sustain me and give me
consolation. Spread before me the table of your word, and I shall draw
near to take from it strength with which I may boldly oppose all the
power of the devil, that his devices may gain no hold on me. Anoint
my head with the oil of gladness and with the blessed sanctification of
the Holy Spirit. Pour out for me a drink from your own cup that I may

never forget myself and that I may never deny you. Let your Holy Spirit alone reign and hold sovereign sway within me. Let your kindly mercy never leave me as long as I live. I shall dwell forever in your house, being gathered into your flock, within the fold of your grace and your gifts, O my God, who art the sovereign Shepherd and Giver of all good things. Amen.

—*A Swiss Reformed Psalter, 1558*

258 ## *For Guidance*

O Good God, lead us by the power of thy Holy Ghost unto such unfeigned repentance that we may not prefer terrestrial things unto thee or unto thy word, or unto the care we ought to have for our souls, but rather, that at all times we may seek thy kingdom and the righteousness thereof above all things in the world.

And so lead us, O Lord, that we may not be like unto the horse or mule that have no understanding, nor like unto dogs and swine, that trample the pearls and holy things under their feet, but grant us to be wise as serpents, and innocent as doves, and patient as lambs; but above all things, that we may take delight in hearing thy voice, the voice of our heavenly Shepherd, to believe and obey it, to the end that the fruit of the womb, the fruit of our fields and of our cattle, of our sheep and oxen may be blessed; and that we may be blessed in our going out and in our coming in.

—*Church of Zurich, 1693; alt.*

259 ## *For Peace of Heart*

O God, the King of kings, whose glory is incomprehensible, whose majesty is infinite, whose power is incomparable: keep your servants in peace, and grant that we may be so dependent on the certitude of your promises, that whatever may come upon us, we may remain firm in faith, living righteously and without reproach in the midst of the church which Jesus Christ has won through his precious blood. Amen.

—*Augustin Marlorat, 1506–1562*

## Intercession: For the Church

O Lord God Almighty, King of saints, who hast chosen Zion for thy habitation and thy rest forever: regard, we beseech thee, with special favor and benediction, thy holy church in all lands and nations. Pour out thy Spirit upon thy ministering servants, that they may truly be the salt of the earth and the light of the world; and after having turned many to righteousness, may shine as the brightness of the firmament and as the stars for ever. Bless thy people with all spiritual blessings and grant that they may daily grow in grace and in the knowledge of our Lord and Savior Jesus Christ. Heal all divisions and distractions among believers, and so unite them in truth and love, that they may be of one heart and of one soul, keeping the unity of the Spirit in the bond of peace. Extend the borders of thy kingdom, and give to thy Son the uttermost parts of the earth for his possession. Hasten the time when at the name of Jesus, every knee shall bow, and every tongue confess that he is Lord, to the glory of God the Father. Amen.

*—German Reformed Church in the USA, 1857*

## At the Ending of the Day

O God, all powerful, take me this night under thy protection. Let my weary nature be refreshed by easy and quiet sleep; and, by thy grace and providence, bring me at last through all the trials and temptations of this world to a blessed end; that so I may die in peace, rest in hope, and rise to glory, through Jesus Christ our Lord. Amen.

*—Henry Harbaugh, 1817–1876*

262

## A Prayer at Thy Uprising

Most loving God and tender Father, we thank thee for our sweet sleep
and comfortable rest, which thou hast given us this night passed. And
forasmuch as thou hast commanded us, by thy holy word, that no
one should be idle, but all occupied in good and virtuous exercises,
everyone, according to their calling, we most humbly beseech thee
that thine eye may attend upon us, and daily defend us in perils,
and govern all our studies and labours, that we may spend this day
according to thy blessed will, in praising thy holy name, through Jesus
Christ our Lord. Amen.

*—Possibly by Robert Waldegrave, ca. 1554–1604; alt.*

263

## For Freedom from Sin

Although we be sinners, O Lord, yet we are thine.
And therefore we beseech thee to separate our sins from us,
which would separate us from thee,
that we may be ready to every good
as we are to evil.
Teach us to remember our sins,
that thou mayest forget them;
and let our sorrow here prevent the sorrow to come.

Let not thine enemies prevail against thee,
to take us from thee.
But make thy word unto us like the star
which led unto Christ.
Make thy benefits like the pillar
which brought to the land of promise.
Make thy cross like the messenger

which compelled guests to the banquet,
that we may always look upon thy Son,
how he would speak and do,
before we speak or do anything.

Keep us in that fear of thy majesty,
that we may make conscience of all that we do,
that we may count no sin small.
Let not our hearts at any time be so dazzled,
but that in all temptation we may discern
    between good and evil,
between right and wrong,
between truth and error,
and that we may judge all things as they are,
and not as they seem to be.

               *—Henry Smith, ca. 1550–1591; alt.*

## For Confidence in God 264

This new day, my Lord, I desire to bless thee for the many mercies I
enjoy. Sanctify every trial I meet with, whether in temporal or spiritual
concerns. Thou, Lord, who seest me, seest that I am surrounded with
many difficulties. But nothing is too hard for thee: thou art able to
support and deliver. Be pleased in thy good time to put a new song
into my mouth. I know, O my God, thou canst not err. Be a present
help to me, and uphold me with the right hand of thy righteousness.
Let me confide in none but thee, for none else is worthy of confidence.
Thou art my friend, my covenanted God: my all for time, my all for
eternity, my joy, my rest, and crown of rejoicing. In prosperity and in
adversity, I desire to have my heart wholly fixed on thee. Lord Jesus,
come to me, and as thou hast heard me, still look with love and pity
upon me, and revive and comfort my drooping soul.

               *—Frances Cunningham, 1743–1811; alt.*

## Intercession

Dear Father, for Christ's sake, I beseech thee to take from me and from
all others for whom thou wouldest that we should pray, all envy, pride,
arrogance, disdain, hatred, and all suspicion. Grant unto us mercy,
humility, patience, meekness, long-suffering, gentleness, peace, charity,
and love. Comfort the feeble. Relieve the poor. Help the fatherless.
Heal the sick. Bless the afflicted. Show thy great mercy upon all poor
prisoners, and deliver them in thy good time. Remember thy pity
towards strangers, captives, widows, and such as are oppressed.

*—John Bradford, 1510–1555; alt.*

## Before Beginning Work

Eternal and ever-blessed God,
this day do I surrender myself to thee.
I renounce all former lords that have had dominion over me,
and I consecrate to thee all that I am, and all that I have:
> the faculties of my mind,
> the members of my body,
> my worldly possessions,
> my time and influence over others,
to be all used entirely for thy glory,
and resolutely employed in obedience to thy commands.

To thee I leave the management of all events,
and say without reserve,
"Not my will, but thine be done,"
rejoicing with a loyal heart in thine unlimited government.
Use me, O Lord, I beseech thee,
as an instrument of thy service.

*—Philip Doddridge, 1702–1751; alt.*

## To Adore, Love, and Fear Thee     267

Lord,
lead me unto acquaintance with thee.
Give me eyes to see thee,
ears to hear thy lovely voice,
taste to relish thy sweetness.
Give me faith which answers all.
Give me a heart to love thee,
choose thee,
embrace thee,
repudiate every other thing for thee.

O let not my own praise, credit, or worldly interest
be dear to me in comparison of thee.
Let me for thee,
be content to pass for a cipher, nothing,
a contemptible object.
Nay, for thee,
let all other things be such to me.
Give me to adore thy holiness, purity.
Give me to love thy goodness,
to tremble and fear before thy sovereignty,
omnipotency, immensity, and omniscience.
O give me to adore, love, and fear thee
in all these.
O grant that I may rest on thy all-sufficiency,
committing myself to thy wisdom and faithfulness,
and let that infinite incomprehensibleness and eternity,
in thyself and all thy attributes
strike me
with a holy reverential admiration.

—*Hugh Rose, ca. 1633–1686; alt.*

## *For Self-Forgetfulness*

O thou eternal and ever-blessed God, teach me to be poor in spirit, mourning for sin, hungering and thirsting after righteousness. Make me patient in suffering and faithful in thy service. Let the mind that was in Christ Jesus be also in me. Give me some measure of his self-forgetfulness. Forbid that I should constantly brood on my own sorrows, unmindful of those whose pains are more intense, whose burdens are heavier, whose loneliness more forlorn than mine. I thank thee that whatever I lack, I am rich in Christ. In him I am complete, and he is mine forever. Not life nor death, things present nor things to come, shall separate me from thy love which is in Christ Jesus our Lord. For this, help me to sing hallelujah.

—*David J. Burrell, 1844–1926; alt.*

## *Be Mindful of Your Compassion*

Lord, I am human, and I talk to you as to a human being.
Are you forgetful? Do you forget your very self?
Would you not forget yourself if you forgot your goodness?
Your goodness alone has created the world,
humankind with it, and your church,
    composed of human beings.
Despite storms, the world exists for humankind,
even with humankind annoying you all the time,
every day.
The church is composed of human beings,
and they continually attack it.
Everything moves towards its end,
everything towards destruction, and yet still endures,
through you, not of itself.
So what have I said to you now, Lord?
Be mindful of your compassion,
    and be mindful of your goodness.

Lord, tiny dream though I am,
I know that all will go into dissolution.
I know it, Lord.
This whole universe will fall into the abyss.
Your looking on us keeps us,
turning your gaze from us would bring us to confusion.
Your caring for us is our salvation,
your forgetting us, perdition.
You chose the church eternally, before the world was made,
so that it might be in the world.
Indeed, Lord, it is for the church that you made the world.
O what mindfulness!
At the end of an eternity,
you turn to and create this universe,
and in this universe, you sow the seed of your church.
Lord, do you forget?

Would you forget, you, who forget nothing
through all eternity?
You promise aid for your church,
your Christ, your dear Son.
The world forgets you,
but you never forget it.
You take Abraham,
from Abraham a son,
and from his sons a race.
The world attacks it through endless centuries
and moves along, going astray in all directions.
At the time preordained, the time established before the ages,
your Son came to be born,
despised by the world and by ourselves:
your Son, my Savior!
Your Son, in whom you behold me.
You see me there, in him, my God;
I am not afraid that you will forget me.

*—Philippe Duplessis-Mornay, 1549–1623; alt.*

## *Intercession: For Creation*

Lord and Creator, in your committed love, you have entrusted to us your good gifts and your precious creation. You have called us to make the earth subject to us. In all this, do not let us try to live without you. Keep us from spoiling what you have made; help us to cherish it in due responsibility to you; to whom alone honor and worship belong.

*—The Evangelical Reformed Churches in*
*German-speaking Switzerland, 1972*

## *At the Ending of the Day*

Praise be to the Lord my God,
who has let me complete yet another day to his glory.
My God! in your grace and for the sake of my dear Lord
            and Savior,
Jesus Christ, and by his innocent suffering,
pardon me for all my wrongdoings known and unknown,
in thought, word, and deed.
Protect me from all danger.
Give me a gentle sleep, a joyful awakening,
and eternal blessedness. Amen.
The grace of the Father give me direction,
the wisdom of the Son give me life,
and the power of the Holy Spirit give me light!
My Creator, remain with me!
My Redeemer, help me!
My Comforter, dwell in me and refresh me!
The Lord bless and keep me,
the Lord make his face to shine upon me,
and give me peace.
Amen. Amen. Amen.

*—America,* Heidelberg Catechism and Prayers, *1752; alt.*

## Adoration

More love to Thee, O Christ,
　　　More love to Thee!
Hear Thou the prayer I make
　　　on bended knee:
This is my earnest plea.
More love, O Christ, to Thee,
　　　More love to Thee!

Once earthly joy I craved,
　　　Sought peace and rest;
Now Thee alone I seek,
　　　Give what is best:
This all my prayer shall be,
More love, O Christ, to Thee,
　　　More love to Thee!

Let sorrow do its work,
　　　Send grief and pain:
Sweet are Thy messengers,
　　　Sweet their refrain.
When they can sing with me,
More love, O Christ, to Thee,
　　　More love to Thee!

Then shall my latest breath
　　　Whisper Thy praise;
This be my parting cry
　　　My heart shall raise,
This still its prayer shall be,
More love, O Christ, to Thee,
　　　More love to Thee!

—*Elizabeth Payson Prentiss, 1818–1878*

## Elder Burnbrae's Prayer

Almighty Father,
we are all thy poor and sinful children,
who grew tired of home and went away into the far country.
Forgive us, for we did not know what we were leaving,
or the sad heart we were giving our Father.
It was weary work to live with our sins,
but we would never have come back
had it not been for our Elder Brother.
He came by a long road to find us,
and a bitter hard labor he had, before he set us free.
He has been a good Brother to us,
and we've been a heavy burden to him.
May he keep a firm hold on us, and guide us in the right road,
and bring us back if ever we go astray,
and tell us all we need to know, until the evening comes.
Gather us in then, we pray thee, and all whom we love,
with not one child missing,
and may we sit down forever in our own Father's house. Amen.

—*John Watson, 1850–1907; alt.*

## Elder Burnbrae's Prayer

(original version)

Almichty Father,
we are a' Thy puir and sinfu' bairns,
wha wearied o' hame and gaed awa' intae the far country.
Forgive us, for we didna ken what we were leavin',
or the sair hert we gied oor Father.
It wes weary wark tae live wi' oor sins,
but we wud never hev come back
had it no been for oor Elder Brither.
He cam' a long road tae find us,

and a sore travail He had afore He set us free.

He's been a gude Brither tae us,

and we've been a heavy chairge tae Him.

May He keep a firm haud o' us, and guide us in the richt road

and bring us back gin we wander,

and tell us a' we need tae know till the gloamin' come.

Gither us in then, we pray Thee, and a' we luve,

no a bairn missin',

and may we sit doon for ever in oor ain Father's House. Amen.

—*The prayer appears in Watson's novel,* Beside the
Bonnie Brier Bush *(1894); alt.*

## *For Constancy in Faith* 274

My Eternal God! Thou hast created me as eternal spirit. Thou hast
molded me in the likeness of thine image. Out of thine own self hast
thou given me that which is thine essence that I might be a copy and
representation of thine image among all creatures. Thou didst send
me forth and place me in this wonderful world, full of wealth and joy,
beauty and treasures, innumerable things of desire, but at the same
time also filled with poverty and need, pain and suffering, numberless
things which make us tremble and from which we would fain flee. I
pray thee, Father, that in this world—this world of desires and fears—
I may stand firmly beside thee and remain in thee. Not for anything let
me surrender thee, thou who art my all, my highest treasure. Though
I lose all under the sun, mayest thou remain in all thy fullness so that
I may rejoice in the thought that, having lost all that is of the world, I
am nevertheless rich in possessing thee, my God.

I implore thee not to harden my heart in the face of the
outward changes of my destiny. If thou givest joys and the goods of
this world, enable me to show forth true gratitude; and if thou dost
take away things precious to me, may I, humbly bowing my head, give
them back to thee. May the close of every prayer of mine, spoken or
silent, be, Grant me to remain in thy love. To those who love thee all
things are for their good. Amen.

—*László Ravasz, 1882–1967*

## *Intercession: For Neighbors*

Lord, you have made us for one another; you give us a mission to watch each person whom you have given us today as a neighbor. Give us the right thing to say; show us the right thing to do, to meet one another's needs. We pray to you for all the people you have entrusted to us. We pray for those who are dear to us, wherever they may be. We pray to you for those who work with us. We pray to you for all the members of your church, for the healthy and sick, the joyful and sorrowing, the strong and the weak. We pray to you to keep us all, for Christ's sake. Amen.

*—Netherlands Reformed Church, 1955*

## *For the Day's Work*

O God of light, who hast preserved me and brought me from the darkness of this night, shine into my heart this day and ever by thy blessed and Holy Spirit, that I may be enlightened and led into all truth, that I may walk faithfully, as the child of light before thee and in the place that thou hast set me, casting away the works of darkness and doing and performing diligently those things that thou hast required of me either to the praise of thy Name or to the comfort of my brothers and sisters. Grant this, good Lord, I humbly beseech thee, for Jesus Christ's sake. Amen.

*—John Field, 1545–1587; alt.*

## Invocation

Come, Lord Jesus, come,
for lacking thee,
I am no day nor hour in quiet.
Thou art my joy
without whom my table is empty.
Let others seek what they will
instead of thee.
Nothing doth nor shall please me,
but thou my God,
my hope and eternal salvation.
—*Henry Smith, ca. 1550–1591; alt.*

## Adoration

O Lord our God, how excellent is your name in all the earth.
We come to you knowing that you are holy and righteous,
you are high and lifted up,
you are unchangeable.
You alone are worthy to worship.
We stand before you in reverence, and honor your greatness.
We praise you for your great powers and wisdom
and your providence in all your creation.
We praise you that we are not animals, birds, or fish,
but that we are human beings;
we are like you.
We praise you for your love

and that your grace is stronger than your anger.
We praise you for what you are;
through Jesus Christ our Lord.

—*Presbyterians of the Republic of Vanuatu, 1990; alt.*

## *Confession*

O Lord God! Thou art the eternal all-sufficient God, a being everywhere present and every way perfect, whom I desire to reverence at all times. Thou hast directed me in thy word to pray to thee as my Father in heaven, and when I am in the closet and have shut the door, so that no other eye can see me and that no other affairs may disturb me, then to pray to thee who seest in secret, hoping in thy goodness and mercy to reward me openly.

I acknowledge myself unworthy of the least favor from thee. I have sinned against heaven and in thy sight, and my sins have been often repeated and greatly aggravated. I have been worse than the ox or ass, which know the hand that feeds them. Whereas I have not known the God from whom all my blessings come. Thou hast nourished and brought me up, but I have rebelled against thee. I have been sadly unmindful of thee and neglectful of my duty to thee, and by vain imaginations, sinful and profane words and ungodly actions, done great dishonor to thy Name.

I have greatly sinned against the laws of justice and mercy. I have done and spoken wrong things and perverse things, sometimes, if I could, to the injury of my neighbor, and the pain and grief of my relations, friends, and acquaintance.

God, be merciful to me a sinner, and blot out all my past transgressions. Grant me the remission and pardon of my sins through the blood of Christ, the blood of the everlasting covenant. I desire this forgiveness through faith in his Name.

—*Samuel Wright, 1683–1746*

*Prayers from the Reformed Tradition*

## Comfort

Speak low to me, my Saviour, low and sweet
From out the hallelujahs, sweet and low,
Lest I should fear and fall, and miss Thee so
Who art not missed by any that entreat.
Speak to me as to Mary at Thy feet!
And if no precious gums my hands bestow,
Let my tears drop like amber while I go
In reach of Thy divinest voice complete
In humanest affection—thus, in sooth,
To lose the sense of losing. As a child
Whose song-bird seeks the wood for evermore,
Is sung to in its stead by mother's mouth,
Till, sinking on her breast, love-reconciled,
He sleeps the faster that he wept before.

*—Elizabeth Barrett Browning, 1806–1861*

## Intercession

Father of mercies and God of all comfort: we bring to Thee in faith
and love all those from whom their heart's desire has been withheld:
those who have no home, and those who have no friendship; those
who are unhappy, and those who have lost heart; those who find faith
difficult, and those for whom the way of life is hard; those who are
sick, and those who are bereaved. O Thou Companion of the lonely,
Comforter of the mourner, Guide of the perplexed, Thou inexhaustible
Source of solace and strength and blessing: suffer none of Thy tried
children to rebel as though Thou hadst forsaken them, but turn them
to Thee for succour, and in Thy love bring them to light and peace.

*—Church of Scotland, 1928*

From *Book of Common Order of the Church of Scotland* (1928). Reprinted by permission of Oxford University Press.

# *At the Ending of the Day*

Good Father, pardon my sins past, and for thy own Name's sake be merciful unto me. Receive me this night into thy custody and safe protection. Let thy arms of love embrace me, thy grace comfort me, and thy continual favor defend me from all perils. In thy name, Good Father, I yield myself unto my rest. Let thy Holy Spirit keep the door of my heart, and the holy angels attend about my bed for safety, for Christ Jesus, thy dear Son's merits. Amen.

O Lord, increase our faith.

—*John Norden, 1548–1625; alt.*

## Invocation

Blessed are you, O Father,
Lord of heaven and earth. (Matthew 11:25)

Father, most wise,
intelligence beyond us,
deepest mystery,
and highest truth.

O heavenly wisdom,
perfect in simplicity!

Reveal yourself to us, O Father,
in the name of your Son
for to him you have delivered all things
and no one knows you except in him.

Reveal yourself to us, O Father,
in the name of your Son
for he is gentle and lowly in heart
and we would take his yoke upon us
and learn of him. (Matthew 11:29)

For yours is the Kingdom,
the power and the glory,

Father,
Son, and
Holy Spirit.

Forever one God. *Amen.*
—*Hughes Oliphant Old, contemporary*

## *For Refreshment*

O thou that commandest the clouds above and openest
the windows of heaven,
remember and refresh this parched wilderness wherein I live
with showers of grace,
that we may not be as the heath in the desert
which seeth not when good cometh,
nor inhabit the parched places of wilderness.
O Lord, thou hast caused the heavens above me
to be black with clouds.
Thou openest the celestial casements from above,
and daily sendest down showers of gospel-blessings.
O that I might be as the parched earth under them!
Not for barrenness, but for thirstiness.

*—John Flavel, ca. 1630–1691; alt.*

## *Manna*

While they wandered
in the wilderness, Lord,
you fed your people, the children of Israel,
with the gift of manna from the skies,
bread falling from heaven—new every morning—
sufficient for the day,
and only for that day,
to be eaten in joy and thanksgiving
and never stored up for tomorrow.
And for those who doubted
and sought to hoard
your bread of life,
their store turned foul by morning.

Early in this morning, Father,
I rise to gather the fresh manna
of your love.
Fill me now to overflowing
with the strength, the grace, and the truth
I will need for the tasks ahead.
Then go with me
to ensure that
I give these gifts away,
that I spend them all
as currency for this day,
keeping nothing for myself,
guarding no store for the morrow,
sharing your gifts
in all that I do,
all that I am—
lest like the manna of old,
stored love turns stale,
and poisons its possessor.

—*J. Barrie Shepherd, b. 1935*

## Intercession: For Our Opponents

286

Open our hearts to your love, so that we may be free from touchiness, jealousy, and bad temper. We pray to you for the people with whom we have any complaint, for those with whom we are in any enmity, or who have got us blamed, and so made our life difficult. Give us the power to meet them with the will to be reconciled.

—*The Evangelical Reformed Churches in
German-speaking Switzerland, 1972*

# For Perseverance through the Day

Our God, Father and Savior: as you have graciously brought us through the night to this present day, grant in your kindness, that we may use all of it in your service, to think, say, and do nothing except to please you and obey your good will. Make all our works glorify your Name and help our neighbors in their life of faith.

In your grace, you make your sun shine upon the earth to give us light for the life of this world. Even so, by the light of your Spirit, illumine our understanding and our souls, to turn us to the true path of your righteousness. Whatever tasks we take up, make it our chief purpose and intent to walk in your fear, to serve and honor you, to seek all our happiness and well-being in your blessing, and to put our hand to nothing but what is pleasing to you.

As we work for the needs of our bodies and of this present life, let us also look beyond this, to the life of heaven, which you have promised to your children. May it please you to protect us both in body and soul, to strengthen us against all temptation, the devil, and to free us from all dangers that may confront us.

Since nothing good is truly begun unless it is persevered in, kindly take us into your holy keeping, not only this day, but all our life long. Continue and increase your grace within us daily, until you have brought us into full union with your Son, Jesus Christ our Lord, who is the true sun of our souls, shining day and night, without end and forever.

To prepare us to receive such merciful gifts from you, graciously forget our past faults and forgive us in your boundless mercy, as you have promised to all who call on you with an honest heart. For all such people, as for ourselves, we pray to you in the Name of your Son, Our Lord Jesus Christ, as he taught us to pray, saying: Our Father . . .

Also, Lord, grant us grace to persevere in your holy faith, which you have planted in our hearts by your mercy. Increase it and make it grow within us, day by day, until it comes to its fullness. This faith we confess, saying: I believe in God the Father. . . .

—*Jean Calvin, 1509–1564; alt.*

## *Adoration* 288

Eternal, Sovereign God, whose greatness rises above the heavens, you that have founded the earth and spread forth the span of heaven: we bow before you and worship your holy majesty, for you are our Creator and Benefactor. Your faithful goodness provides for all our needs, your inexhaustible patience still allows us time to turn to our salvation.

We thank you for the redemption of our souls in Jesus Christ, for the ceaseless gifts of your mercy, and for the living hope of eternal glory.

We bless you for the continual help which you grant to your church, and for the certain assurance you have given it that the powers of hell shall never prevail against it.

Powerful and most good God, our hearts are filled with joy and hope in the expectation of the glorious salvation which you have kept for that day when your Son shall take possession of his kingdom, where sin and death shall be no more, and where you shall be all in all.

And since we have come here to seek strength and peace in the teachings of your word, let them never be made ineffectual by our trust in ourselves, by indifference, by unbelief. Keep far from us the distractions that hinder us. Silence within us those voices which would hinder us from hearing yours, and compose our distracted spirits so that they may be totally given to the worship we wish to offer you, through Jesus Christ our Lord. Amen.

—*Reformed Church of Berne (Switzerland) 1955*

## I Do Not Want Anything But Thy Love

I am thy slave, O God. I am only dust and ashes. I can do nothing by myself. I have nothing about which to boast unto thee. I do thank thee for thy great love with which thou hast commanded me to love thee—even with all my heart and soul. As thy slave I do not have that kind of love, but thou canst give it to me.

I do not want anything but thy love, for the more I have the more I am happy. Give me enough that I may love my neighbor as myself, that I may endure any kind of suffering, and that I may gladly die if need be. I do not ask for my flock wisdom, honor, or money; but I do ask that, through thy great Grace, they may be saved. Amen.

—*Boon Mark Gittisarn, fl. 1930–1960*

## For Freedom from Bondage

O Almighty God, who hast planted in us a desire to be freed from the bondage of things seen and temporal, grant that we may be increasingly delivered from their yoke, and that we may be truly and always free. Reveal unto us the power of those things which are not seen and eternal.

—*Scotland,* Home Prayers, *1879*

## For a New Heart

O Thou dear God,
take from us our hard hearts,
our stony hearts, our impenitent hearts,
our distrusting and doubtful hearts,
our carnal, our secure, our idle,
our brutish hearts,
our impure, malicious, arrogant,
envious, wrathful, impatient,
covetous, hypocritical, and selfish hearts;
and in place thereof,

give us new hearts,
soft hearts,
faithful hearts, merciful hearts,
loving, obedient, chaste, pure,
holy, righteous, true, simple,
lowly and patient hearts,
to fear thee,
to love thee,
and trust in thee for ever.
    —*John Bradford, 1510–1555; alt.*

## *Out of Thy Fullness*

292

O Lord, thou only art my sun
from whose beams I must receive saving light.
Thou art my head
from whom I must get spiritual life.
Thou art the root
from which I must receive sap and growth.
Thou art the fountain
from which I must draw living water.
Thou art the treasure
from which I must obtain the riches of grace.

Without thee, I am nothing,
I have nothing, I can do nothing.
To thee then must I go for all my supplies,
and out of thy fullness receive grace for grace.
Lord, thou hast enough to supply many worlds of needy souls,
for the sun is not so full of light,
nor the sea so full of water,
as thou art full of grace and mercy to needy creatures.
And as thou art full, so I am assured thou art free
and willing to communicate thy fullness.

In spite then of all objections and difficulties,
forward to thee I will go,
and cast myself down at thy feet.
If I perish, I perish.
Oh! Did ever any perish
at mercy's door?

—*John Willison, 1680–1750*

## 293    *Intercession: For the Church*

O Lord, Almighty God! Through your Spirit you have brought us in
unity of faith into your one Body, and you have commanded this Body
of yours to give you praise and thanks for the goodness and generosity
in which you gave up your only-begotten Son, our Lord Jesus Christ,
to death for our sin. Grant us to hold so faithfully to this that we may
never dishonor this pure truth by any disobedience or falsehood. Grant
us also to live such innocent lives as befit your Body, your kindred and
your children, so that those who do not believe may come to know
your name and glory. Lord, protect us, so that your name and glory
may never be blasphemed because of the way we live. Lord, increase
our faith, that is, our trust in you, in every way, for you live and reign
as God for ever and ever! Amen.

—*Huldrych Zwingli, 1484–1531*

## 294    *At the Ending of the Day*

Lord, bless and defend us from all evil. And whilst we sleep, do thou,
O Father, who never slumbrest nor sleepest, watch over thy children,
and give a charge to thy holy angels, to pitch their tents round about
our house and dwelling, to guard us from all dangers; that sleeping
with thee, we may in the morning be awakened by thee, and so being
refreshed with moderate sleep, we may be the fitter to set forth thy
glory in the duties of our callings.

—*Lewis Bayly, 1565–1631; alt.*

## The Morning Light Is Come

Now the shades of night are gone;
Now the morning light is come;
Lord, we would be thine today,
Drive the shades of sin away.

Make our souls as noonday clear,
Banish every doubt and fear;
In thy vineyard, Lord, today,
We would labor, we would pray.

Keep our haughty passions bound
Rising up or sitting down,
Going out or coming in,
Keep us safe from every sin.

When our work of life is past,
O! Receive us then at last;
Labor then will all be o'er,
Night of sin will be no more.

—*Possibly by Samson Occom, 1723–1792*

## For the Taste of Divine Love

Thou hast touched my soul with thy Spirit, O most Beloved,
and draweth me to thee.
So by thee doth she run after thee,
O thou Fountain and Rest of loves.
Her loves begin and end in thee.
O let my soul ever be tasting of thy loves,

and ever love thee by tasting them!
Give me the flagons of the new wine of the kingdom,
which may lift up my soul above herself in her loves,
and give her better loves than her own,
wherewith to love him that is far better than herself.
Yea, let her drink plentifully
that she may be mounted up in a divine ecstasy,
above her carnal and earthly station,
that she may forget the low and base griefs and cares
and distractions of carnal and worldly love,
and by an heavenly excess,
be translated into an heavenly love
to embrace her beloved
who is the Lord from heaven.

Let my love rest in nothing short of thee,
Neither let it be content merely to rest in thee,
but kindle it,
enflame it,
enlarge it,
that it may rest largely in thee.

—*Francis Rous, 1579–1659; alt.*

297 ## *A Prayer That God Will Never Hide His Face from Us*

Thy favor, O Lord, which thou showest unto us weak and unworthy
creatures, is as an unfathomable sea of love. Thou becomest a suitor
unto us. Thou biddest us to seek and to see thy face. Thou, the
most beloved seemest to make love unto us. Thou, the most mighty
Creator callest us, thy weak creatures, unto thee. And shall we,
hateful, deformed, and vile wretches stand in conceit, thinking that
we are lovely and beautiful because thou, great Jehovah, absolute in

all perfection, dost entreat us? Thou sayest, "Seek my face." It is as if thou saidst, "Come and see me. Come and receive me. Come and dwell with me."

But when I consider thy greatness, thy majesty, and glory, thy power and omnipotence, I cannot but fear, considering what I am. I desire to hide myself from thee as Adam did, rather than to intrude into thy presence; to cover my nakedness with the fig leaves of shameful absence rather than come into thy presence, since I am naked of all spiritual virtues.

Should I come into thy presence, O most powerful and holy Lord God, in the bespotted garments of mine own corruptions? Then mayest thou well stand with the burning sword of thy fury to keep me from the sweet paradise of thy loving presence, amiable indeed to them whom thou makest worthy, but most fearful unto such as have not on the wedding garment of the righteousness of Jesus Christ. If thou observest the self-righteousness of the best, and deal with them accordingly, who can see thy face and live? Who dare to seek thy face as worthy?

But since it hath pleased thee to call me, though unworthy, and to accept me as worthy, how can I but give all diligence to attend thy call? Should I stand consulting with flesh and blood whether I should seek thy face and live or remain out of thy favor and perish eternally?

Thou sayest, "Seek my face." O that my heart could truly answer and faithfully seek thy face. For of my own power I cannot. Though my spiritual part be willing, my carnal part is weak. I desire to seek and to find thee, for with thee is the well of life. Thine eyes are upon them that fear thee, and thine ears open unto their cry. Show me therefore the light of thy countenance, and turn thy face towards me that I may see it, in thy favor and loving-kindness.

—*John Norden, 1548–1625; alt.*

# For the Protection of the Good Shepherd

O quicken me, thou that art the fountain of life and call out of heaven, thy dwelling place, that my wandering soul may hear the voice of her Shepherd and follow thee whithersoever thou leadest. Of thy tender compassion, take me up upon thy shoulders and carry me gently into thy fold again, for thieves have stolen me away, and have bound my feet so that I cannot go. They watch for me until thou art gone, then they carry me away quick from thy pastures. O do thou therefore deliver me and give me thy helping hand.

I desire, I look, I call, I cry for thy assistance. O blessed Savior that hast granted so many petitions upon earth: fulfill, I pray thee, my desire, not for health nor strength nor riches nor honor, nor for food, nor apparel, but for thy heavenly grace and inspiration.

Deliver me, O Lord, from the snares of the hunter and preserve me from the hand of mine enemy who lieth in wait for my spiritual life and laboreth for my everlasting destruction. Then shall I praise thee for thy great goodness, and magnify thy name for giving me conquest over my adversary that is too strong for me. To thee I fly for succor till this tempest be overpast. Hide me, I pray thee, under thy shield and buckler, that none of the fiery darts of Satan take hold on me. Good Lord, for the love thou bearest unto humanity, for thy Son's sake, who hath taken our nature upon him: grant that I may not be tempted above my strength, and that in all temptations I may fly unto thee as a horn of my salvation, yielding thee most humble and hearty thanks.

—*Henry Smith, ca. 1550–1591; alt.*

## Intercession

Most merciful Father, we entreat thee for our brothers and sisters
throughout the earth. Pity and deliver the oppressed from the hand of
the oppressor. Succeed every effort in favor of virtue and liberty. Dispel
the dark clouds of ignorance, both political and religious. And hasten
the time, we beseech thee, in the revolution of human things, in the
improvement of the human mind, in the progress of knowledge, in
the perfection of society, and above all, in the extension and obedience
of the gospel of Christ, when liberty, civil and religious, shall be
universally enjoyed and rightly improved; when the reign of peace
shall commence upon earth, when the Redeemer's kingdom shall fully
come, when there shall be one sheepfold and one Shepherd.

—*Ashbel Green, 1762–1848; alt.*


## For the Day's Work

300

Eternal God, everloving Father who committest to us the swift and
solemn trust of life, whom to serve is perfect freedom and joy; we
praise Thee for calling us into the service of Jesus Christ Thy Son our
Lord. The hour for serving Thee is always present. Help us now to lay
aside all passion, indolence, and fear, and to yield to Thy claim by the
help of Thy Holy Spirit.

Even the humblest work is glorious and the roughest places are
plain, when they are consecrated by Him who has washed his disciples'
feet, and has gone the way to Golgotha. Give us grace to follow Him
wherever He calls us, and thus let us glorify Thee, who art ever to be
praised and worshipped. Amen.

—*Presbyterian Church of Ghana, 1966*

301 *For God's Transforming Light*

To say of you, my God, my Father and King, that which you alone know infinitely better than I—in myself I know I do it imperfectly; for I cannot praise you as I ought, or thank you for the benefits I receive, or confess the wrong which causes me remorse. I cannot make satisfaction, whatever my striving nor attain by my own efforts to the haven of grace—grace by which I believe you will save all who by faith have placed in you their trust and comfort. Apart from you none has fulfilled the law. Of itself, our works are of such ill quality that the best of them is bad, dirty, and foul. Therefore, seeing that there is no bound to be seen either in your goodness or my wrong, let the one who cannot praise you at all, praise you by silence—that much I understand.

Blind me with your great light, whose nature, form, and fashion my spirit cannot comprehend by reference to its own, but its effects are such that to the deepest level of its power to grasp and apprehend, my spirit sees that all its good flows from that light, even when it understands nothing of that light's intensity, or whether it is great, or how or why.

The more the blindness falls from my spirit's eyes, the more it has the power to behold, the more it confesses that its earthly sight is unworthy to see the whole of your heavenly splendor. To wish to see it is too proud a desire, but to absorb within itself what is mine, by means of its gentle rays—for that I pray you, so that my stubborn sins' bonds may be loosed.

—*Marguerite of Navarre, 1492–1549; alt.*

## For Pardon and Renewal

O Eternal God and Heavenly Father, if I were not taught and assured by the promises of thy gospel and the examples of Peter, Mary Magdalene, the Publican, the prodigal child, and many other penitent sinners that thou art full of compassion and ready to forgive the greatest sinners, who are heaviest laden with sin, I should despair for mine own sins, be utterly discouraged.

But O my God, I humbly beseech thee by the mercy of Jesus Christ, deal not with me according to my deserts, but freely and fully remit unto me all my sins and transgressions. Wash me clean from them with the virtue of that most precious blood which thy Son Jesus hath shed for me. For he alone is the Physician, this blood only is the medicine that can heal my sickness. And give me, I beseech thee, thine Holy Spirit which may assure me of mine adoption, enlighten my understanding, purify my heart, rectify my will and affections, and so sanctify me throughout, that my whole body, soul, and spirit may be kept unblamable until the glorious coming of my Lord Jesus Christ.

*—Lewis Bayly, 1565–1631; alt.*

## For Safety

O God our Father, who hast redeemed us with the precious blood of thy dear Son; grant us thy grace that we may consecrate ourselves to thy service. Arm us against temptation, and deliver us from all perils of body and of soul. Be thou our refuge and strength, a hiding place from the wind, and a covert from the tempest; that, whatever dangers may surround us, our hearts and minds may be kept in peace, and we be brought in safety to our journey's end. Enable us ever to hold faith and a good conscience, lest we make shipwreck of the soul; and when we have finished the voyage of life, grant us an abundant entrance into the haven of eternal rest; through Jesus Christ our Lord, who liveth and reigneth with thee, O Father, in the unity of the Holy Ghost, ever one God, world without end. Amen.

*—Church of Scotland, ca. 1910*

## For Grace to Love

O Sweet Jesus, when I desire grace to fulfill thy commandment of love and charity, where shall I take my pattern but from thee, such a Lover as is Love himself? For whom didst thou not love? Thou didst love thy disciples as a kind schoolmaster doth his scholars, and cherish them as a good father doth his children. Thou didst stoop down to wash their feet, who were not worthy to untie thy shoe. Thou didst restore Peter, who had abjured thee. Thou didst forgive James and John who asked too much of thee. Even thy persecutors and crucifiers had thine earnest prayers on the cross before thou didst arrange for thy mother or pray for thyself. Yea, thy holy hands did wash the unclean feet and thy sacred lips did touch the profane mouth of Judas, who betrayed thee and sold thee for thirty pence.

O thou Fountain of love, thou that dost drench those that love thee in the stream of thy pleasures, and anointest even thine enemies with the oil of compassion, and hast loved humanity with an everlasting love: grant that my love may be out of a pure heart and of a good conscience and of faith unfeigned. Thou that wouldest be betrayed with a kiss, and didst hasten Judas on with his task, lest he should be too slack, give me grace to die in thy favor and bring me to life.

O kindle my desires to thee. Inflame my heart with thankfulness to thee. Inspire my soul with the fire of thy zealous love to thee, that for thy love to me, I may evermore love thee above all things, and my neighbor as myself.

*—Thomas Sorocold, 1561–1617; alt.*

## Intercession

BLESSED Lord, who for our sakes wast content to bear sorrow and want and death; grant unto us such a measure of Thy Spirit that we may follow Thee in Thy courage and self-denial, and help us by Thy great love to succour the afflicted, to relieve the needy and the destitute, to share the burdens of the heavy-laden, and to see Thee in all who are poor and desolate; who livest and reignest with the Father and the Holy Spirit, one God, now and for evermore. AMEN.

—*Church of Scotland, 1940*

From *Book of Common Order of the Church of Scotland* (1940). Reprinted by permission of Oxford University Press.

## Thanksgiving for the Faithful Departed — 306

O LORD God, the Light of the faithful, the Strength of those who labour, and the Repose of the blessed dead; we give thee thanks for Thy saints who have witnessed in their lives a good confession, for all the faithful departed, and for those dear to our own hearts who have entered into rest. . . . . Grant us grace so to follow their good example, that we may be one with them in spirit, and, at the last, together with them, be made partakers of Thine eternal kingdom; through Jesus Christ our Lord. AMEN.

—*Church of Scotland, 1940*

From *Book of Common Order of the Church of Scotland* (1940). Reprinted by permission of Oxford University Press.

## At the Ending of the Day — 307

O thou that dwellest in unapproachable light, keep us thy servants during the darkness and silence of the night from all evil, whether of the body or the soul; for we know not what enemies and dangers encompass us about. And, when the night and darkness of this dying life are passed away, grant that we may awake to behold the light of thine eternal glory in the kingdom of heaven, with all thy saints; through him that loved us and hath redeemed us with his precious blood, Jesus Christ our Lord. Amen.

—*Robert Lee, 1804–1868*

308

## Adoration

My Divine Savior,
I see the prints of thy hands, of thy feet, of thy side.
I see the streams of blood issuing out from them,
streams of mercy for me.
I adore thee, I embrace thee, O my Savior, O my God!
Give a clear shine into my soul,
fill it with thy fear and enlighten it
with thy knowledge;
shed abroad thy love into it,
make it to partake of thy holiness and happiness.
And when it shall leave its frail body,
let it reign with thee for ever and ever.

—*Anonymous, a French Reformed woman, d. 1690*

309

## A Morning Prayer for a Family

O Lord our God, we desire with all humility and reverence to adore thee. Thou art good to all, and thy tender mercies are over all thy works; and thou art continually doing us good, though we are evil and unthankful. O look upon us now and be merciful to us, as thou usest to do unto those that love thy name.

Thou art the God of all the families of Israel, be thou the God of our family, and grant, whatever others do, we and ours may always serve thee, that thou mayest cause the blessing to rest on our house. Lord, bless us, and we are blessed indeed.

We humbly thank thee for all the mercies of the night past, and this morning, that we have laid us down and slept, and waked again, because thou hast sustained us; that no plague has come nigh our dwelling, but that we are brought in safety to the light and comforts of another day.

We have rested and are refreshed, when many have been full of tossings to and fro till the dawning of the day. We have a safe and quiet habitation, when many are forced to wander and lie exposed.

We confess we have sinned against thee. We are guilty before thee. We have sinned and have come short of thy glory. We have corrupt and sinful natures, and are bent to backslide from thee, backward to good, and prone to evil continually. We are too apt to burden ourselves with that care which thou hast encouraged us to cast upon thee.

We are very much wanting in the duties of our particular relations, and provoke one another to more folly and passion than to love and good works. We are very cold and defective in our love to thee, weak in our desires towards thee, and unsteady and uneven in our walking with thee. We are at this time much out of frame for thy service.

We pray thee to forgive all our sins, for Christ's sake, and be at peace with us in him who died to make peace, and ever lives, making intercession.

Lord, we commit ourselves to thy care and keeping this day. Watch over us for good. Compass us about with thy favor as with a shield. Preserve our going out and coming in.

Lord, plead thy cause in the world: build up thy church into perfect beauty. Let the reformed churches be more and more reformed, and let everything that is amiss be amended. And let those that suffer for righteousness' sake be supported and delivered.

Do good in these nations. Bless all that are in authority. Guide public counsels and affairs. Overrule all to thine own glory. Let peace and truth be in our days and be preserved to those that shall come after us.

Be gracious to all our relations, friends, neighbors, and acquaintances, and do them good according as their necessities are. Supply the wants of all thy people. Dwell in the families that fear thee and call upon thy name. Forgive our enemies and those that hate us. Give us a right and charitable frame of spirit towards all people and all that is theirs.

Visit those that are in affliction and comfort them. Be unto them a very present help. Recover the sick. Ease the pained. Succor the tempted. Relieve the oppressed, and give joy to those that mourn in Zion.

Be gracious to all that are dear to us. Let the rising generation be such as thou wilt own, and do thee more and better service in their day than this has done.

Do for us, we pray thee, abundantly above what we are able to ask or think, for the sake of our blessed Savior Jesus Christ, who is the Lord our righteousness. To him with the Father and the eternal Spirit be glory and praise, now and for ever. Amen.

—*Matthew Henry, 1662–1714; alt.*


<sub>310</sub>

## *For Guidance*

O Father of lights, open mine eyes to see what my true happiness is. Point out the road clearly that leads to it and never suffer me to depart from it. Send forth thy light and thy truth. Let them lead me and bring me to that new heaven and new earth wherein dwelleth righteousness. Guide me with thy counsel while here, and afterward, receive me to glory.

—*William Leechman, 1706–1785*

## Let Me Be Received

Accept, O Lord, this imperfect sacrifice,
and cover the faults of it
with the perfections of that great High Priest,
who by the eternal Spirit did offer himself without blemish.
Let me be received as a living sacrifice,
holy and pleasing to thee,
which is our reasonable service.
Crucify, O Lord, this old man,
that this body of sin may be brought to nothing.

*—André Rivet, ca. 1573–1651; alt.*

## For the Day's Work

Protect, direct, and bless us this day in all our lawful ways and labors,
that in the evening we may return thee joyful thanks, through Jesus
Christ our only Savior, in whose words we sum up all our prayers:
Our Father . . .

*—Richard Baxter, 1615–1691*

313

## Adoration

Alas, my God, none could be found like you, who deign to preserve
your servants whom you have redeemed as well as created. It is your
will to test them in many ways, to show forth your graces in them
more and more, in manifold delights, riches, and honors, and then
through pains, sicknesses, labors, fears, shames, losses, distresses,
sorrows, as you set them to work in your vineyard, the better to
establish your mighty works within them.

But as you observe their souls, and in so doing behold the
unbearable travail of their hearts, you face them, without denying the
rightness of your doings, by covering the errors of those for whom you
have poured out tears and laments in order to recover all by love, and
have chosen to keep for yourself their hells, their punishments, their
griefs.

*—Marguerite of Navarre, 1492–1549; alt.*

314

## For Repentance

O my Sovereign Lord, I have sinned against thee and committed
abominable acts. But I repent in dust and ashes. O God, who searchest
the heart, the number and greatness of my crimes are not hid from
thee, and thou understandest what I ought to do and to be, to obtain
pardon. O Lord, I seek thy infinite mercy that desirest not the death of
sinners, but rather that they should turn and live.

Turn me, O God, and grant me the grace of repentance. Thou
art able to change this stony heart and cause it to yield penitent tears.
Give me instead of this hard heart another, fashioned after thine own
image, an heart that may be inflamed with love and zeal for thee.

O my Redeemer, thou hast completed the work of my salvation
by spilling thine own blood to atone for us. Continue that good work
in us. Sanctify my soul and body, and make me a new creature. Mortify

this flesh that the life I shall lead may be in imitation of the holy Jesus. Take possession of me by the direction and government of thy blessed Spirit that I may detest and shun all appearances of evil.

But chiefly, let charity influence my affections and actions, for such sacrifices are acceptable to thee. Assist me, therefore, in the performance of what thou requirest from me, and accomplish in me thy good work that at thy coming I may not be surprised or troubled, being diligently employed in thy service.

—*Charles Drelincourt, 1595–1669; alt.*

## *Prayer for Christ's Intercession* 315

Father, we would willingly ask thee for nothing but what thy Son already asks thee for. We would willingly request nothing at thine hands but what thine own Son requests beforehand for us. Look upon the Lamb as he had been slain, in the midst of the throne. Look upon his pure and perfect righteousness and that blood with which our High Priest is entered into the highest heavens and in which for ever he appears before thee to make intercession. Let every blessing be bestowed upon me which that blood did purchase, and which that great infinite Petitioner pleads for at thy right hand. What canst thou deny thine own Son? For he hath told us that thou hearest him always. For the sake of that Son of thy love, deny us not.

—*Isaac Watts, 1674–1748*

## *For Union with Christ*

Most wise and most Holy God, Who in creating our humanity hast most wonderfully dignified it, and in the Incarnation of Thy Son hast still more wonderfully glorified it: so reform us that in our humanity we may be one with Him, and so direct us that in all our thoughts and actions we may reflect His likeness. Help us to build our faith upon such sure foundations, that in the time of tempest we be not shaken, nor in the hour of death, overcome, nor in the day of judgment, rejected.

—*James Burns, 1875–1948*

James Burns, *A Pulpit Manual Containing Forms of Prayers used in the Conduct of Public Worship* [1914]. Used by permission of James Clarke & Co.

## *Intercession: For All Who Suffer*

Father, may your will be done.
Your Son's cross shows
that suffering does not have to be meaningless.
Grant that all who have to suffer
may learn this, and know it for themselves.
Do not be silent when they cry out to you.
Be close to them with your consolation.
Bless those who stand at their side to support them.
You alone are our life.

—*Germany,* Evangelical Hymnal, *1996*

## *Thanksgiving for Ordinary Saints*

God of all people,
not only the achievements of the great,
but also the kindness of the humble
has touched and influenced our lives for good.
For the ordinary saints
who helped your kingdom
take root and grow among us,
we praise you:
mothers and grandmothers,
fathers and grandfathers,
common heroes
and unsung servants of the kingdom,
who have let us see Jesus.
We bless you for our fellowship with those
whom you have called to greater life,
and we prize the company
of those who still live around us.
Lord, find a place for all of them in paradise,
and bring us with your saints
to glory everlasting.

—*Church of Scotland, 1994*

## *At the Ending of the Day*

The night is thine, O Lord,
and during its silent and defenseless hours,
we cast ourselves on thy sleepless providence.
Do thou accept and bless us
for the sake of the divine Mediator, Jesus Christ. Amen.

—*John Morison, 1791–1859; alt.*

320

## Praise

Glory be to thee, O God the Father,
> that thou shouldst find a way for the recovery
> of undone sinners.
Glory be to thee, O God the Son,
> who hast loved me and washed me from my sins
> in thine own blood.
Glory be to thee, O God the Holy Ghost,
> who by thine almighty power hast turned about my heart
> from sin to thee.

*—Joseph Alleine, 1634–1668; alt.*

321

## Thanksgiving

Accept, O God, our thanks and praise
for all you have done for us.
We thank you for the splendour of the whole creation,
for the beauty of this world,
for the wonder of life,
and for the mystery of love.
We thank you for the blessing of family and friends,
and for the loving care which surrounds us on every side.
We thank you for setting us tasks
which demand our best efforts,
and for leading us to accomplishments
which satisfy and delight us.
We thank you also for those disappointments and failures
that lead us to acknowledge our dependence
on you alone.

Above all, we thank you for your Son Jesus Christ:
for the truth of his word and the example of his life;
for his steadfast obedience,
by which he overcame temptation;
for his dying, through which he overcame death;
for his rising to life again,
in which we are raised to the life of your kingdom.
Grant us the gift of your Spirit,
that we may know Christ and make him known;
and through him, at all times and in all places,
may give thanks to you in all things.

—*Uniting Church in Australia, 1988*

## Sinner's Plea

322

God of mercy,
behold what a poor, blind, dead, hardened, unclean,
guilty creature, what a naked, empty, helpless
creature I am.
Look upon my sin and my misery
and let thine eye affect thine heart.
One deep calls to another,
a depth of misery cries out to a depth of mercy.

My misery speaks my curses.
My bones speak.
My perishing soul speaks,
and all cry in thine ears:
Help, Lord;
God of pity, help and heal me,
help and save me.
Come unto me, for I am a sinful man.
O Lord, I dare not say

as once it was said,
"Depart from me, for I am a sinful man."
Come, Lord, for I am a sinful man.
Thou couldst never come where there is more need.

My misery saith, "Come."
My wants say, "Come."
My guilt and my sins say, "Come."
And my soul saith, "Come."
Come and pardon.
Come and convert.
Come and teach.
Come and sanctify.
Come and save me:
Even so, come, Lord Jesus!

*—Richard Alleine, 1611–1681; alt.*

323

## *Do Not Reject Me*

O God, Father of mercies, save me from this hell within me. I acknowledge, I adore, I bless thee, whose throne is in heaven, with thy blessed Son and crucified Jesus, and thy Holy Spirit, and also, though thou slay me, yet will I trust in thee. But I cannot think that thou canst hate and reject a poor soul that desires to love thee and cleave to thee, so long as I can hold by the skirts of thy garment, until thou violently shake me off, which I am confident thou would not do, because thou art love and goodness itself, and thy mercies endure forever.

*—Robert Leighton, 1611–1684*

Most holy and loving God: we pray for the leaders of the nations of this world: that they may have wisdom beyond their intelligence, and compassion beyond their fear; that governments of whatever kind may be just and righteous and merciful.

We pray for victims of injustice: for the unemployed, the underemployed, the underpaid, the unappreciated, for the abandoned, the unloved, the abused—whether by persons or systems, for people on the fringes of society, the edges of sanity, the borders of survival. . . .

We pray for people in particular need . . . for refugees and exiles, for those without shelter because of storm, or fire, or flood, or war; for those who are ill in body, mind or spirit; for those in prisons of their own or others' making.

We pray for the children of this world: may their eyes be bright with hope; may their voices ring with laughter and song; may they be loved and disciplined, and loved and taught, and loved and fed and loved. May their dreams be of peace for the whole human family.

We pray for those who mourn the death of loved ones: comfort and sustain them by your Spirit. We remember before you especially those servants of Christ who have served faithfully and well in our denomination, who have died this past year, and who now sing your praise in the church triumphant. For their witness among us, we give you praise. For their living faith, we give you thanks. For their love, we rejoice.

We pray for loved ones who support us by their prayers and by their faithfulness. As we are aware of a cloud of witnesses surrounding and upholding us, so may we be a cloud of witnesses for your church, listening to your voice and speaking your word.

O God of mercy, grant us the willingness to be your instruments to answer our prayers; in the name of Jesus Christ, the living, life-giving Head of the church. Amen.

—*Jane Parker Huber, b. 1926; alt.*

# For God's Care through the Day

Oh thou that carriest the winds in thy fist:
so take care of me
that the waves of the sea or of worldly desires
may not swallow me up.
As we cannot fathom sometimes the depth of the water,
so we cannot fathom or reach the height of thy divine
           counsels.
For unsearchable are thy judgments
and thy ways are past finding out.
Thou who carriest forth,
graciously return home in safety thy poor creature,
that I may bless thee in the land of the living
and in the congregation of thy people.
All this and whatever else is needful
I ask for the sake of Jesus Christ my Redeeming Lord,
to whom with the Holy Spirit of grace
be glory, honor, dominion, praise
now and for ever. Amen.

—Mariner's Divine Mate, *Boston, 1715; alt.*

## Approach

326

Who am I, Lord, that I should make any claim to thee or have any part or portion in thee? To despair would be to disparage thy mercy, and to stand off, when thou biddest me come, would be at once to undo myself and rebel against thee. Therefore, I bow my soul to thee and with all possible thankfulness accept thee as mine and give up myself to thee as thine. Thou shalt be sovereign over me, my King and my God. Thou shalt be my portion, O Lord, and I will rest in thee.

—*Joseph Alleine, 1634–1668; alt.*

## Thanksgiving for God's Care

327

Early, O Lord, I was cast upon thy care, and thou hast never ceased to care for me. Thou hast been to me as a shepherd. Thou hast prepared a table before me. Thou hast made my cup to run over. In sorrow thou hast restored my soul. Thy mercies have been new to me every morning, and thy faithfulness every night. If I should endeavor to reckon up thy loving-kindnesses, they are more than can be numbered. Bless the Lord, O my soul, and let all that is within me be stirred up to bless thy holy name.

I look back this day, O heavenly Father, with heartfelt gratitude for the many tokens of thy tender mercy which blessed my early life. Thou gavest me the great blessing of parents who taught me thy law, who earnestly prayed for my welfare, who led me with them to the holy hill, and who ceased not to set before me all the blessings which thou hast promised to those who are faithful to thee amidst the temptations of this life.

Thou also hast made a way for me to that station and those prospects which I now enjoy. Often, indeed, have I failed to mark thy providential hand in the events of my lot, but thou hast still watched over my ways with more than a parent's care, and I can now see that thy pity and great love have delivered me from a thousand dangers of which I was not aware, and have led me amidst all the changeful scenes of this life to the good and gracious purposes which thou hast ordained for me.

—*Thomas Wright, 1785–1855*

328

## *For Forgiveness and Divine Communion*

Lord, I humbly beseech thee to forgive all my sins; to pour into my heart the gift of the Holy Ghost, and to enable me to abide steadfast in my calling.

Satisfy the longings of my soul with that bread of God which is the life of all who eat it. And let there be such a spiritual participation of thy blessed body and blood, that I may dwell in thee, and thou in me, and that having life, I may have it more abundantly.

Show me that thou art an all-powerful God, and that where thou art pleased to manifest thyself, there is heaven, there is a temple, there, an altar, there, divine communion. And while thy servant in a humble dependence on thy promises, with a bended knee and with a contrite heart waits upon thee, reveal thy mercy and thy loving-kindness, and overflow her soul with the cleansing and reviving streams of thy redeeming grace. Make me to know that I am thine, and that nothing shall ever separate me from thy love, divert me from thy service, or finally, prevent my admission into the realms of unchangeable felicity.

—*Martha Laurens Ramsay, 1759–1811; alt.*

# To Christ, the Bridegroom of the Soul

Lord, grant me help from above to run with patience that race which thou hast, Lord, appointed me to run with perseverance in true godliness unto the end,

>           that when my Bridegroom comes,
>                   I may be dressed
>           with him to go unto that
>                   marriage feast;
>           And being fitly trim'd
>                   may meet my dear
>           and gracious Lord
>                   where I shall never fear
>           more to displease him,
>                   but delighted be
>           in fresh communion
>                   to eternity.
>           O blessed Lord, how hast
>                   thou sweetened grace
>           In making me to behold
>                   thy heavenly face.
>           How beautiful dost thou
>                   appear to thine,
>           on whom thou mak'st
>                   thy glorious face to shine.
>           Inflame my heart, Lord,
>                   with more heavenly fire,
>           And fill my heart with love,
>                   more to aspire.
>           Through grace, dear Lord,
>                   thou hast made love to me,
>           More sweet and pleasant
>                   than all wines can be,

by sweetness blest
    and put in gracious store,
given to those poor souls
    which will implore
thy heavenly blessings.
    O let thy love then fill
my soul with songs
    of praises to thee still;
if drops of love
    thus pleasant are to thee,
what will the oceans
    in thy presence be?
    *—Sarah Davy, ca. 1638 – ca. 1699*

330

## *Intercession: For the Church*

O God, we pray for the prosperity and increase of thy kingdom on the coming day. Assist thy ministering servants who have to preach the word of life. Renew their commission. Send them forth in thy strength. Baptize them with thy Spirit; touch their lips with celestial fire, so that thy word out of their mouth may be sharp and powerful, and abundantly successful in the conversion of sinners, the edification of the saints, and the glorious perfecting of the church of Christ, which he bought with his own blood.

*—George Smith, 1803–1870; alt.*

# At the Ending of the Day

As you have made this day, O God,
you also make the night.
Give light for our comfort.
Come upon us with quietness and still our souls,
that we may listen for the whisper of your Spirit
and be attentive to your nearness in our dreams.
Empower us to rise again in new life
to proclaim your praise,
and show Christ to the world,
for he reigns forever and ever.

*—Presbyterian Church (U.S.A.) and the Cumberland
Presbyterian Church, 1993*

# Part 2

## Prayers for
## Occasional Use

# BEFORE READING THE WORD

Read not, but first desire God's grace
to understand thereby.

—*Geneva Bible*

## *A Prayer for the Readers of God's Word*                    332

O Living God and Merciful Father, which by thy mighty and everlasting
word didst command all the whole world and all things therein to be
made, and by and by, they, through the mighty power thereof, were all
most perfectly made, and this, for our sake: give me and all people grace
always to laud and praise, for ever to extol and magnify thy most godly
high prudence in the creation of things, and thy eternal providence, in
most decently ordering and disposing the same.

By thy word, Lord, thou in thy prophets hath prophesied many
strange and wonderful things, to human wit seeming clean impossible.
Yet, at the time appointed, thy infallible truth hath and will accomplish
and bring them all to pass. Thy word is everlasting and true: heaven
and earth shall perish rather than one jot promised in thy word not be
fulfilled. Thy word is thy determinate will. Thereby we know what thy
pleasure is, what we should observe and follow, and what we ought
to omit and avoid. In short, thy word and gospel is thy power unto
salvation to as many as believe in thee by it.

But my heart, Oh Lord, is so disobedient, so hard and stony,
that of myself, I can neither love thy word nor willingly embrace thy
fatherly benevolence offered me therein. Neither can I understand thy
secret mysteries nor take the consolations promised me in it, so that of
myself, I cannot but most miserably hate mine own salvation. Wherefore

I humbly beseech thee, O most merciful Father, for thy Son Christ's
sake: look upon mine infirmity with the eyes of thy mercy and work in
me a love and fervent desire to hear and read thy holy word and sacred
Scriptures, and that in hearing and reading of it, I never stumble, but
may truly understand the right sense and meaning of it; understanding
it, may undoubtingly believe it; believing it, may earnestly follow it in
all faithfulness and obedience, always bringing forth such fruits as shall
become a true Christian, and that I may ever, in all my doings, seek thy
honor and glory. Amen.

—*Huldrych Zwingli, 1484–1531; alt.*

333

## A Prayer to Be Said Before
## Studying or Reading Scripture

O heavenly Father, whatever I am, whatever I have,
whatever I know, it is only by thy free grace.
I commit into thy hands only my salvation.
If my knowledge be small, yet I doubt not
that I am the child of thy everlasting kingdom.
Therefore by thy mighty power I shall grow,
when it shall be thy good will and pleasure
to a more full and riper knowledge
as of a more perfect age,
wherein my faith shall be fully able to comprehend
  and perceive
the breadth, depth, height, and largeness
of thy great mercies and gracious promises.

O Lord, do thou whatsoever shall please thee,
to open unto me and all the rest of thy elect servants
  and children

who depend upon thee, as much of the light of thy
        countenance
as may be most for thy glory and for our comfort,
yea, and at such time as shall seem good to thy wisdom
and fatherly mercy.
I rest only in thy hands, O my God,
asking thee to increase my knowledge of thy holy word,
whereby I may know thy good will and pleasure.

Give me, O Lord, thy Holy Spirit,
to conduct me and lead me all the days of my life,
that in sincerity of faith and pureness of living,
thy glorious Majesty may be magnified in me forever.
Grant this, O Father, for thy dearly beloved Son,
our Savior Jesus Christ,
to whom with thee and the Holy Ghost,
be all honor, glory, and praise, world without end. Amen.
        *—Edward Dering, ca. 1540–1576; alt.*

## For Obedience    334

O Lord, whose word is a two-edged sword to cut down all things
that shall rise up against the same, the majesty whereof shaketh the
heavens and the earth: grant that, our proud and vain affections
being cut down, we may with reverence read it, and humbly in
obedience submit ourselves unto it, through Jesus Christ our Lord.
So be it.
        *—From Eusebius Paget's Short Questions and Answers, 1579; alt.*

### *That the Word May Be Written in Our Heart*

O Gracious God, and merciful Father, which hast vouchsafed us the rich and precious jewel of thy holy word: assist us with thy Spirit, that it may be written in our hearts to our everlasting comfort: to reform us, to renew us according to thine own image, to build us up, and edify us into the perfect building of thy Christ, sanctifying and increasing in us all heavenly virtues. Grant this, O heavenly Father, for Jesus Christ's sake. Amen.

*—Geneva Bible*

### *For Wisdom*

Eternal God, most gracious and merciful in Jesus Christ: make me as a newborn babe to desire the sincere milk of thy most sacred word. Grant that I may rejoice at it, as one that findeth a great spoil. Let it be better unto me than thousands of gold and silver. Open my heart, as thou didst the heart of Lydia, that I may even with a kind of hunger and greediness attend to the things which are delivered. Clear the eyes of my mind and anoint them with that precious salve of thy Spirit, that the scales of ignorance may fall from them, and that I may see the wonders of thy law, even thy hid wisdom, which my nature of itself is not able to discern. And because thou hast promised to guide the humble in thy way and to reveal thy secret to the meek, take from me, I pray thee, a proud heart. Teach me to become a fool in myself, that I may be wise in thee.

*—Samuel Hieron, ca. 1576–1617; alt.*

## To Bear the Fruit of the Word

Thy word, O Lord, is the seed and we are the ground.
And whereas there are many sorts of evil ground,
there is only one good,
and that is wherein thy word, taking deep root,
bringeth forth fruit accordingly.
O Lord Jesus, thou that art the good husbandman,
make good the ground of our hearts
and take forth from the same
all harmful and unprofitable weeds—
such as worldly cares and pride,
and make such place for the word to enter,
that inwardly to our own soul
and outwardly to the world
it may appear we are not idle nor unprofitable hearers.

*—Peter Howat, ca. 1567–1645; alt.*

## For Understanding

O Father of light, who hast been pleased to vouchsafe unto us poor
miserable sinners, who by nature sit in darkness and in the shadow of
death, the light of thy word to direct us through the darkness of this
world, unto the light of glory; we beseech thee for Jesus Christ's sake
to pardon all our sins, and to open the blind eyes of our understanding,
that we may rightly comprehend thy word, and give us grace rightly
to apply thy word unto our own hearts, and to yield all holy obedience
thereunto, so that we may honor thee in this world, and be honored
by thee in the world to come, through Jesus Christ our Lord and only
Savior. Amen.

*—William Gouge, 1578–1653; alt.*

## For the Companionship of the Word

O let thy word be a light unto my feet
and a lamp unto my path.
When I go, let it lead me,
when I sleep, let it keep me,
when I awake, let it talk with me.
Give me the seeing eye, the hearing ear,
the understanding heart.
Make thy word like fire,
and like a hammer that breaketh the rock in pieces.
Oh let thy word be powerful to kill sin,
and to convert my soul unto thee.

*—Nathanael Vincent, ca. 1639–1697; alt.*

## For the Nourishment of the Word

O God, feed us in the green pastures of thy holy word, and lead us to the still waters of the comfort of thy Holy Spirit. Quicken thou our souls, O Lord, and bring us to life everlasting, through our Lord Jesus Christ.

*—Church of Zurich, 1693; alt.*

## For Discernment

Lord, thou who knowest all things:
do thou search and try me;
for amid this confusion of heart and life,
I cannot, without uncommon aid,
distinguish between light and darkness,
reality and delusion,

common and uncommon operations of thy Spirit.
Enable me candidly to compare my heart and life
with thy word,
and to draw a just conclusion.

—*John Brown, 1722–1787; alt.*

## *Praise of God's Word*

342

(based on Psalm 119)

O Lord, open thou mine eyes,
that I may behold wonderous things out of thy law.
O let me not wander from thy commandments.
Enable me to hide thy word in my heart,
so that I may not sin against thee.
Thy word is a lamp unto my feet,
and a light to my paths.
Thy word is very pure;
therefore it is the delight of my soul.
It is true from the beginning;
and every one of thy righteous judgments endureth forever.
I will never forget thy precepts;
for with them thou hast quickened me.
I have sworn, and through Christ will perform it;
that I will keep thy righteous judgments.
I love thy commandments above gold,
yea above fine gold.
Seven times a day do I praise thee,
because of thy righteous judgments.

—*Abigail Abbot Bailey, 1746–1815; alt.*

## 343      *To Embody God's Word*

Lord, help us to understand thy word, as we read it, and to live it.
May we make it a lamp to our feet and a light to our path. May its
great ideals and principles build themselves into our character, and be
exemplified in our lives. Only as we follow thy lead can we hope to be
happy or to develop as we ought to. Be thou ever with us, and keep us
ever under thy control. Amen.

*—Francis J. Grimké, 1850–1937*

## 344      *For Openness to Grace*

Almighty God, grant us your Spirit, that we may rightly understand
and truly obey your Word of truth. Open our hearts that we may love
what you command and desire what you promise. Set us free from
private distractions that we may hear and from selfish pride that we
may receive the promise of your grace. Through Jesus Christ our Lord.
Amen.

*—Christian Reformed Church in North America, 1987; alt.*

## 345      *For the Hallowing Power of the Spirit*

Come upon us now, O Holy Spirit,
and give us holy thoughts which are translated into prayer,
holy prayers which are translated into love,
and holy love which is translated into life;
for the sake of Christ Jesus our Lord. Amen.

*—Uniting Church in Australia, 1988*

# COMMUNION PRAYERS

### *Looking with the Eye of the Heart*                346

Oh God,
we praise thee for all the goodness thou hast wrought towards us.
Now that we are assembled round this table, do thou be with us.
While we see the bread broken in our presence,
may the eye of the heart be looking at the body of the Lord Jesus
as broken on the cross for us.
And when we see the wine poured into the cup,
may the ear of the heart be listening
to the voice of the Lord Jesus saying,
"This cup is the new covenant in my blood,
which was shed for the remission of sins."
Let not what the Apostle says be applicable to us:
never may we eat and drink condemnation to ourselves.

Forbid that we should take nails
and fasten the Lord Jesus again to the cross.
Once he has been put to pain for us, may that suffice.
May we never take the spear of sin and pierce again his side,
thus crucifying him afresh, and putting him to an open shame.
In partaking of this sacred feast,
may our hearts be warmed,
may our love to the Savior be made greater,
and may our faith be made stronger.

> —*Anonymous, fl. 1830, a Polynesian Congregationalist man; alt.*

## *For Christ's Indwelling*

Come and dwell in my heart, blessed Child of the Eternal, and as you come in, bring salvation and life as your companions. Lift up your heads, O gates, and the King of glory will come in.

—*Walloon Synod of the Netherlands Reformed Church, 1730*

## *Here I Am, Lord*

O Lord, I am not my own.
I never was, never can be, never desire to be so,
and hope and promise never to act as if I was.
Truly, I am thy servant.
Thou hast loosed my bonds.
Thine I am by creation, thine by purchase, thine by covenant.
I confess and triumph in this relation,
and acknowledge all the duties resulting from it.
I have sworn and cannot repent,
that I will keep thy righteous statutes.

Here I am, Lord.
What wilt thou have me to do?
Deal with me and mine as seemeth good in thy sight.
Thy will and not mine shall be the rule of my desires and actions,
and thy glory my supreme end.
'Tis thine to command and dispose,
mine to obey and submit.
Thou hast bought me with a price,
even with the precious blood of thine own Son,
of which the sacramental wine is a memorial.
I therefore, in gratitude bound,
present my whole self, body and soul, to thee,
a living sacrifice, holy and acceptable,
which is my reasonable service,
with a full purpose of heart to glorify thee with both.

—*Henry Grove, 1684–1738; alt.*

O Heavenly Father,
since we desire to receive the Holy Supper of our Savior,
praised over all,
and so to proclaim his death:
draw our souls to you,
robe us in the splendor of faith and holiness,
awake in us the spiritual hunger and thirst
for the friendship of our Savior
and for the heavenly gifts that he has obtained for us
by his passion and death.
Satisfy our souls with your goodness
through the power of this blessed feast.
Grant us the strength
to progress from grace to grace
until we come to you
and enter your glory.

*—Church of Bern, 1761; alt.*

## For Faith                350

O God, through your messenger, than whom none greater has arisen
among those born of women, you graciously showed that your Son
is the Lamb who takes away our sins. Grant us now to call upon you
through the Lamb; and when we cry, "Lamb of God, you take away
the sins of the world; have mercy upon us!" then in your kindness,
pardon all our guilt. He suffered, so that through him we might always
draw near to you; he chose to be bound by our weakness, that in
him we might be made strong; he gave himself as food, that by his
nourishment we might grow into the fullness of his stature. Draw our
hearts, O Lord, by the light of your grace, that we may draw near
worthily, that is, with true faith, to this most sacred banquet of your
Son, where he is both host and feast.

*—Huldrych Zwingli, 1484–1531*

## For Confidence and Joy

O Lord Jesu, who callest me to thy table, be pleased to meet me and bring me to it thyself. Give me the two wings of faith and love to raise my heart to thee.

O Son of God, who hast given thyself for me, and dost at this time give thyself to me, open thou my heart to receive thee; give me holy affections to entertain thee, that with a confidence tempered with humility, and a joy full of holy trembling, I may receive this high mystery of my salvation, yea, that I enjoy thine own self really and truly.

O thou that wouldst be conceived in the Virgin's womb, be conceived again in my heart, that hereafter I may live with thy life.

O thou that wouldst die for me, make me now feel the efficacy of thy death in the comfort of my soul and the mortification of my sinful affections.

O thou that art risen from the dead, and ascended to heaven, work a resurrection of holiness in my heart, and a lively faith to ascend to heaven after thee, there to embrace thee and hold thee, while I take with my hand the outward elements of bread and wine. O Bread of life, come feed my soul. O Holy Ghost, give me the true taste of these great mercies. And for the fruits of thy bounty, let me ever return the fruits of my love and thankfulness.

—*Pierre Du Moulin, the Younger, 1601–1684*

## The Wedding Feast of the Lamb

Lord Jesus, who have loved me with an eternal love, who came to visit me in my stinking grave, and who gave me life when I was dead in my faults and sins: grant me to be received at your table like Lazarus restored to life.

And since, my Lord, you have absolute rights over me, having bound me to you in kinship, closer than Boaz to Ruth the Moabite woman, let me find grace in your eyes. Speak to your creature, speak to my heart and console me. Hold out to me the hem of your garment. And allow me to eat with your servants and to drink out of your vessels. Oh, that I may browse in your meadow and bear in my heart the seed of life eternal, in expectation of enjoying the freedom of your whole house, when in heaven above you at last consummate that marriage, the promise of which you intend to confirm again today in the presence of your people. Oh how happy are those who are called to the wedding feast of the Lamb. Amen.

—*Charles Drelincourt, 1595–1669*


## To the Divine Physician 353

Seeing it is thy blessed pleasure to come to sup with me and to dwell in me, I cannot but for joy burst out and say, "What is man that thou art mindful of him, and the Son of Man, that thou so regardest him?" Whatever favor thou vouchsafest me in the abundance of thy grace I will freely confess what I am in the wretchedness of my nature.

I am, in a word, a carnal creature whose very soul is sold under sin, a wretched man compassed about with a body of death. Yet, Lord, seeing thou callest, here I am. And seeing that thou callest sinners, I have thrust myself in among the rest. And seeing that thou callest all with their heaviest loads, I see no reason why I should stay behind.

O Lord, I am sick, and whither should I go but unto thee, the Physician of my soul? Thou hast cured many, but never didst thou meet with a more miserable patient: for I am more leprous than Gehazi, more unclean than Magdalene, more blind in soul than Bartimaeus was in body. For I have lived all this while, and never seen the true light of thy word.

Cure me, O Lord. Though I have sins and sores, yet, Lord, so abundant is thy grace, so great is thy skill, that if thou wilt, thou canst with a word forgive the one and heal the other. And why should I doubt thy good will, when to save me will cost thee now but one loving smile, who didst show thyself so willing to redeem me, though it cost thee all thy heart-blood, and now offerest so graciously unto me the assured pledge of my redemption by thy blood?

If Elizabeth thought herself so much honored at thy presence in the womb of thy blessed Mother, that the babe sprang in her belly for joy, how should my soul leap within me for joy now that thou comest by thy holy sacrament to dwell in my heart for ever? Oh what an honor is this, not that the Mother of my Lord, but my Lord himself should come to visit me! Indeed, Lord, I confess with the faithful Centurion that I am not worthy that thou shouldest come under my roof, and that if thou didst but speak the word only, my soul would be saved.

Yet, seeing it hath pleased the riches of thy grace, for the strengthening of my weakness, to seal thy mercy unto me, in all thankful humility, my soul speaks unto thee with the blessed Virgin: "Behold the handmaid of the Lord. Be it unto me according to thy word." Knock thou, Lord, by thy word and sacraments at the door of my heart, and I will, like the publican, with both my fists, knock at my breast, that thou mayest enter in. O Lord, by thine almighty power, enter in and dwell there for ever, that I may have cause with Zacchaeus to acknowledge that this day, salvation is come unto mine house.

I resign the whole possession of my heart unto thy sacred majesty, entreating that I may not live henceforth, but that thou mayest live in me, speak in me, walk in me, and so govern me by thy Spirit, that nothing may be pleasing unto me, but that which is acceptable unto thee, that finishing my course in the life of grace, I may afterwards live with thee for ever in the kingdom of glory. Grant this, O Lord Jesus, for the merits of thy death and bloodshedding. Amen.

*—Lewis Bayly, 1565–1631; alt.*

<h2>354     Complete Thy Mercy in Me</h2>

This is thy Body, O blessed Savior, and this is thy blood.
Thine was the smart, but mine the ease;
thine were the sufferings, but mine is the mercy;
thine were the stripes, but mine is the balm;
thine were the thorns, but mine is the crown;
thine was the death, but mine is the life.
O complete thy mercy in me!
Come Holy Jesus, come and take possession of my soul.
Purify me with thy precious Body and blood.
Cleanse me from all filthiness of flesh and spirit;
that being fitted for thy habitation it may please thee
to abide with me forever. Amen.

*—Henry Harbaugh, 1817–1876*

## For Faithfulness

My God, you have been so kind as to give me your Son to die for my salvation: your word has taken hold of me; your sacrament has just assured me of this; and my soul triumphs in the awareness of so great a grace. Forever you shall be my hope, my consolation, my joy, and my soul will seek its happiness in none but you alone. For my part, O my God, I promise you an obedience more faithful and a love more fervent than I have ever shown you up to this hour. My heart is ready, O my God; I shall bless you, I shall celebrate you eternally. King of saints, who is there that will not fear you and magnify your Name? For you only are holy, and all the nations shall come and worship you. Yet, O Fount of grace, keep steadfast in my heart the awareness that you inspire in me this hour. Lord, do not allow the world to succeed in leading me astray. Do not allow my passions to grow stronger anew within my bosom. Help me according to your promises, sustain my weaknesses, correct my failings. Take me by the right hand, guide me by your counsel, until just as you have accepted me at your table here below, I may be summoned also to the wedding of the Lamb in paradise, where I shall bless you into the ages of ages, with the angels and the saints. Amen.

—*Raimond Gaches, ca. 1615–1668*

## Thanksgiving

Most merciful Father, we render unto thee all thanks, praise, honor, and glory that it hath pleased thee of thy great mercy to grant unto us miserable sinners such excellent benefits and privileges as to be received into the fellowship and company of thy dear Son Jesus Christ our Lord. Yea, by this means, we are thy adopted children, and he is made our elder brother. Yea, O Lord, we come nearer than so: He is our Head, and we are the members of his mystical Body. And all this proceeds from thy gracious goodness and compassion. For thou hast delivered him to death to give us life. Thou hast made him a sacrifice for the necessary food and nourishment of our souls. Thou gavest way to the piercing of his sides, from whence issued water and blood, that we might know how we came cleansed from our sins and redeemed from damnation. Yea, O Lord God, thou hast presented us in this sacrament the whole tragedy of his Passion that we, out of his sorrows, might recover joys; out of his groans, might be comforted; out of his sighs and tears, might have ours put into his bottle; and out of his death, be presented to life everlasting.

We beseech thee then, O heavenly Father, to grant us this request: that thou never suffer us to become so unkind as to forget such worthy benefits, but rather make a sure impression of them in our hearts for ever, and let the virtue and strength of his Spirit ever be found in us, by which we may be confirmed and established so that we may not only prevail against all our spiritual enemies, but continue also in confessing thy goodness, reformation of our lives, and performance of all good duties, to the glory of thy Name; through the same Christ Jesus our Lord, to whom with thee, O Father, and thy Holy Spirit, be all glory and praise, now and for ever. Amen.

—*Michael Sparke (compiler)*, The Crums of Comfort, *1629 ed.; alt.*

<hr>

357

## *Gratitude*

Lord,
you have put gladness in our hearts,
you have satisfied our hunger with good things.
In giving all, you have not withheld from us
your own dear Son, your very self:
how can we withhold anything from you,
our Lord and our God?
Renew us day by day with the gift of your Spirit,
that we may give ourselves completely
to your service,
and walk with joy in the footsteps
of Jesus Christ our Lord.

—*Church of Scotland, 1994*

## For Vigorous Faith

Heavenly Father, we give you everlasting praises and thanks that you have bestowed upon us, poor sinners, so great a benefit—that you have drawn us into the communion of your Son Jesus Christ our Savior, whom you surrendered to death for us and whom you give to us as food and nourishment for eternal life. Grant us now this benefit also: that you will never allow us to become forgetful of these truths, but that rather, having them imprinted upon our hearts, we may grow and thrive vigorously in faith, a faith committed to all good works; and that in so doing we may order and direct our whole human life to the exaltation of your glory and the upbuilding of our neighbor, through the same Jesus Christ your Son, who in the unity of the Holy Spirit lives and reigns with you eternally. Amen.

—*Jean Calvin, 1509–1564*

## Maranatha

Lord Jesus, thy word is sweet, thy sacraments sweet, and all thine ordinances are sweet, through thy sweetness, yet they satisfy not fully. Thou art more sweet and soul-satisfying than all.

I love thine appearing, I long for thy coming. Thou hast said, "Behold, I come quickly"; and my heart echoes, "Even so, come, Lord Jesus." Amen.

—*Francis Roberts, 1609–1675; alt.*

# The Church's Year

### 360
## *The Coming of the Lord*

Most holy God, whose firm promises cannot fail and whose Son Jesus Christ is the promised Messiah and Savior, prepare us for his advent and rule through humble, teachable, and penitent hearts; in the name of Jesus Christ, our Lord. Amen.

*—Horton M. Davies, contemporary*

### 361
## *For Readiness to Receive Christ*

Almighty God, Father of our Lord Jesus Christ, in the fullness of time light arose over a dark world in the birth of your Son at Bethlehem. He came and he shall come. The doors of our heart are too small to receive this King of glory. All is too weary and cold for us to be ready to meet him. So, we beg you, come into our hearts with your Holy Spirit, so that everything which resists the coming of your Son may be done away with, and a clear path be opened for him. Make us into one people, ready in the day of his appearing. Yes, Lord Jesus, come quickly. Amen.

*—Netherlands Reformed Church, 1955; alt.*

*Prayers from the Reformed Tradition*

## For Grace to Recognize Jesus

Lord God, dear Father in heaven, you have sent your Son Jesus Christ
as our Savior. We thank you for this. Help us to understand what it
means to be redeemed from sin and saved from death. We shall never
know his righteousness and lordship unless you awaken us by your
Holy Spirit to love him. Grant that we may not take offense at his
unimpressive servant form. Let us not fail to hear his quiet voice nor
hope too little in his hidden kingdom. Help us to believe and trust that
he is in very truth our Savior and the Savior of all the world. Amen.

*—The Evangelical Reformed Churches in
German-speaking Switzerland, 1974; alt.*

## Am I a Wise Virgin?

O thou great Searcher of hearts, I am one of those virgins who have
taken a lamp and am come forth to meet the Bridegroom of precious
souls. Am I a wise, or am I a foolish one? Have I taken my lamp
without oil? O let me not live at the least uncertainty. Arouse me
out of my spiritual slumber. And with me, all Christians, for we all
slumber and sleep. O arouse us before the midnight cry comes, that
we may now arise and trim our lamps, while oil is to be had.

O my God, let us not be mistaken. I beg for others, as for my
own soul, that we may not be found foolish virgins at last, and while
we are gone to buy, thou come, and those who are ready go in with
thee, and the door be shut.

O let not me nor any of thine rest secure in past attainments,
but all watch. For we know not the day nor the hour wherein the Son
of Man cometh.

Prepare me, Lord, for that grand and awful moment when thou
who hast taken on thee human nature shall come in thy glory and all
the angels with thee, and thou shalt sit on thy throne of glory and
before thee shall be gathered all nations. Thou shalt separate them
from one another as a shepherd divideth his sheep from his goats.

O then let me stand on thy right hand and not on the left. O then, unworthy as I am, let me, of thy boundless sovereign grace, hear thee bid me come, hear thee pronounce me blessed of thy Father, and called to inherit the kingdom prepared for thine from before the foundation of the world.

—*Sarah Osborn, 1714–1796; alt.*

## *Adoration*

God of glory,
because you disturb our expectations
with troublesome greetings,
and news of unwanted, improbable events;
because we cannot control nor predict
the unveiling of your power
and its flaring to perfection
in a baby born to die;
because you enable us at last
to accept your promises
and to build our lives upon them,
with Mary, faithful and trusting,
we rejoice and await the unfolding of your plan
through Jesus Christ our Savior.

—*Diane Karay Tripp, b. 1954*

## *For Transformation* 365

Lord Jesus, do not for a moment let me today contemplate your birth with any idle gazing, like a passerby stopping to look at some rich tableau, or like someone curious about things new or old, taking pleasure in reading or recounting some famous history; but, looking upon your glory with uncovered face as in a mirror, let me be transformed into the same image, from glory to glory, as by your Spirit. As I watch you being born, let me learn to be reborn and to begin a new life. For if anyone be in Christ Jesus, they must also be made a new creature.

Lord Jesus, in your incarnation, I detect the true model of my regeneration. For as you were conceived by the Holy Spirit without any human agency, we too, who by your grace are God's children, are certainly not born of flesh or blood, but we are born of God. You rested, conceived at one unique moment, in the womb of your blessed Mother, but each day you are conceived in the hearts of your elect, through the preaching of the word and the secret operation of your Holy Spirit.

Almighty and All-beneficent Spirit, who intervened in the conception of God's Son, and by overshadowing the holy Virgin caused her to conceive bodily this great God and Savior: possess my soul in like manner, and display your power upon me, in such a way that I may conceive him spiritually, and that I may be able to say with the apostle, "I live no longer, but Christ lives in me." Grant us to do the will of the heavenly Father, so that our Lord may hold out over us the hands of his grace, and that he may acknowledge us as his mother, brothers, and his sister. You have made us hearers of your holy and divine word. Grant us so to keep and obey it all the days of our life, so that we may forever be counted among the number of the blessed.

—*Charles Drelincourt, 1595–1669*

# Nativity

I know you well: you vanquished hell
As conqueror and king
Though you appear as baby here,
A poor and wormlike thing.

You left the throne, your Father's own,
To join us from above,
That God might be eternally
Our Father, through your love.

No man on earth defiled your birth,
No sin in your conception,
So that our blot by sin begot
Might turn into perfection.

Our sorry fall to dirty stall
Sent you from heaven's throne,
Thus making clean a place serene
For those who are your own.

All night you lay on pricking hay,
A crude and dusty nest,
That my soul may, one blessed day,
Find softer, sweeter rest.

The air was cold, the wind was bold
O Jesu, at your birth,
That your love's art might warm my heart
And all the chilly earth.

The gloomy night increased your fright
And plaintive misery,
So that a bright, amazing light
Might ever shine on me.

A sweet salt tear, O Savior dear,
Makes moist your tiny face,
So that my eye, forever dry,
May sparkle with your grace.

Your little hands in little bands
Are bound as with a string,
That I may be forever free
From sin and from its sting.

Your lips of red for sinner's dread
Bring comfort sure and sweet;
The serpent's head shall be downtread
By your bedimpled feet.

Your perfect eyes, I realize,
Are small, but they can see;
For with love's grace in this dark place
They turn and look on me.

O Bridegroom small, laid in a stall,
Make glad my waiting heart;
O infant wee, be born in me
And nevermore depart.

      —*Jacobus Revius, 1586–1658*

# *Thanksgiving*

O Great God, dwelling in light inaccessible: you chose to conform yourself to our weakness and to cover the rays of your glory with the veil of our poor fleeting nature, so that we might draw near with confidence to the throne of your glory. You wished to teach us that your kingdom is not of this world. You wished to make our faith more enlightened and miraculous. For if you had come at the head of a victorious and triumphant army, bristling with thunder, surrounded by flames, clothed in splendor, flesh and blood would have advised me to take your side. You wished to confound the glory of this world and to sanctify poverty by your example. In short, Lord, it is we who enjoy all the benefit of your incarnation and of your being made of no account. For the child has been born for us; to us the Son is given.

Merciful Savior, you came down into the lowest parts of the earth, but it was to raise us to the highest place of the heavens. You robed yourself in our mortal darkness in order to clothe us in your light and immortality. You wished to share in human nature in order to make us sharers in your divine nature. You clothed yourself in our flesh, in order to clothe us in your Spirit. You made yourself Son of Man, so that we might have the power to become children of God. You took the form of a servant, to free us from the fetter of the devil, and to make us "kings and priests" to God your Father. You had yourself registered in Caesar's roll, so that our names might be inscribed in your book of life, and our portrait might be forever on the palm of your hand.

You came down here as a stranger, but in order to make us fellow-citizens of the saints and members of God's household. People shut the doors of Bethlehem in your face; no place was found for you in the inn, but this was in order to open to us the gates of your holy city and to prepare for us a place in your heavenly Father's house, where there are many dwelling places. You were born in a stable, but this was in order that we might one day be lodged in the mansion of angels and archangels. You were wrapped in swaddling-clothes in order to gird us with strength and to cover our brow with a crown. You lay in a manger in order to raise us up to the palace of heavenly glory and to make us sit upon a throne. You chose to babble as a baby in order to teach us the language of angels. You sucked on the breasts of your mother in order to slake our thirst with the milk of understanding and to comfort us with the breasts of your consolation. In short, you chose to weep in order to wipe away our tears.

*—Charles Drelincourt, 1595–1669*

## *For Grace to Accept Jesus and to Share His Work*     368

Most gracious Father, we bless Thee that Jesus came into the world as a little child, and grew up in our midst, with all our human needs and human sorrows. We thank Thee that He came into the world as light in the midst of its darkness, as peace in the midst of its strife, as love in the midst of its bitterness, and as life in the midst of its death. We pray Thee that He may be born anew in all our hearts, that by faith we may receive Him, and by love open wide the doors of our hearts to His most gracious incoming. Unite us, we beseech Thee, with Him in duty and in sacrifice, in compassion and in helpfulness, in hope and in charity. Teach us to do His works, and grant that more and more He may come into the world, and cast out every bitter wrong, and bring in the blessed reign of peace and good-will.

*—James Burns, 1875–1948; alt.*

---

James Burns, *A Pulpit Manual Containing Forms of Prayers used in the Conduct of Public Worship* [1914]. Used by permission of James Clarke & Co.

# A Christmas Prayer for Lonely Folks

Lord God of the solitary: look upon me in my loneliness. Since I may not keep this Christmas in the home, send it into my heart.

Let not my sins cloud me in, but shine through them with forgiveness in the face of the child Jesus. Put me in loving remembrance of the lowly lodging in the stable of Bethlehem, the sorrows of the blessed Mary, the poverty and exile of the Prince of Peace. For his sake, give me a cheerful courage to endure my lot, and an inward comfort to sweeten it.

Purge my heart from hard and bitter thoughts. Let no shadow of forgetting come between me and friends far away; bless them in their Christmas mirth; hedge me in with faithfulness, that I may not grow unworthy to meet them again.

Give me good work to do, that I may forget myself and find peace in doing it for thee. Though I am poor, send me to carry some gift to those who are poorer, some cheer to those who are more lonely. Grant me the joy to do a kindness to one of thy little ones; light my Christmas candle at the gladness of an innocent and grateful heart.

Strange is the path where thou leadest me. Let me not doubt thy wisdom, nor lose thy hand. Make me sure that eternal love is revealed in Jesus, thy dear Son, to save us from sin and solitude and death. Teach me that I am not alone, but that many hearts, all round the world, join with me through the silence while I pray in his name: Our Father . . .

—*Henry J. van Dyke, 1852–1933; alt.*

## Intercession: For the Forgotten

O GOD, who before all others didst call shepherds to the cradle of thy
Son: Grant that by the preaching of the gospel the poor, the humble,
and the forgotten, may know that they are at home with thee; through
Jesus Christ our Lord. **Amen.**

*—Church of South India, 1963*

## Intercession: For Children

ALMIGHTY and most blessed God, who heard with pity the cry of
the holy innocents, we pray thee for all infants and little children
everywhere; that thou wilt preserve them from all cruelty, and nourish
in them for ever the sweet innocency of their faith and trust; through
Jesus Christ our Lord. Amen.

*—Colin F. Miller, 1911–1988*

From *Prayers for Parish Worship* by Colin F. Miller (1948). Reprinted by permission of Oxford
University Press.

## Intercession: For Those Who Mourn

ALMIGHTY and most blessed God, who heard with pity the cry of
the women wailing for their children, be with all who mourn their
dead everywhere; especially with any such as are known to ourselves,
whom, with all those near and dear to us, we name in the silence of
our hearts before thee. (*Silence*) Be with them, we beseech thee, and
help them; through Jesus Christ our Lord, to whom, with the Father
and the Holy Ghost, be all glory, dominion, and power, world without
end. Amen.

*—Colin F. Miller, 1911–1988*

From *Prayers for Parish Worship* by Colin F. Miller (1948). Reprinted by permission of Oxford
University Press.

## Intercession: For the Exiled and Homeless

ALMIGHTY and most blessed God whose Son was a fugitive into Egypt, we pray thee for all travellers, exiles, wanderers, and homeless folk; that thou wilt ever be with them to lead them as thou didst lead Mary and Joseph and the infant Christ; through the same Jesus Christ our Lord. Amen.

*—Colin F. Miller, 1911–1988*

From *Prayers for Parish Worship* by Colin F. Miller (1948). Reprinted by permission of Oxford University Press.

## *Adoration with the Magi*

The Magi came from the East to seek the King of Israel. And we, Lord, your poor children, few and scattered through all parts of the world, shall we not also gather in your holy temple, to live forever happy in the shadow of your scepter?

They came from the East to worship him. And I, Lord, shall I be content only to look upon you and to rejoice in your love, without yielding to you the homage due to your divinity? O peerless Child, how I adore you with my whole heart! For you are my Redeemer and my God, my life and my happiness.

Yet, Lord, do not let me appear before your face empty. After the example of your Magi, I bring you gold and incense from my store. Let me make a sweet smelling sacrifice to you, for the relief of your poor members. But above all, let me present to you a faith more precious than fine gold, prayers and praises sweeter than incense, a heart more incorruptible than myrrh.

And, Lord, let me not only fall down before you in all humility, and worship you with the Magi, but allow me, I beg you, to take you in my arms, like Simeon. And not only to take you in my arms, but to hold you in my bosom, and to lodge you in my heart.

The shepherds, having worshiped the Lord Jesus, and the Magi having offered him their presents, went away again; and Simeon, having taken him in his arms, blessed him and gave him back to his mother. But for me it is impossible to leave my Savior. He is so joined and united to my heart, that neither life nor death could separate him from it. I shall not let him go until he has led me into the banquet hall prepared on high in heaven since the foundation of the world.

My Father and my God, let me live in you, let me die in you, let me dwell eternally with you. I am weary of this life, its pleasures are stale and bitter for me. Lord, let your servant (handmaid) go in peace, according to your promises. For my eyes have seen your salvation.

*—Charles Drelincourt, 1595–1669*

## *Great Enough to Be Lowly* 375

O Lord God, we thank Thee that when Thou didst remember the poor, telling the shepherds at their labour the wonder of the birth of Christ, Thou didst not forget the wise and the rich, but hadst a message and a messenger for them also. Looking higher than the common track of mean pursuits, pleasure, and ease, and what money can buy, searching not for their ideals in the dust; their eyes beheld Thy star, and they were great enough to be lowly enough to follow Thy sign, till it led them to the bed of a little babe's poverty. They laid their gifts and treasures at His feet, but we thank Thee, O God, that first they laid their hearts, with all their pride and wisdom, there. Help us to follow their example, and this day to give into Thy keeping all we have and all we are, and all we hope to be, that Thou mayest give us Thy precious love, which all earth's money cannot buy, through Jesus Christ our Lord.

*—Lauchlan MacLean Watt, 1867–1957*

376  ### *For Insight*

Lord Jesus Christ,
on the mountain top Peter, James, and John
looked upon the majesty of your glory,
and from the mystery of a cloud
heard a voice declaring you to be God's Son.

Though we do not live on mountain tops,
grant that we too may glimpse your glory.
In the mundane predictability of our life,
may there be for us moments
when sight gives way to insight,
and the paths of earth
become the road to heaven.

—*Church of Scotland, 1994*

## Approach

Holy and righteous God, grant that we may acknowledge our sins that we made a burden for our Savior, and awaken in us heartfelt penitence and sorrow for them. O God, cause the love of Christ so to constrain us, that we may not refuse, in discipleship to him, to suffer rebuke, contempt, or persecution for his name's sake, if so you judge to be good and necessary for your glory and for the testing and clarifying of our faith. Make us then mindful that the servant is no greater than the master and the disciple is no greater than the teacher.

*—Biel, Switzerland, in* Reformed Churchbook, *1889 ed.; alt.*

## Confession

O God, our God, the law of love you remind us of makes us know the gravity and number of our faults. You have summoned us to follow the holy and righteous One on the way of renunciation, but we have preferred to walk the easier way of self-seeking and of doing our own will. We have been proud, ambitious, hard, haughty, and full of ourselves. And here, now, we have come to ourselves, not happy, but empty-hearted, frustrated, and troubled.

O God, have pity on us. Break the pride that makes us slaves; set us free from the egoism that is destroying us. Sanctify us by your Holy Spirit, so that we may live for you and walk in the communion of Jesus Christ your Son our Lord, to love as he loved us. So be it.

*—Reformed Church of Berne (Switzerland), 1955*

## Hoping in God Alone

O Lord, you are our God, and we are but earth and dust. You are our Creator, and we the work of your hands. You are our Shepherd, and we your flock. You are our Redeemer, and we the people whom you have redeemed. You are our Father, and we your inheritance. Be pleased therefore not to punish us in your fearsome wrath, but discipline us graciously, and preserve the work you have begun in us by your grace, so that the whole world may know that you are our God and Savior. For through your grace we have the very same covenant which you established of old with your people Israel, yet made far more glorious and mighty between you and us by the hand of Jesus Christ our Redeemer, the covenant which you have inscribed for us with his own blood and confirmed by his holy suffering and death.

Therefore, O Lord, we renounce ourselves and all human hope, and seek our sole refuge in this blessed covenant of grace, through which our Lord Jesus Christ reconciled us eternally with you by giving his body on the cross, once for all, as the perfect sacrifice.

Look, O Lord, on the face of your Anointed and not on our sins, so that your wrath may be stilled by his intercession, and your countenance may shine upon us to give joy and blessedness.

*—Church of the Electoral Palatinate, 1684*

## *Intercession*

Almighty and merciful God, although we are unworthy even to open our mouths to pray for ourselves, nonetheless, since you have commanded us to pray for the whole Christian church and for all in authority and indeed, for all humankind, we call upon you, therefore, for all the churches and all servants of the church, that you would give your blessing to the preaching of your holy gospel, and send forth faithful servants to your harvest.

Be pleased, on the other hand, to drive out all false teachers, ravening wolves, and hirelings who seek their own glory and advantage and not the glory of your holy Name and the salvation and blessedness of needy souls.

We call upon you also for all governments of the world. Give your grace to all in authority so that they may direct their entire government to the reign of Jesus Christ the King of kings over themselves and their subjects, and to the progressive destruction, through them as your servants, of the kingdom of the devil, which is the kingdom of all shame and disgrace, so that under them we may lead a peaceful and quiet life in all godliness and honor.

Further, we call upon you for all our brothers and sisters suffering persecution under the tyranny of the enemies of your truth, that you would be pleased to comfort them with your Holy Spirit and save them in your grace.

O Lord, do not allow your Christian world to be wholly laid waste: do not allow the memory of your Name to be blotted out from the earth, nor the enemies of your truth, together with other unbelievers, to gloat that you are despised and blasphemed. Yet when it is your divine will that your believers should give their lives for testimony to your truth and for the praise of your name, then be pleased to grant them constancy to the last drop of their blood.

We call upon you also for all to whom you send grief, poverty, imprisonment, sickness, childlessness, and other trials. Comfort them as you know their needs require. Give them endurance and patience. Ease their grief for them, and finally, have mercy upon those who languish in darkness and error, and lead them into the light of your truth through Jesus Christ our Lord. For these and all other needs, we call upon you as our faithful Lord and Savior Jesus Christ himself has taught us: Our Father . . .

*—Church of the Electoral Palatinate, 1684; alt.*

381

## For Grace to Share Jesus' Patience

O Man of sorrows, but mirror of patience, what week of pains was this to thee? What a Good Friday was that for me? What days of sorrows were then one after another to thee? And yet with what patience didst thou pass over them? Patient, when Caiaphas despitefully used thee, patient, when Pilate so unrighteously judged thee, patient, when false Judas so cunningly and treacherously saluted thee, designating thee to be taken; again patient, when thou didst carry thine own cross, patient, when the crown of thorns drew blood from thy sacred head, and patient when all others reviled, reproached, spitted, scoffed, and abused thee.

O thou that so patiently and peaceably, mildly and meekly, truly and willingly didst carry painful and pangful, heinous and heavy sorrows for me: I beseech thee, let thy patience discharge my impatience and let thine infirmities strengthen my weakness, inform my ignorance, comfort my sadness, kindle my love, discharge my fear, and moderate my anger.

O Lord, grant me patience to bear thy holy will in all things.

—*Thomas Sorocold, 1561–1617*

382

## On Palm Sunday

O Lord Jesus, who as on this day didst enter into the city of Jerusalem in the midst of the acclamations and praises of a multitude of people, and of thy disciples, who spread their garments in the way, and who followed thee, carrying branches of palms in their hands: give us grace to prepare the way for thee by all kinds of good works, to present thee with the fruits of righteousness, to serve thee constantly, and to rejoice without ceasing in thy salvation.

O Lord, who wast pleased to be praised by the children as on this day, that cried in the temple "Hosanna to the Son of David"; grant that in imitation of their innocence and simplicity, we may worthily celebrate thy praises this day and all our days. Grant that when thou shalt come from heaven at the last day, we may meet thee in the air, and enter with thee triumphant and victorious in the heavenly Jerusalem, into the temple and palace of thy glory. Amen.

—*Church of Neuchâtel, Switzerland, 1712*

## MONDAY OF HOLY WEEK

O God most blessed, who by Thy Spirit didst so reveal to Mary of 383 Bethany the end of the sorrows of her Lord that she anointed Him beforehand to His burial: mercifully work within us a like discernment and the same reverent devotion. Grant us, we pray, such a sense of the amazing love of our Lord and Saviour, that we may count no treasure too costly to lay at His feet. Help us so to live in the joy of His fellowship and so to crown Him with the homage of our hearts, that He may esteem us friends indeed. Deliver us from the fear of men and self-distrust, so that we may not hold back any gift or service to which His love shed abroad in our hearts may move us, but may hear now and obey Thy call to better things: for the love of Thine only Son, Jesus Christ our Lord.*

—*Church of Scotland, 1928*

*Alteration prohibited by copyright.

From *Book of Common Order of the Church of Scotland* (1928). Reprinted by permission of Oxford University Press.

### 384        *For Newness of Life*

O God, from whom Judas received the punishment of his sad end, and the penitent murderer received the reward of his confession and repentance: grant us the mind and attitude that belong to a state of grace; and, as the Lord Jesus Christ, in his bitter suffering, gave to them both according to their deserts, be pleased also to give us grace in our understanding, so that we may cast away from us the old error and put on the dress of righteousness, in the name of your Son, who reigns with you eternally. Amen.

*—Johannes Oecolampadius, 1482–1531*

---

## WEDNESDAY OF HOLY WEEK

### 385        *For Union with Christ*

Source of everlasting grace, who hast not left us without thy holy image in our humanity: fill us with the mind that was also in Christ Jesus, who thirsted only to do thy will and finish thy work, and declined no cup of sorrow from thy hand. Fix our eye upon the shadow of the cross which he has left upon every human path, and make us one with him in patience, in pureness, in love, in trust, in divine forgiveness, in entire self-sacrifice. Dying with him to earthly thraldom and mortal fears, may we rise with him to heavenly life, and set our affections on things above. Amen.

*—John Hunter, 1848–1917*

## For Submission and Trust

O Christ, who in Gethsemane
      Didst all alone in anguish pray,
"Father, if it be possible,
      Let this cup, Father, pass away,"—

O holy Christ, who rose serene,
      Sublime in victory to cry,
"Not as I will, but as Thou wilt!"
      Let us in faith on Thee rely.

Did not the stars in far off space,
      Upon their silver axes pause
To hear those words? Was not the air
      Calmed by the myst'ry and its cause?

O Christ, veiled in Humanity!
      O Victor over deepest woe!
When we, like Thee, endure the pain,
      Let us, like Thee, submission know.

Grant us a vict'ry like to Thine
      O'er all the storms that rage within.
Teach us, O Christ, we humbly pray,
      The trust that fain would conquer sin.

And when life's discords all are hushed,
      Blended in perfect harmony,
Call us, O pitying Son of God,
      Take us, O blessed Christ, to Thee!
         —*H. Cordelia Ray, ca. 1849–1916*

## *Adoration*

It is for us, O Lord, our God and Father, that Christ has suffered and died. We adore in Him Thy redemptive love. Jesus has come down to us, to lift us up to Thee; He has clothed Himself with our wretchedness, in order to fill us with His riches; He let Himself be bound with ropes, that our chains should be broken; He let Himself be condemned by human judges, that we should be declared just before Thy throne; He has taken our sin upon Himself, to clothe us with His holiness; He has partaken of our anguish, that our hearts should be filled with His peace; He has tasted our sadness, that we should ever sing with joy; He has entered into our death, that He might draw us with Himself into His eternal glory.

Almighty God, we bow down before Thee in deep humility and thankfulness, and adore Thy immeasurable love. Amen.

—*Presbyterian Church of Ghana, 1966*

## Adoration 388

Remembering thy resurrection, Lord Jesus, I worship thee, who art holy, who alone art without sin. I fall down before thee, who wast crucified; I praise and glorify thee, who art risen from the dead. For thou alone art my God and besides thee I know no other; and of thy name alone will I make mention.

Thou art risen indeed. Hallelujah.

Through thy glorious resurrection, O Lord Jesus, great joy has come to all thy people. Wherefore I bless thee, O Lord; I celebrate thy blessed resurrection. For thou hast abolished death, and brought life and immortality to light.

Thou art risen indeed. Hallelujah.

Although thou wast laid in the grave, O thou Eternal, yet didst thou spoil the power of hell. Thou didst rise victorious, O Christ my God, bringing resurrection to all that, living, believe in thee, and to all that, dying, sleep in thee.

Thou art risen indeed. Hallelujah.

*—Henry Harbaugh, 1817–1876; alt.*

## To Walk in Newness of Life 389

Grant, O Lord, that like as Christ our Lord was raised from the dead by thy glory, so we also, who are buried with him by baptism unto death, may be continually raised from the death of sin, and walk in newness of life; through the same our Lord Jesus Christ. Amen.

*—Henry Harbaugh, 1817–1876*

Almighty, merciful God, we give you praise and thanks that you gave your dear Son Jesus Christ as a gift to us, who died for the sake of our sins and rose again for our justification and overcame all our foes: death, sin, the devil, and the world, won and restored righteousness and life for us.

We ask that by the power of your Holy Spirit you would awake us ever more and more from the death of sin to a new life so that we may indeed perceive within ourselves the power of the resurrection of Christ Jesus, and with every passing day we may be more truly incorporated into him, until at last our mortal bodies also may be raised from the dust, reunited with their souls, conformed to his glorified and splendid body, and dwell with him in eternal joy and splendor.

Give your blessing also to the preaching of your holy gospel; destroy every work of the devil; strengthen all ministers of the church, and those in authority over your people. We pray you therefore . . . that you would grant those in authority grace and unity to govern their subjects according to your divine will and pleasure, so that righteousness may be advanced and wickedness prevented and punished, so that we may complete the course of our life in quiet rest and blessed peace in all godliness, as befits Christians.

Strengthen all weak and troubled spirits, and send us your peace, through Jesus Christ our Lord, who has taught us to pray in this manner, Our Father . . .

—*Church of the Electoral Palatinate, 1684; alt.*

## 391      *A Prayer for the Evening of Easter Day*

Eternal, mighty God, let your holy name be blessed from age to age and let your church proclaim your greatness and mercy in every place. On this day, turning our eyes to the triumphant Jesus, we give you thanks for the work of our salvation, and we worship the One who for our sakes surrendered himself to death and who is alive into the ages of ages.

O God, you decreed that your people Israel should celebrate Passover on the day when you brought them back from the land of bondage by your mighty hand and your outstretched arm. We too, set free by you from a different slavery, snatched from condemnation, raise to you our praises, for you are the Redeemer of our souls, and our salvation comes from you.

You led Israel across the deep waters, and they drew back to let Israel pass. In vain their enemies sought to pursue them; you blew upon them and the sea covered them. Lord, display the same power towards us; fight for us as you did for your people of old. When the floods threaten us, stop them. When our enemies surround us, scatter them. Save us when we are in danger of sliding into the abyss, and set our feet firmly on the rock of ages.

You were with Israel and led them when they made their weary way in the desert. Your cloud led them by day and your pillar of fire gave them light by night. For them the manna came down from heaven and water sprang from the rock. In your righteousness you chastised them but in your mercy you took pity on them and led them into the land of promise, to the places where you had prepared their dwelling. We too who are voyagers upon this earth, which is so often laid waste, await from you the water that refreshes, the bread that nourishes. Be our shelter in the heat of the day and our light in the darkness. Guide us, protect us, and lead us into the heavenly Canaan, into the eternal rest of your redeemed.

Lord, you have already listened to our prayer. You have fed us at the table of the bread of life and your word has been opened up before us, like an inexhaustible spring where our souls can slake their thirst. O Eternal One, all your good gifts are upon us. Teach us to use them with gratitude and for your glory. We shall take in our hand the cup of salvation and shall declare your holy name. We shall offer you the sacrifice of our praises and adoration. We shall live for you alone, O God, you that have redeemed us. Accept our vows. Grant us to remain faithful to them. Our hope is in you, living God, for time and eternity. Amen.

*—Reformed Church of France, 1897*

## *Praise*

O Holy and Divine Savior, as thou hast suffered for my sins and art risen again for my justification, thou art also ascended up into heaven to prepare a place for me. Thou art willing that I should be admitted into thy noble and divine palace, that I should be where thou art, that I may behold thy glory, which thou hast enjoyed with God the Father before the creation of the world. O sweet and merciful Lord, what cause have I to fear to go to heaven, since thou art there seated in the highest glory and felicity and stretchest out thy merciful hand to receive me!

Thou art the same yesterday and today and thou shalt always be the same for ever. Thou hast been pleased, for my salvation, to lie in a manger and to be nailed to a cross. Thou hast given thy soul for my ransom and hast spilt thy precious blood to wash and cleanse me from my sins, and to mark me a way that I might enter into thy holy sanctuary. In the midst of all that glory and light with which thou art now clothed, thou hast not thought it a scorn to acknowledge me as thy brother or sister and a member of thy mystical body. It is for my sake that thou appearest before thine heavenly Father, and it is for me that thou offerest up unto him prayers and supplications.

O wonderful Lord, it is in thy power to give me the things which thou hast merited by thy sufferings and which thou desirest for me by thy prayers and intercession, for all power is given unto thee in heaven and on earth.

—*Charles Drelincourt, 1595–1669; alt.*

## Thanksgiving

It is right and fitting, our joy and our salvation, that we should at all times and in all places give thanks to you, O Lord, Holy Father, almighty, everlasting God, through Christ our Lord.

We praise and give you thanks for your Spirit: who in the beginning moved over the face of the waters and without whose breath every living creature dies, inspired the prophets of old and filled them with power to speak your Word, overshadowed the Virgin Mary and made her womb the dwelling place of your Son, descended as a dove upon him and anointed him with grace and truth, appeared as tongues of fire upon the apostles, and armed them with power to become faithful witnesses to the resurrection of your Son; who gives us second birth and makes us living temples of his presence, who fills with life, guides and sanctifies, the entire church; Therefore with the whole company of saints in heaven and on earth we worship and glorify you, God most holy, and we sing with joy:

"Holy, Holy, Holy Lord, God of power and might, Heaven and earth are full of your glory. Hosanna in the Highest!"

*—Church of the Servant, Grand Rapids, Michigan; Christian Reformed Church in North America, 1984; alt.*

## For the Gifts of the Spirit

Almighty and most glorious Lord God, who as on this day didst send down thy Spirit upon thine apostles in cloven tongues as of fire: vouchsafe unto me the light of his inspiration and inflame in me the fire of his love.

Lord Jesus Christ, who baptizest with the Holy Ghost and with fire: make me partaker of his holy anointing and seal me unto everlasting salvation.

Holy Ghost, the Spirit of the Father and of the Son: sanctify my whole spirit and soul and body. Vouchsafe unto me the distributions of thy heavenly gifts; come down upon me in thy glory and take up thy habitation in my heart henceforth and for ever. Amen.

*—Henry Harbaugh, 1817–1876*

## 395 *For Life in the Power of the Triune God*

O Lord God Almighty, before the mountains were brought forth, or ever thou hadst formed the earth and the world, even from everlasting to everlasting, thou art God. We bow our hearts in humble reverence, and adore thee as the Father of an infinite majesty, the Father of our Lord and Savior Jesus Christ, the Father of mercies and the God of all comfort. For when the fullness of time had come, thou didst send thine only begotten into the world, that whosoever should believe on him might not perish, but have everlasting life. Thou didst declare him to be the Son of God with power, and thy voice was heard, saying, "This is my beloved Son, in whom I am well pleased: hear ye him." Grant us grace, O Lord, to receive him, to hear him, to obey him, to love him with all our heart and soul, and reconciled to thee through his peace-making blood, to call thee Abba, Father.

O Lord Jesus Christ, thou eternal Son of the eternal Father, God of God, light of light, life of life, aid us to keep ever before our minds the comfortable mysteries of thy deep humiliation, thine immaculate birth, thine innocent, bitter, and shameful death on the cross, thy victorious resurrection from the dead on the third day, thy triumphant ascension and exaltation at the right hand of the Father. O Lord, grant us grace to watch with joy, every hour and every moment, for thy glorious second coming in the clouds of heaven, as the righteous judge of the quick and the dead.

O Holy Ghost, proceeding from the Father and the Son, thou Lord and giver of life, who in the beginning didst move with creative energy upon the face of the waters, who didst overshadow the Virgin Mary, and cause her to conceive and bear the Savior of the world, grant that we, born again of water and of the Spirit, may rise to newness of life, and becoming more and more closely united to our blessed Lord, at last attain unto perfection in Christ Jesus.

O Holy and ever-blessed adorable Trinity, Father, Son, and Holy Ghost, one only, true, eternal God: guard, defend and uphold thine oppressed and struggling church in all parts of the earth, and bring us all in thine own good time out of the waves of this troubled life to the glad shores of everlasting felicity, where we will join in the song of saints and angels: "Holy, holy, holy is the Lord God Almighty, which was, and is, and is to come, world without end." Amen.

*—German Reformed Church in the USA, 1857; alt.*

## For Renewal and Unity

396

O Lord, you gave one Shepherd to your scattered sheep to bring them, by the sacrifice of his life, to you and to one another. Be pleased to bring them together into one fold, through the power of your Holy Spirit. We ask your forgiveness for the divided state of the one catholic church. We ask your forgiveness for our ingratitude for the liberation and enrichment which you brought us through the Reformation. You gave to your church the assurance of salvation and set the conscience free from the burden of human failure. But we confess to you our narrowness of heart, double-mindedness, small faith, our failures in self-denial and love.

Make us thankful anew. For you do not cease to call us, even now, to have one heart, for the sake of the breadth and length and depth of your love in Christ which, with all the saints, we can comprehend only in part.

Lord, lead all that belong to you to live the faith of their own baptism, and bring them out of narrowness into the openness of your truth, so that they may seek what unites and abandon what divides; so that they may truthfully make their own the prayer of their Lord and Savior: that they may all be one, even as you, Father, are in him and he in you, that they also may be one in you and in your Son through the Holy Spirit, so that the world may believe that you have sent Christ. Amen.

*—Kornelis Miskotte, 1894–1976; alt.*

<hr>

397

### Prayer for the End of the Year

Most holy and merciful God, you are the strength of the weak, the rest of the weary, the comfort of the afflicted, the Savior of sinners and the refuge of your children at all times; lend your ear to our supplications and come to our help, we pray.

When our faith wavers and our love grows cold, when we lose the vision of you and your presence seems less real to us, when we are tempted to follow unworthy, evil ways, and sin loses its gravity in our eyes, when duty is difficult, work painful, and our burdens very heavy, when the uncertain future fills our minds and in our fears and anxieties we forget your eternal love and compassion, when the final darkness engulfs us and our hearts and bodies fail and all human help is useless, then, heavenly Father, help us and save us. Amen.

*—Reformed Church of Berne (Switzerland), 1955*

398

### A Prayer for New Year's Day

ALMIGHTY Father, we pray Thee graciously to lead us through the uncertainties of this new year of our earthly pilgrimage. Protect us from the dangers of the way; prepare us for the duties, the trials, the joys, and sorrows that await us; and grant that each change the year brings with it may bring us nearer to Thyself, and to the eternal joy and rest that await the faithful in Thy blessed and glorious presence; through Jesus Christ our Lord. AMEN.

*—Church of Scotland, 1952*

Suppose you saw the heavenly hosts of saints and
angels praising God in the presence of his glory.
You belong to the same family and society as they
and are learning their work, and must shortly
arrive at their perfection. Strive therefore to
imitate them in love and joy, and let your very
souls be poured out in praises and thanksgiving.

—*Richard Baxter, 1615–1691; alt.*

### DECEMBER 26: ST. STEPHEN

### *For Constancy* 399

As we honor on this day, O Lord God, the memory of thy blessed
martyr, St. Stephen; grant unto us grace, we beseech thee, to follow
his faith and charity; that however sorely tried by the contradiction
of sinners, we may be able, like him, to look steadfastly up to heaven,
and to commend even our enemies to the pardoning mercy of our only
Mediator and Advocate, Jesus Christ: to whom with thee and the Holy
Ghost, be honor and glory, world without end. Amen.

—*Reformed Church in the United States, 1866*

400

## For the Conversion of the World

Almighty God, in the change from Saul the Pharisee to Paul the apostle and martyr you have shown us the power of the Holy Spirit to transform human lives. We pray that the light of the risen Christ may dawn upon all those who have not yet come to faith; and we remember those known to ourselves . . . . Grant that they may recognize Christ as their Lord and their Saviour, and be born into new life through the power of the Spirit; in the name of Jesus Christ our Lord.

—*Church of Scotland, 1980*

JULY 22: SAINT MARY MAGDALENE

401

## *SAINT MARY MAGDALENE*
## *(July 22)*

MERCIFUL and gracious God, who didst deign to make Mary Magdalene the first witness and herald of the glorious resurrection of thy Son; grant unto those who have fallen into the torment and captivity of sin to hear that wondrous voice of Jesus, which is able to subdue and cast out all evil passions: that there may be none without hope of mercy, or beyond help of grace; through the same Jesus Christ our Saviour. *Amen.*

—*William Orchard, 1877–1955*

## *Thanksgiving* 402

God of the spirits of all flesh, God of Abraham, of Isaac, and of Jacob; thou that rememberest the blood of the righteous Abel, and the blood of all thy prophets and martyrs; we bless thy holy Name, and render our unfeigned thanks to thee, for all the witnesses to thy truth and works, which thou hast raised up from the beginning unto this day. We bless thee for all those to whom thou didst give promises, and grace to believe the same. We thank thee for the prophets of old, especially for the greatest of all, the forerunner of our Lord. We thank thee for the grace which thou didst give unto the Virgin Mary, whom all generations bless, that she did become the mother of the Lord. We thank thee for the apostles, prophets, martyrs, and confessors of thy truth. We thank thee for all who have faithfully served thee in their day and generation, into the fruit of whose labors we are entered. We thank thee for all the dead who rest in thee, and for all thy living saints upon the earth. And, we beseech thee, grant unto us here present, that we may imitate their good example, faithfully serving thee all our lives, and being ready at all times to bear witness to thee, even unto the death.

Hear us for the sake of Jesus Christ, to whom, with thee, O Father, and the Holy Ghost, one God, be glory for ever. Amen.

—Catholic Apostolic Church, ca. 1899; alt.

# *Confession*

O Lord our God, gracious and full of compassion, slow to anger and of great mercy: with contrite hearts we confess our sin and seek thy pardon. We are unworthy of the heritage thou hast given us in thy Church; we have not shown the courage and patience of those who went before us in the way of Christ; nor have we earnestly contended for the faith which was once delivered to the saints. Though thou hast numbered us among thy people, and called us with an holy calling, we have been faithless and disobedient. Yet blessed be thou, O God, whose mercy covers all our sin. Forgive us, we beseech thee, for his sake who died for us and rose again, our Lord and Saviour, Jesus Christ. Amen.

—*James M. Todd, 1912–1977*

---

## November 30: St. Andrew's Day

# *To Be Witnesses*

Almighty God, as Andrew the apostle was the means of bringing Simon Peter to a knowledge of the living Christ, grant that we too may use every opportunity to share our faith with others; and as Andrew gave up his career and home to serve his Lord, grant that we too may be willing to make any sacrifice, and to renounce those things which hold us back from true commitment; in the name of Jesus Christ our Lord.

—*Church of Scotland, 1980*

# The Stations of Life's Journey

### For a Pregnant Woman to Use

405

O good God, seeing that I have through thy blessing conceived, make me wise in well-ordering myself, that I do nothing that may in anyway prove prejudicial to my child, either while I bear it in my womb, or afterwards, but that rather I may provide all things requisite for it at the time of birth and afterwards.

—*William Gouge, 1578–1653; alt.*

### Approaching the Birth

406

Be present with me in my labor, O Lord.
Help me, most merciful God, and mightily deliver me.
Let thy power, might and love be no less manifested
in the delivery, than in the forming of thy creature,
that being through thy goodness made a glad and joyful
       mother,
I may obtain perfect strength again,
and live to praise and please thee forevermore. Amen.

—*John Norden, 1548–1625; alt.*

# The Birth of a Child

Almighty and most merciful Father, from whom we come and to whom at the last we go: visit us with a special sense of thine overshadowing Presence, and make us feel that all our household, sick and well, young and old, are safe in thy keeping. We reverently receive the child born into our house as the gift of thy hand, and devote *him/her* thankfully to thee. Sustain and guard *him/her* in *his/her* utter helplessness, and enable us so to surround *him/her* with love and care that *he/she* may live as thy child, and serve *his/her* generation according to thy will. Cause thy goodness and mercy to follow *him/her* all the days of *his/her* life; and at the end bring *him/her* to dwell with thee in everlasting joy and felicity; through Jesus Christ our Lord. Amen.

—*Presbyterian Church in Canada, 1919; alt.*

# For New Parents: "A Prayer for the Hour"

Blessed Father, we confess that we are not very experienced in coping with anxiety. Help us not to live in terror of what might happen but to entrust ourselves and our child (children) to you. Help us to accept the risk at the heart of life and to share the courage you revealed when you sent your Son to teach and save us. We want to learn to depend more on you. In Jesus' Name. Amen.

—*Elwyn A. Smith, b. 1919*

Reprinted from A SPIRITUAL EXERCISE FOR NEW PARENTS by Elwyn Smith, copyright © 1986 Fortress Press. Used by permission of Augsburg Fortress.

# For the Baptism of a Child

Merciful and gracious, slow to anger and full of compassion, hast thou shown thyself this day to us and to our dear child. With peaceful confidence may we now commit him/her to thy fatherly arms; with what joyful hope may we bring him/her up before thee, seeing that he/she has been received into thy church, that thou hast taken it upon thee to care especially for him/her, and settest heaven before him/her as his/her true home.

We thank thee, O God, whose name is love, and we beseech thee now to fulfill unto this child all thy promises, according to thy faithfulness, and to keep thy covenant to be a Father unto us, and we shall be thy sons and daughters. Grant that henceforth he/she may be a true member of the body of Christ. Keep him/her evermore in the possession and enjoyment of all the good gifts secured to him/her in the holy ordinance of baptism; and do thou also help him/her to keep the covenant with thee, and in the obedience of faith to present himself/herself as an offering well pleasing unto thee.

Help, Lord, we pray thee, that he/she may be brought up in all faithfulness and godliness, to the honor and praise of thy holy name. Help us, his/her parents and friends, so that we may do unto him/her, as an heir of thy kingdom, all that is needful for his/her well-being. And do thou bless all our labor, and hear all our supplications; and grant that we and this child may be admitted into the heavenly inheritance which thou hast promised to all believers through Jesus Christ our Lord. Amen.

—*Norman MacLeod, 1812–1872; alt.*

## *For Children*  410

Son of the Father, who chose to become a child so that you could be a Savior and Helper for children, and became so truly like them that you had to grow in size and wisdom, and were tempted like them in every way: we entrust to you our children, in all their childish weakness and sin. Form their hearts according to your will, so that they may come to love your Father's house and his word as you loved them, and love and honor their parents as you loved and showed obedience to your earthly parents, but to your Father above all. Hear us for your dear Name's sake. Amen.

—*Netherlands Reformed Church, 1955*

## 411         *For Those Who Seek to Marry*

O Heavenly Father and Fountain of all blessing, by whose providence I am now come to maturity of years, made able to perform the essential duties of marriage, and freed from such noisome and contagious diseases as might bring prejudice to a bedfellow: seeing it hath pleased thy divine wisdom to sanctify marriage, I humbly beseech thee to pardon all my sins past, and to provide for me a meet yoke-fellow: meet in age, estate and condition, but especially in piety. Keep therefore mine heart, I pray thee, from being bewitched with beauty of face or comeliness of person. Turn my mind from covetousness and greedy desire of wealth. Let me first have assurance of a spiritual union with the Lord Jesus, that from him, as an Head, I, as one of his members, may receive ability to do good for that mate which thou hast provided for me; and that the said mate may have capacity to receive good from me, and ability to do good for me. Let it be not only a professor of the true religion, but also a lively member of Christ's mystical body.

Lord, in whose hand the hearts of all are, to turn them whither it pleaseth thee, set my heart and that of the mutual helper which thou hast provided for me, upon a fear of thy name. Give us grace in so weighty a business to proceed according to the direction of thy word, and with a consent of such as have charge over us, and with the advice of wise and godly friends. As it is through thy gracious dispensation an occasion of rejoicing, so may our rejoicing be in thee, O Lord.

Make me therefore, I heartily entreat thee, wise in enterprising a matter of such importance, lest instead of rejoicing, I find cause of mourning. Hear me, O Lord, I beseech thee, in this my humble and earnest prayer, for thy Son, my Savior Jesus Christ's sake, to whom with thee and thy Holy Spirit be all honor and glory now and for ever. Amen.

—*William Gouge, 1578–1653; alt.*

## A Prayer for Husbands and Wives

O most mighty and most merciful Lord God, who, by thy wise-ordering providence hast made us two one flesh, and joined us together by the nearest and firmest bond of all, which is marriage: so knit our hearts together, we humbly beseech thee, that matrimonial unity may ever be kept inviolable between us. Let thy fear so possess our hearts, that we may keep our bodies the temples of the Holy Ghost, and be so watchful over our company, our diet and apparel, and over everything that we take in hand, that we be in no way drawn to sin, but rather, yielding due benevolence one to another, we may mutually delight one in another. So link our hearts together by mutual love, even such love as may keep the unity of the Spirit in the bond of peace, that there be no jealousies, no offenses, no contentions between us.

Make us also, we pray thee, mutually provident one for another, that we may do each other good. Make us ever willing to dwell together, and when there is just cause of absence for a time, let us take all occasions of testifying our mindfulness of each other and longing desire after each other. And, good Father, so pour upon us the spirit of supplication, that we may always, without ceasing, call upon thee, the fountain of all blessing.

And now we earnestly beseech thee to make us, whom thou hast made one flesh, to be one spirit, joint members of the mystical body of Christ, and so sanctify our fellowship, that we may truly rejoice in each other, and bless thee from our hearts for each other.

Bless us with children, and bless us in them. Bless us with a competent estate, and with all needful gifts and graces. Keep us from wishing any hurt to each other and from wishing anyone ill. Give us, we beseech thee, not only a mind to wish one another well, but also ability and willingness to do good for each other, in our souls, bodies, estate, and good name.

Lord, we beseech thee to make us one heart and mind, in giving hospitality according to our ability, unto such people as come to our house, whether kindred or others, holding grudges against no one; and in relieving the poor also, lest we should by unmercifulness cause many curses to rest upon our house. These and all other duties, enable us, O God of power, to perform. Pardon all our sins, we most humbly beseech thee, and that, for Jesus Christ's sake, in whom and by whom, through the assistance of thy Holy Spirit, we desire that thy name may be glorified by us and others, now and for ever. Amen.

—*William Gouge, 1578–1653; alt.*

*Prayers from the Reformed Tradition*

## For the Healing Touch of Christ

O Christ, who sufferedst Thy hands to be pierced, so healing for our wounds might flow from them: Create within us such assurance of Thy love, and such hope in Thy power, that we may hide no hurt from Thine eyes, neither withhold any pain from Thy touch; that we, who have groaned in solitude, may be blessed by the fellowship of Thy sufferings, and we, who have been broken, may be made whole; through Thy mercy, who livest and reignest with the Father and the Holy Spirit, one God, world without end. Amen.

*—John U. Stephens, 1901–1984*

## For Strength

O Lord, I need your strength. I am weak, but you are strong. I am sick, but you are the source of all healing. You know how I feel, for you have suffered far more pain than I will ever know.

Lord, it's hard to wait patiently for you to renew my strength. Allow me to share the strength of others and lean on them while I wait. Allow me to experience your strengthening presence and to rest in you. Enable me to find that strength which is possible even in weakness. And, should I never be strong again, give me the grace to be content with weakness, hardship, and disease, for when I am weak, because of Jesus Christ, then I am strong. Amen.

*—Neil Weatherhogg, b. 1939; alt.*

## *In Health, I Don't Know How to Be Yours*

O my Lord, I want to bless You for the state of sickness,
because it is so easy then to be a little child and
to let myself be taken by the hand.
I want to bless You because, stretched out like this,
I am really subjected to Your power, unable to escape
or to do anything other than what You will.
How good it is, O my Savior, thus to be Your servant!
Since, alas, I am not strong enough to obey You always
when I can dispose of my life and my time, I bless You for
giving me these days when I cannot flee. Since in health I
don't know how to be Yours, I bless You for this sickness
when nothing can separate me from Your presence.

—*Michel Bouttier, b. 1921*

## *Before Taking Medicine or Medical Treatment*

O Merciful Father, who art the Lord of health and of sickness, of life
and of death, who killest and makest alive, who bringest down to the
grave and raiseth up again: I come unto thee as to the only Physician
who canst cure my soul from sin and my body from sickness. I desire
neither life nor death, but refer myself to thy most holy will.

O Lord, in this my necessity, I have sent for thy servant, the
physician, who hath prepared for me this medicine, which I receive as
means sent from thy fatherly hand. I beseech thee therefore, that as by
thy blessing on a lump of dry figs, thou didst heal Hezekiah's sore so
that he recovered, and by seven times washing in the river of Jordan,
didst cleanse Naaman the Syrian of his leprosy and didst restore the
man that was blind from birth by anointing his eyes with clay and
spittle, and sending him to wash in the pool of Siloam, and by
touching the hand of Peter's wife's mother, didst cure her fever, and
didst restore the woman that touched the hem of thy garment from her
bloody issue; so it would please thee of thy infinite goodness and
mercy to sanctify this medicine to my use, and to give such a blessing
unto it, that it may, if it be thy will and pleasure, remove this my
sickness and pain, and restore me to health and strength again.

*Prayers from the Reformed Tradition*

Lord, let thy blessed will be done. For I submit to thy most holy pleasure. Only I beseech thee, increase my faith and patience, and let thy grace and mercy never be wanting unto me, but in the midst of all my extremities, assist me with thine Holy Spirit, that I may willingly and cheerfully resign up my soul, the price of thine own blood, into thy most gracious hands and custody. Grant this, O Father, for Jesus Christ's sake, to whom with thee and the Holy Ghost, be all honor and glory, both now and evermore. Amen.

*—Lewis Bayly, 1565–1631; alt.*

## Now Thou Callest Me by Sickness 417

Oh, my God, I humbly pray,
receive my soul by thy free mercy in Jesus Christ,
my Savior and Redeemer,
for Christ has died for me
and for all my sins in this world committed.
My great God hath given me long life,
and therefore I am now willing to die.
Oh Jesus Christ, help my soul.
Oh, pardon me and help me.
Lord, thou callest me with a double calling,
sometimes by prosperity and mercy,
sometimes by affliction,
and now thou callest me by sickness.
Let me not forget thee, O my God.
I give my soul to thee, oh my Redeemer, Jesus Christ.
Pardon all my sins, and deliver me from hell.
Oh do thou help me against death,
and then I am willing to die,
and when I die,
oh help me
and receive me.

*—Thomas Waban, fl. 1646–1720; alt.*

## Prayer for Healing

**418**

Eternal God, for Jesus' sake, send your Holy Spirit upon your servant; drive away all sickness of body and spirit; make whole that which is broken. Grant deliverance from the power of evil, and true faith in Jesus Christ our Lord, who suffered on our behalf but also rose from death so that we, too, could live. In his name we pray. Amen.

*—Reformed Church in America, 1987; alt.*

## Thanksgiving for Recovery

**419**

All glory be given to thy name, O Lord, who art the great and powerful Physician. Thou didst hearken to the requests of our family, and heal my dear father (mother, brother, sister, etc.), when he (she) was smitten with sickness, and brought very low. Let me ever remember that thou art a God hearing prayer, and trust in thee at all times. Let me call upon thee in a day of distress, and let all our lips be filled with thy praises. Amen.

*—Isaac Watts, 1674–1748*

## For Assurance of God's Healing Power

**420**

Most gracious God, source of all healing: we give thanks to you for all your gifts but most of all for the gift of your Son, through whom you gave and still give health and salvation to all who believe. As we wait in expectation for the coming of that day when suffering and pain shall be no more, help us by your Holy Spirit to be assured of your power in our lives and to trust in your eternal love, through Jesus Christ our Lord. Amen.

*—Reformed Church in America, 1987*

## Prayer for Family and Friends of the Dying

Almighty God, our creator and redeemer,
you are our comfort and strength.
You have given us our *sister/brother* N.
to know and to love in our pilgrimage on earth.
Uphold us now as we entrust *her/him*
to your boundless love and eternal care.
Assure us that not even death
can separate us from your infinite mercy.
Deal graciously with us in our anguish,
that we may truly know your sure consolation
and learn to live in confident hope of the resurrection,
through your Son Jesus Christ our Lord.

*—Presbyterian Church (U.S.A.) and the Cumberland
Presbyterian Church, 1993*

## Prayer with the Family at the Time of Death

Lord Jesus,
we wait for you to grant us your comfort and peace.
We confess that we are slow to accept death
as an inevitable part of life.
We confess our reluctance to surrender
this friend and loved one into your eternal care.
You, Lord Jesus, know the depth of our sorrow;
you also wept at the grave of your friend Lazarus.
Let the Holy Spirit come upon us now,
the Comforter you promise.
Grant us your love and peace
as we reach out to comfort one another.

Be our companion as we live through the days ahead;
and even as we mourn,
may all that we feel, think, say, and do
bear witness to our faith.
Amen.

*—Uniting Church in Australia, 1988*

423

## *Prayer upon the Death of One's Beloved*

O my God, I acknowledge that there is nothing certain nor unchangeable on earth but thy precious and holy promises. Thou hast snatched out of my embraces and pulled from my bosom my greatest darling and most intimate friend. Thou hast opened my heart and torn it, and thou hast separated me from myself, so that my life is but a burden and pain to me.

He (or she) was my greatest joy and my sweetest comfort. The day that took him (or her) away overwhelmed me in a sea of grief.

O God of all comfort, remove all these vain displeasures that consume me, deliver my soul from this unmerciful grief and torment that it suffers, and from these troubles that are more than human. Give me grace to remember that the least things as well as the greatest are governed and ruled by thy wise providence, and that the good and the evil proceed from thy divine appointment. Give me grace to consider that thou dost hold in thine almighty hand the keys of life and death, and thou alone dost cast us in the grave, and liftest us up from thence again.

The person for whom I lament was close to me, like another myself and was also thy creature, thy child, and a member of our Savior's mystical body. We believe we have the right of disposing of our handiworks and that which we have bought with our money; and hast not thou, O God, the liberty to dispose of that which thou hast created after thy likeness? Thou hast a Son who is the brightness of thy glory and the express image of thy person, whom thou hast not spared for me, and shall I, Lord, refuse thee my heart? Thou hast taken up into heaven the person whom my soul loved, to crown him (or her) with a glorious and ever happy immortality. Shall his (or her) rest occasion my displeasure? Can I be so cruel as to wish him (or her) out of thy embraces and the ravishing enjoyment of thy favor and eternal life, to deliver him (or her) again into the torments of mortality?

Thou hast taken from me what I highly valued on earth, that I might look up to heaven whither he (or she) is departed from me. Grant me therefore grace to put to an end all these sighs, groans, and tears, and spend no longer my time and my breath lamenting my loss. Grant that I may imitate the piety, zeal, faith, constancy, and all other virtues of such as thou hast admitted into thine eternal rest, and crowned with everlasting joy and happiness. Amen.

—*Charles Drelincourt, 1595–1669; alt.*

## When a Child Has Died                                              424

Holy God,
your goodness is everlasting,
and your mercies never fail.
Yours is the beauty of childhood
and yours is the fullness of years.
Comfort us in our sorrow,
strengthen us with hope,
and breathe peace into our troubled hearts.
Assure us that the love in which we rejoiced for a time is
        not lost,
and that this child is with you,
safe in your eternal love and care.
We ask this in the name of Jesus Christ,
who took little children into his arms and blessed them.
Amen.

—*Cumberland Presbyterian Church and the*
*Presbyterian Church (U.S.A.), 1986*

# When a Child Has Died

Our Father in heaven,
we are shocked into silence:
a mother and a father
who loved their child
have lost her/him;
a little brother and a little sister
played with her/him—
and now she/he is not there any more.

The house is so quiet
now that her/his voice is heard no longer,
so empty now that she/he doesn't live there any more.
We are strangers in our own city,
who cannot find our way home.
The world looms dark and cold;
where shall we find comfort?

Dear Father in heaven,
open our eyes to the light of your love,
wake us with the warmth of your word.

We recall the baptismal candle
that was kindled for N., the light of Christ*

Lord, let light shine for N.
and for us
and for all the children in the world.
Amen.

—*J. C. Wit-Ribbers, b. 1933*

------

*Omit where use of the baptismal candle is not customary.

## At the Death of a Parent

Father, I have so much to be thankful for today. My father/mother lived long enough for me to know him/her. Strengthen me now for the responsibility that I inherit today. If in your Providence, I am ever entrusted with a high and honorable title of parenthood, may I so live that I may be an unfailing source of wisdom, security, and encouragement to my children.

Remove the guilt of my grief today. From this loss, I find that I could and should have done more. But I am not perfect. You know this, and my father/mother knew this. I thank you for flooding this moment of my life with divine forgiveness. You are righting every wrong and I thank you.

As the fruit of the love of my father and mother, I shall live on. I dedicate and commit myself to live honorably and respectfully so that the remainder of my years brings no disgrace to my family's name. I rejoice and thank you for Christ's promise of eternal life. "He who lives and believes in me shall never die." "In my Father's house there are many mansions."

I am strengthened now by your word: "When my father and mother forsake me, then the Lord will take me up." I know that sorrow never leaves us where it finds us. I remember it is not what happens to me in life but how I react to what happens to me that is supremely important. Now, God, you will be constantly my heavenly parent. "Weeping may endure for the night, but joy comes in the morning." Amen.

—*Robert H. Schuller, b. 1926; alt.*

## For the Bereaved

O living God, you share all our griefs; give a meaning to that which defies our understanding. Shine upon our night.

You alone can show us that we are not abandoned to chance or fate, not even in what seems revolting or senseless to us, but that all things can work together for the good of those who love you.

Lord, grant that our brothers and sisters may perceive your message even through their sufferings. May their sorrow challenge them to discover the help of your mercy, and to hope more fervently for your kingdom.

May their sadness make them more open to your compassion, and help them to live in your strength alone. Be near to those who are suffering this day. Surround them with the love which you bear to your children, through Jesus Christ our Savior.

—*Reformed Church in France, 1963*

428 ### *In Bereavement*

Dear Lord God,
you know what we need even before we ask you.

Our heart is grieving because N. has died.
In our despair we call upon you,
God of the living and the dead,
you that dwell on high
and look into the depths,
have mercy upon us.

We draw near to you with fear
to entrust to you our dear departed.
Be mindful of his/her name
and accept him/her in your mercy.
Let him/her partake of your peace
and gather him/her up with all the children of humankind
that have fallen asleep in Christ.

We thank you for N.'s life.
You wove him/her in his/her mother's womb.

You caused him/her to come forth into the light
and led him/her through the darkness of death.
Let him/her therefore rest
in expectation of your kingdom
that is to come.

Be near to the living who are here
to share their sorrow
and to seek comfort in you.
Do not be ashamed to be our God.
Stand by us in these days of sorrow,
so that we may hold to our faith in all simplicity.
For the sake of your Son, Jesus the Messiah, our Lord,
who gave his life for us,
send us your light and your truth,
so that we may not fear death.

Lay us as a seal upon your heart,
as a seal upon your arm.
In you we have taken refuge.

Now the evening has drawn on
and the night is at hand.
But we, who praise you
for the light of creation,
look forward to the new dawn
when the sun of righteousness,
Jesus Christ,
shall arise upon us all.
Amen.

—*J. C. Wit-Ribbers, b. 1933*

# A Prayer for the Night

Lord Jesus, in the night my grief comes back, pouring over me, and I cannot help myself. I ask you now to send your Spirit into my mind and heart and affirm your love for me. Let me not awaken to tears but to thoughts of your care; and if I weep, let my tears draw me closer to all who grieved for you when you were taken from them. Lord, let the return of the morning be a sign to me of your rising. Give me hope in the restoration of the whole world when there will be no more death, no more separation, and no more tears. In Jesus' Name. Amen.

—*Elwyn A. Smith, b. 1919*

## In Age and Weakness 430

O Eternal God, Almighty and Merciful Heavenly Father, which hast been my hope from the first day of my life and during all the course of the same, and until this great age hast by infinite ways caused me to feel thy providence, care, and protection: thou art he to whom I have recourse, my God, my glory, my salvation. My legs are feeble, but I lift up myself upon the wings of my thoughts, even unto thee, who art my strength in infirmity, my light in the great darkness of my understanding, my life in death which encompasseth me about, beseeching thee to be pleased to forget the sins of my youth and to have no more remembrance of my transgressions, but remember thy faithful promises, to look upon the wounds and sufferings of thy Son, my pledge and Savior, for whose love, be pleased to pardon mine iniquities.

Suffer me not, O my God, forever to cast thee off and forsake thee. Be pleased to anoint the eyes of my soul with the salve of thy Spirit, that I may continually behold thee, and that acknowledging myself a poor way-faring man and a stranger in this world, as all my forebears were, I may earnestly aspire to thee, and to the country where the blessed are, and where thou hast prepared a place for all thine elect.

Grant that I may see myself delivered out of the waves and storms of the dangerous sea of this world. O Lord, teach me to know mine end and the number of my days, to the end that seeing that the flourishing state of this human life hath no abiding, but is encompassed with sorrows and oppressed with labors and pains, most dangerous when we least feel them, I may give myself to the study and exercise of that wisdom which doth teach me to renounce the world and myself, and to meditate upon the heavenly happiness of thy kingdom, to the end that my heart may be where my treasure is, with the Head and Spouse of the church, and where thou hast prepared for them which love thee, incomprehensible joys, through Jesus Christ, thy Son, my Redeemer. Amen.

—*Simon Goulart, 1543–1628; alt.*

Aged Simeon waited patiently for death.
But as soon as he had seen the Savior of the world
and embraced him, he ran to meet death.
He prayed to God most earnestly to receive him
into his glorious rest.

Since death brings thee nearer to thy Redeemer,
perfects this blessed union and casts thee into the
very fountain of life, instead of being frightened
at it and grieved when it comes to thee, thou
shouldest then rejoice and be transported above
measure with gladness.

—*Charles Drelincourt; 1595–1669; alt.*

431

## Confession

O Thou unknown, Almighty Cause
    Of all my hope and fear!
In whose dread presence, ere an hour,
    Perhaps I must appear!

If I have wandered in those paths
    of life I ought to shun—
As something, loudly in my breast,
    Remonstrates I have done—

Thou knowest that Thou hast formed me
    With passions wild and strong;

And listening to their witching voice
    Has often led me wrong.

Where human weakness has come short,
    Or frailty stept aside,
Do Thou, All-Good! for such Thou art,
    In shades of darkness hide.

Where with intention I have erred,
    No other plea I have,
But, Thou art good; and Goodness still
    Delighteth to forgive.

          *—Robert Burns, 1759–1796*

## *Preparing to Go to God*       432

O Heavenly Father, who art the Lord of all flesh, and hast made us and hast appointed us the time to come into the world, and, so having finished our course, to go out of the same, the number of my days, which thou hast determined, are now expired, and I am come to the utmost bounds.

O Lord, for fear of displeasing the world, I have given way unto sins and errors, and for desire to please my flesh, I have broken all thy commandments, in thought, word, and deed. But, O my Lord and my God, for Jesus Christ, thy Son's sake, take pity and compassion on me, who am the chief of sinners. Blot all my sins out of thy remembrance, and wash all my transgressions out of thy sight with the precious blood of thy Son. O Father, for his death and passion's sake, acquit and deliver me.

Strengthen, O Christ, my faith, that I may put the whole confidence of my salvation in the merits of thy obedience and blood. Increase, O Holy Spirit, my patience. Lay no more upon me than I am able to bear, and enable me to bear so much as shall stand with thy blessed will and pleasure. O Blessed Trinity in unity, my Creator,

Redeemer and Sanctifier: vouchsafe that as my flesh doth decay, so my inward nature may more and more by thy grace and consolation, increase and gather strength.

O Savior, put my soul in readiness, that like a wise virgin, having the wedding garment of thy righteousness and holiness, she may be ready to meet thee at thy coming with oil in her lamp. Marry her unto thyself, that she may be one with thee in everlasting love and fellowship.

I thank thee, O Lord, for all thy blessings both spiritual and temporal, bestowed upon me, especially for my redemption by the death of my Savior Christ. I thank thee that thou hast protected me with thy holy angels from my youth till now. Lord, I beseech thee, give them a charge to attend me till thou callest my soul, and then to carry her, as they did the soul of Lazarus, into thy heavenly kingdom.

Grant, O Lord, that my soul may draw nearer unto thee, and that I may joyfully commend my soul into thy hands as into the hands of a loving Father and a merciful Redeemer, and at that instant, O Lord, graciously receive my spirit. In all that I may do, assist me, I beseech thee, with thy grace, and let thy Holy Spirit continue with me unto the end and in the end, for Jesus Christ's sake, thy Son, my Lord and Holy Savior, in whose name I give thee the glory, and beg these things at thy hand, in that prayer which Christ himself hath taught me, saying: Our Father . . .

—*Lewis Bayly, 1565–1631; alt.*

433
## *For Union with Christ*

O Mighty and Merciful Lord, the Son of righteousness and Fountain of living water, thou hast not only died for me, but thou art pleased to live in me, that I might one day live for ever with thee. Thou hast, of thy pure mercy, chosen me for thy child and hast made me a member of thy mystical body, flesh of thy flesh, bone of thy bone, and caused me to be a partaker of thine Holy Spirit. God has given thee the Spirit without measure, that of thy fullness we might receive grace for grace.

By the means of this blessed and infinite Spirit that abides in my soul, I am united to thee in a more perfect manner than the tree is to the root that bears it, or the child to its mother that nourisheth it in her womb, or the members of the human body to the head that gives them life. As nothing can pluck me out from thine hand, there is nothing that can separate me from thine heart. Whether I live or die, I am thine, my Lord and my God.

Lord Jesus, since thou hast granted me the spirit of thy grace, enlightened my soul with thy divine knowledge, and caused me to know the way of life; since thou hast given me to taste of the heavenly gift of the powers of life to come, and hast vouchsafed to me the first fruits of thy glory, so that I already feel heaven in my soul; since I behold thee with the eyes of my faith, I embrace thee with all my affections. That thou mayest dwell in my heart, perfect in me the work of thy grace and bring me at last to thy eternal glory. "Lord, now lettest thou thy servant depart in peace, for mine eyes have seen thy salvation." Amen.

—*Charles Drelincourt, 1595–1669; alt.*

## *Ready for God*

434

O Lord, now draw near unto my soul and redeem it, for the time is at hand wherein I shall taste of the cup of death. Now therefore is the acceptable time for thee to receive my soul in the multitude of thy mercies, which are wonderful. Therefore do I trust under the shadow of thy wings. My soul cleaveth unto thee, for thy right hand upholdeth me. My soul thirsteth for thee, my flesh longest greatly after thee, whose loving-kindness is better to me than life, for from thee cometh my salvation.

Have mercy upon me, O God, have mercy upon me, for my soul trusteth in thee, and under the shadow of thy wings will I trust, till this my final affliction be overpast.

My heart is prepared, O God, my heart is prepared to come unto thee. Make it constant in thee, because I know that although this body for a time shall wither, yet it shall be in the house of my God as a green olive tree, ever to flourish and be blessed.

Thou, Lord, hast chosen me and hast caused me to come unto thee. My salvation is of thine own free mercy and of thy free and fatherly election. I shall dwell in thy courts for ever and shall be satisfied with the pleasures of thine house, even of thy kingdom of glory. I shall drink of the rivers of thy pleasure, for with thee is the well of life, and in thy light shall I see light.

Let thy good Spirit lead me in the land of righteousness and bring me by thy strength to thy holy and heavenly habitation. Plant me in the mountain of thine inheritance, even in the place which thou hast prepared, and in thy sacred sanctuary which thou hast established, that I may see thy goodness in the land of the living. Let me behold thy face in righteousness, and let me be satisfied with the fullness of the glory of thy countenance, for in thy face is the fullness of joy and at thy right hand are pleasures for evermore.

Into thy hands, O Lord, I commend my spirit, for thou hast redeemed me, O Lord God of truth. Show me a token of thy goodness and favor towards me, that they which wish evil unto my soul may see it and be ashamed, and they that love thy Name, observe it and be confirmed in thee, who hast evermore helped and comforted me.

Increase my faith and prepare my soul to come unto thee. Amen.

—*John Norden, 1548–1625*

<br>

435     *For a Place in the Father's House*

Lord, thou art the common salvation and refuge of thy saints, both strong and weak. All that are given thee by the Father shall come to thee, and those that come thou wilt in no wise cast out. Thousands have been received of thee that were unworthy, just as I. Few of thy members are now on earth, in comparison with those that are with thee in heaven.

Admit me, Lord, into the new Jerusalem. Thou wilt have thy house to be filled. O take my spirit into the number of those blessed ones that shall come from east, west, north, and south and sit down with Abraham, Isaac, and Jacob in the kingdom, that we may together with eternal joy, give thanks and praise to thee that hast redeemed us to God by thy blood.

—*Richard Baxter, 1615–1691; alt.*


## Last Words 436

Father,
into thy blessed hands I commit my spirit.
Sweet Jesus,
into thy blessed hands I commend my spirit.
Blessed Spirit of God,
I commit my soul into thy hands.
Oh most holy, blessed, and glorious Trinity,
three persons and one true and everlasting God,
into thy blessed hands
I commit both my soul and my body.

—*Katherine Stubbes, ca. 1571–1590; alt.*


## Last Words 437

Lord Jesus, receive my spirit.
—*Sarah Huntington Smith, 1802–1836*

# Prayers for Various Needs

438

## For the Gift of the Holy Spirit

Most loving Father, who hast promised good things to them that ask thee, we wait upon thee now for the gift of thy Holy Spirit.

When we pray, when we work, and when we suffer; on the verge of trial, in the midst of perplexity and darkness, and in view of the unknown future, grant us the aid of thy Divine Spirit. Amen.

*—Presbyterian Church in Canada, 1919*

439

## For an Answer to Prayer

O Lord God, thou takest pleasure in those that hope in thy mercies. Thy word is to thy people sweeter than the honeycomb. They keep it as a sweet morsel under the tongue. Since it pleaseth thee so well, they will hope in thy mercy. It is the church's confidence that thou wilt hear. But if thou seemest to slumber, she will waken thee with importunity, she will give thee no rest, her sons and daughters will be thy remembrancers, for they remember that all thou hast done hitherto is that they might set their hope in thee.

Thy servants ask nothing but according to thy will, and it is their confidence that thou hearest them. Therefore we will never leave asking, we will trouble thee day and night and give thee no rest, till thou shalt hearken and hear us and grant our request, till thou shalt perfect what thou hast begun. Then we shall sing the high praises of our God, then Jacob shall rejoice and Israel be right glad, saying "Hallelujah, salvation, glory, honor, and power be unto the Lord our God." Amen, hallelujah.

*—Hezekiah Woodward, ca. 1590–1675; alt.*

## Thanksgiving for Answered Prayer

I have abundant cause, O my merciful Father,
to love thee ardently,
and greatly to bless and praise thee,
that thou hast heard me in my earnest request,
and hast so answered my prayer for mercy
to keep me from decay and sinking.

O, graciously, of thy goodness,
still continue to pity my misery,
by reason of my sinfulness.
O my Redeemer,
I commit myself,
together with my prayer and thanksgiving,
into thine Hand.

*—Jonathan Edwards, 1703–1758; alt.*

## For Confidence and Trust in God

O Lord, by all Thy dealings with us, whether of joy or pain, of light or darkness, let us be brought to Thee. Let us value no treatment of Thy grace simply because it makes us happy or because it makes us sad, because it gives or denies us what we want; but may all that Thou sendest us bring us to Thee, that knowing Thy perfectness, we may be sure in every disappointment that Thou art still loving us, in every darkness that Thou art still enlightening us, and in every enforced idleness that Thou art still using us; yea, in every death that Thou art giving us life, as in His death Thou didst give life to Thy Son, our Saviour, Jesus Christ. Amen.

*—Reformed Church in America, 1915*

442

## For Courage

O SAVIOUR, who didst set Thy face steadfastly to go to Jerusalem to Thy Cross and passion; help us, Thy weak and wavering disciples, to be firm and resolute in doing those things that lie before us. Help us to overcome difficulties and to persevere in spite of failures. When we are weary and disheartened and ready to give in, do Thou fill us with fresh courage and strength, and keep us faithful to our work; for Thy name's sake. AMEN.

—*Church of Scotland, 1940*

From *Book of Common Order of the Church of Scotland* (1940). Reprinted by permission of Oxford University Press.

443

## *For faith in the divine purpose*

O GOD, we thank Thee for the many tokens of Thy gracious presence and leading Thou dost vouchsafe to Thy children. Be pleased to increase within us the spirit of steadfast faith in the eternal wisdom and goodness. In times of perplexity, let us not be fearful and unbelieving; in situations of difficulty, grant us confidence in Thy power; in hours of discouragement, strengthen us by Thy grace; that so we may still press on, and may encourage others also to be faithful, believing that Thy purpose cannot and will not fail.

—*Alexander R. Howell, 1871–1943*

444

## *For Guidance*

O God, direct us in the way we should go. Sometimes we think we know the way, but we are following only our own selfish desires or our foolish impulses. Give us the certainty of Jesus and the will to follow in his footsteps. When we turn aside, warn and correct us. When we are in the right path, encourage us and keep us from stumbling. Give guidance to those who guide us, and may we never disappoint any who look to us for direction, but move steadily forward in the name and spirit of Jesus Christ, our Lord. Amen.

—*Purd E. Deitz, 1897–1987*

## For Peace of Heart

SET free, O Lord, the souls of thy servants from all restlessness and anxiety; give us the peace and power that flow from thee; and in all perplexity and distress, so keep us that we, upheld by thy strength and stayed on the rock of thy faithfulness, may abide in thee now and evermore; through Jesus Christ our Lord. AMEN.

—*England,* A Book of Public Worship Compiled for the
Use of Congregationalists, *2nd ed., 1949*

## For Patience in Adversity

O God of patience and of all consolation, the just dispenser both of calamities and benefits, and that all to one end: as there is nothing in thy word but serveth to our learning and to the guiding of our temporal life, so doth thy word principally insist on this: to lift up our hearts to a firm expectation of eternal life, that amidst the thorns of this world, we may attain constant patience and holy consolation, so that, having done thy will, O Lord, we may reap thy promise. This is the firm pillar of our hope which teacheth us not to love the things of the earth, but constantly to look up into heaven, where our peace and joy doth remain.

But because so holy a resolution doth far surmount our own forces, I beseech thee, my God, to grant me the true patience of the faithful, a meek and moderate heart to bear all adversity, and grant that I may learn to humble the pride of my nature. Going forward, may I rejoice and take comfort in this: that affliction in the house of the righteous is a secret mercy which thou givest, as prosperity with the wicked is a hidden indignation of thy countenance. The present sorrow of thy children is unto them the watch of some future joy at hand. If therefore I bear any sickness or other misery in my flesh, let it be borne with patience. In all other sorrows and griefs that should trouble us, give me grace, my Lord, that I be not moved to bitterness or anger, but that with a quiet mind, I may bear all and tread underfoot the thorns of my life. To this end also touch my heart earnestly with the feeling of thy benefits, lest, as an ungrateful wretch I should forget them.

Whether I walk or stand still, whether I do or suffer, grant, O Lord, that I may always walk as in thy presence, to the glory of thy holy name. May my soul take counsel and be satisfied in thy righteousness, whilst in all patience I wait for my deliverance from all pain, and the perfection of my happiness, at my departure from this carnal habitation, when, according to thy promise, I shall be received into thy kingdom in the company of the angels and saints, there to behold thy glory eternally. So be it.

—*Théodore de Bèze, 1519–1605; alt.*

447

## A Prayer for One Under Spiritual Desertion

O ever blessed and most compassionate Redeemer, who wast in all things tempted like as we are, sin only excepted—O thou Lover of souls, who in the days of thy flesh didst offer up strong cries and tears, and wast heard in that thou fearedst—O thou Restorer of humankind, who wast in such an agony in the garden, that thou sweatest great drops of blood, falling to the ground—O thou almighty High Priest, who, when through the eternal Spirit thou wast about to make thy soul an offering for sin, hadst thy own divinity withdrawn from thee, and didst cry out in the bitterness of thy soul, "My God, my God, why hast thou forsaken me"—O thou, who now sittest at the right hand of the Father, continually to make intercession for us—Look down, I beseech thee, upon me, thy unworthy servant—for thou hast turned away thy face, and lo, I am troubled—Thou hast taken off my chariot wheels, and I drive heavily—Thou hast permitted a cloud to overshadow me, and an horrible darkness, fearfulness, and dread, to overwhelm me, so that my soul would be exceeding sorrowful, even unto death, did I not believe thou wouldst yet turn again and visit me.

But I beseech thee, keep my soul quiet and composed, and for thy mercy's sake enable me only to take pleasure in thee, and patiently wait till I can draw comfort from thee, the fountain of living waters, rather than hew out to myself broken cisterns, that will hold no water.

Enable me to walk by faith and not by sight, and to seek thee in the use of all appointed means, though it be sorrowing; being assured that after three days I shall find thee in the temple; or that thou wilt make thyself known unto me by breaking of bread or in some other way.

Lord, I believe, help my unbelief, that I am now talking with thee as certainly as Mary was, when thou didst converse with her at the sepulchre, though she knew it not—In thy due time reveal thyself again to me, as thou didst to her, and let me hear the voice of my Beloved.

Lord, lift thou up the light of thy countenance upon me; restore me to the joy of thy salvation, and when my heart is duly prepared and humbled by these inward trials, grant me a feeling possession of thee, my God, for the sake of thy dear Son, Jesus Christ our Lord. Amen, Amen.

*—George Whitefield, 1714–1770; alt.*

## *In Time of Perplexity* 448

O God, in these perplexities we see no means here on earth, but our eyes are towards thee. Hear us therefore from thine habitation, and look down, for thou art mighty to raise us up. When human means do fail, it is then that thou displayest thy power, and when we do by our imprudence procure evils to ourselves, thou makest use of our imprudence for our good, that the preservation of thy church be not a work of mortal wisdom, but of thy holy providence.

*—Pierre Du Moulin, the Elder, 1568–1658; alt.*

# Suffering

Gracious and compassionate God, we know you do not will that any should suffer needlessly. Yet confronted by suffering in our own lives and the lives of others, there are many questions we cannot answer. Help us to find peace by resting in your love; teach us to be patient with all that is unresolved within us. Teach us your compassion, that we might not hurt others thoughtlessly, but instead bring light and hope; in the name of Jesus, the suffering Servant Messiah, we pray. Amen.

*—Ruth C. Duck, b. 1947*

# When Tempted

O God, it is thy pleasure to suffer thy dear children to be tempted. But suffer not temptation to prevail against thy Spirit and grace. If temptation be like a torrent of water, to smother, quench, or hide the flame, yet wilt thou never let all the sparks of thy grace be put out in the soul where once thou hast truly kindled it. Lord, suffer not such floods to fall on my soul, where the spark is so small already. O quicken it, and blow it up to a holy flame, most gracious God!

*—Margaret Baxter, 1636–1681; alt.*

# In Time of Trouble

O let it please thee, good Father, to deliver me.
Make haste, O Lord, to relieve me.
Though I be poor and needy, think thou on me.
Thou art my helper and deliverer,
O make no long tarrying.
O my God, why hast thou forgotten me?
Up, my God, why sleepest thou?
Awake, be not far off for ever.
My soul is beaten down, I have no aid, no comfort,

all my consolation is come to an end.
Therefore, rise up, O my succor,
Rise up, O my helper.
Rise up, O my castle.
Rise up, O my refuge.
Rise up and restore me again, thou God of my comfort,
thou my rock and my fortress, my strength, my shield,
the horn of my salvation, and my refuge.

Oh, the remembrance of thy love is sweet.
The experience of thy power comforteth my soul.
It was thou, O Lord, that sentest Elijah food by a raven.
Even so canst thou by unexpected means
send comfort unto thy children.
It was thou that deliveredst Daniel from the lions;
and thou canst deliver us from the cruel ones of the world.
It was thou that directedst the hand of David to kill Goliath.
Thou canst teach our fingers to fight
and withstand them that rise up against us.
It was thou that filledst many thousand people
with a small show of bread and fishes;
and it is thou that canst feed thy servants
that call upon thee.
It was thou that didst save thy three children in the furnace
from the force of the fire;
and thou canst preserve us in the fiery trial of the world.
It was thou that deliveredst Paul and Silas out of prison;
and thou canst deliver thy children out of whatsoever captivity.
It was thou that didst work for Joseph,
so that his imprisonment turned to his promotion;
and thou canst turn all our calamities to our comfort.

It was thou that raisedst me from my mother's breast
unto this estate wherein I am;
and thou canst preserve me, feed me, and hold me up for ever.

Yea, good God, I, even I, by experience, can sing of thy
           goodness:
yea, the goodness of the Lord endureth for ever.
The mercies of the Lord endureth for ever.
The power of the Lord endureth for ever.
Yea, the willingness and the readiness of the Lord
to relieve the afflicted endureth for ever.

When sorrow cometh in the evening, thou, Lord,
sendest joy again in the morning.
When I am in need, thou relievest me.
When I am in danger, thou comfortest me.
When I am sick, thou makest my bed, and curest my disease.
When have I come unto thee and been rejected?
Never hath my complaint been put back, but lovingly heard,
and my petitions granted,
so that I rest assured of thy continual help.
I am forced, good Father, to seek thee daily.
And thou offerest thyself daily to be found:
Whensoever I seek thee, I find thee:
in my house, in the fields, in the temple, and in the highway.
Whatsoever I do, thou art with me:
whether I eat or drink,
whether I write or work,
go or ride, read, meditate or pray,
thou art with me.
Wheresoever I am or whatsoever I do,
I feel some measure of thy mercies and love.

O continue thy loving-kindness towards me for ever,
that all the world may see thy power, thy mercy, and thy love,
wherein thou hast not failed me
and even my enemies shall see
that thy mercies endureth forever.
Lord, increase my faith.

—*John Norden, 1548–1625; alt.*

           *Prayers from the Reformed Tradition*

## Going on a Journey

452

Preserve me, O Lord, in all my ways, and wheresoever I go, guard me with thy hand, that no evil may befall me. All places are under thy eye, and I desire everywhere to remember that God sees me. Make my present journey pleasant and comfortable, and let me consider that I am always traveling through this world towards death and eternity; and when the journey of my life is ended, let me arrive at the gates of heaven and be admitted there for Jesus' sake. Amen.

*—Isaac Watts, 1674–1748*

## Prayer for the Nation

453

Bless this nation with Thy wisdom, O Lord, so that the poor may not be oppressed and the rich may not be oppressors; make this a nation having no ruler except good, a nation having no authority save that of love.

*—Toyohiko Kagawa, 1888–1960; alt.*

## In Time of Persecution

454

O God, the only help and refuge of the afflicted poor, you see the fury of our enemies, who seek for every means to exterminate us. You know how despised and disdained we are by the great ones of this world. Having therefore this sole remedy, we turn our eyes to you, begging you to have mercy on us in the name of your Son Jesus Christ. Amen.

*—Augustin Marlorat, 1506–1562*

## On Behalf of Nations Engaged in War

<sup></sup>455

O Lord God of infinite mercy, we humbly beseech thee to look down upon the nations now involved in war. Reckon not against thy people their many iniquities, for from the lusts of our own hearts come wars and fighting amongst us. Look in mercy on those immediately exposed to peril, conflict, sickness, and death. Comfort the prisoners, relieve the sufferings of the wounded, and show mercy to the dying. Remove, in thy good providence, all the causes and occasions of war; dispose the hearts of those engaged therein to moderation, and of thy great goodness, restore peace among the nations; through Jesus Christ our Lord. Amen.

*—Catholic Apostolic Church, ca. 1899*

## For Peace

456

Holy God, we pray to you for the revelation of the kingdom of Jesus Christ your Son, who must reign until all his enemies are subject at his feet. Grant that those in authority may subject themselves to his lordship of love and justice, so that all people may seek and find their safety, not in the power of weapons, but in that perfect love which casts out all fear, and in the fellowship which you have bestowed upon us through your Son Jesus Christ our Lord. Amen.

*—Netherlands Reformed Church, 1955*

# SENTENCE PRAYERS

We are commanded to pray always and at all seasons . . . while we lie in our beds, while we sit at our tables, or are taking our rest, our souls may go out towards our heavenly Father and have sweet converse with him in short prayers.

*—Isaac Watts; alt.*

Rouse up my drowsy soul to learn from thee,
my Savior, how to pray,
that I may wrestle with thee and weep as Jacob,
never letting thee go
before thou hast blessed me.

*—John Brinsley, fl. 1584–1630; alt.*

457

My gracious Savior, have mercy on me
a miserable sinner,
who am but dust and ashes.

*—Abigail Kenump, ca. 1694–1710; alt.*

458

459

O my Father,
refuse not my petition
to see thy kingdom
and my friends who are dwelling with thee.

—*Haalilio, d. 1844; alt.*

460

Make thy love my continual feast.

—*James W. Weir, 1805–1878; alt.*

461

O my God,
thou who takest away the sins of the world,
forgive my sins,
I beseech thee,
and save my soul for ever.

—*Jedidah Hannit, ca. 1708–1725; alt.*

462

Through darkness and light,
through sorrow and joy,
and by a way we knew not,
thou hast led us;
thou hast done all things well.

—*George Smith, 1803–1870; alt.*

463

Lord, leave me not.
Work all in me and for me,
then work by me.

—*Hezekiah Woodward, ca. 1590–1675; alt.*

O Lord, give me Jesus Christ. 464
> —*Wampas, d. 1651; alt.*

Abba, Father, with thee all things are possible. 465
> —*Sarah Osborn, 1714–1796; alt.*

Thou art all. 466
—*Hezekiah Woodward, ca. 1590–1675; alt.*

O God, have mercy on me. 467
O God, have mercy on me.
O God, have mercy on me.
—*Lydia Ohquanhut, 1710–1715; alt.*

Teach me, O Lord, and direct me where and how 468
to labor for thee.
> —*Helen M. Cowles, 1831–1851; alt.*

Lord, I am wholly at thy disposal; 469
make my way plain:
my resolution is to deny myself if thou callest me:
Here (or anywhere, 'tis no great matter where) I am.
> —*Philip Henry, 1631–1696; alt.*

O Lord, hold me in the hollow of thy hand, 470
and under thy wings let me reside.
> —*James Meikle, 1730–1799; alt.*

471     Lord, make me poor in spirit and rich in spiritual things;
however poor I am in the world, make me rich in faith,
an heir of the kingdom, and I have enough.

—*Sarah Savage, 1664–1752; alt.*

472     Give us, O God, the simplicity of children;
make us willing to be conformed to the birth of thy Son
as well as to his death.

—*Philip Doddridge, 1702–1751; alt.*

473     Holy Spirit, come into my heart.

—*Charlotte Green, d. ca. 1845; alt.*

474     Thou art my portion, my first and last,
my trust and hope, my desire, my all!

—*Richard Baxter, 1615–1691; alt.*

475     Sweet Jesus, let my soul thy garden be,
that thou mayest delight, walk and dwell in me.

—*William Prynne, 1600–1669; alt.*

476     Lord, take me by the hand and lead me in the way I should go.
Let me never depart from thee.

—*Hannah Housman, ca. 1697–1735; alt.*

477     Thou doest all things well.

—*Isabella Graham, 1742–1814; alt.*

# Prayers for Children

O God, reveal yourself to us as you did to your prophet Samuel when   478
he was a child. May we be very still, that we may hear your voice
speaking in our hearts. Tell us what we should do, and help us to do it;
through Jesus Christ our Lord. Amen.

*—John Hunter, 1848–1917; alt.*

O Lord, for the rest of the night I thank you, and also for the light of   479
this new day. Guide me through this day by your presence. Make me
watchful in thought, word, and deed. Keep temptation from me, and
keep me from sin. Help me to do something for you this day. In all
things may I promote your glory and the welfare of other people;
through Jesus Christ. Amen.

*—James I. Good,* Aid to the Heidelberg Catechism, *1904; alt.*

Saviour Lord Jesus!   480
Enable me to love people like you.
And let people enjoy your happiness always
With their hearts filled with truth and joy.

*—C. M. Kao, contemporary; alt.*

481       Good and generous God,
help us not to long for things we don't need,
and help us to share what we do have
with those who have less.
In Jesus' name we pray. Amen.

                  *—Dianne E. Deming, b. 1956; alt.*

## FOR EVENING

482       Lord, as I kneel, this night, to pray,
My burdens at Thy feet I lay.
Refresh me through the night with sleep,
And all my loved ones safely keep.
For Jesus' sake. Amen.

             *—Stuart R. Oglesby, 1888–1977; alt.*

483       Jesus, tender Shepherd, hear me;
        Bless thy little lamb tonight.
Through the darkness be thou near me;
        Watch my sleep till morning light.

All this day thy hand has led me,
        And I thank thee for thy care;
Thou hast clothed, warmed, and fed me;
        Listen to my evening prayer.

             *—Mary Duncan, 1814–1840*

My Father in heaven,                                                      484
you see me in the dark as well as in the daytime.
Stay near my bed when I am asleep.
Please do not let anything hurt me all the night through.
I pray you to forgive me for all the ill I have done today.
O God, make my heart good that I may always love you.
Be kind to (papa and mama and brothers and sisters)
and everybody who is kind to me.
And make me your own dear child, for Jesus' sake. Amen.

*—James O. Dykes, 1835–1912*


O Lord God, make me thankful for all your mercies                        485
          and continue your loving-kindness to me.
Lead me and preserve me all the time;
          night and day let your presence be with me.
I commit myself to you.
Take me for your own and take care of me as your own.
Amen.

*—Richard Alleine, 1611–1681*

# GRACES

"He greatly adored the mercies of God in
every meal."

*—said of Joseph Alleine by his family*

## BEFORE MEALS

486   Lord, the spring and inexhaustible fountain of all good things: pour
out your blessing upon us. Sanctify for our use this food and drink,
the gifts of your kindness.

      Grant that we may, in true thankfulness of soul, always
acknowledge, and with our mouth proclaim you as Father and Author
of all good things.

      Let us so enjoy this bodily nourishment that the chief desire of
our heart may be for the spiritual bread of your teaching, by which our
souls may be fed with growing hope of eternal life ; through Jesus
Christ our Lord.

*—Jean Calvin, 1509–1564*

487   Good God, whatever is set on the table for our refreshment, bless thou
it, and it shall be blessed, through Jesus Christ. Amen.

*—Samuel Bourn, 1689–1754*

Lord Jesus, be our holy guest,
Our morning joy, our evening rest;
And with our daily bread impart
Thy love and peace to every heart.
Amen.*

>  —Henry J. van Dyke, 1852–1933

———
*May be sung to the tune TALLIS' CANON.

O Lord Jesus, who for the comfort and relief of the company at Cana
in Galilee didst not only adorn it with thy gracious presence, but also
turnedst water into wine: be present, we beseech thee amongst us here.
Bless our meats and drinks, which are the gifts of thy liberality, that,
using them with moderation and thanksgiving, they may become
wholesome nourishment to our mortal bodies. Amen.

>  —Thomas Sorocold, 1561–1617

For all your kindly gifts, good Lord,
Your love be blessed, your Name adored. Amen.

>  —Netherlands Reformed Church, 1955

Bless us, O Lord, in what we are about to receive;
and give us grace to enjoy everything in thee,
and thee in everything;
for Christ's sake.
Amen.

>  —Jeremiah H. Good, 1822–1888; alt.

492      With free and bold hearts,
let us give thanks and honor to God,
who, in kindness, has made us his heirs,
and blesses these gifts
to feed and nourish us:
to Father, as to Son and Holy Spirit,
be glory given.

        *—Sixteenth-century Huguenot grace; alt.*


493      Lord,
may we share this meal
with the same joy,
thankfulness,
humour and awareness
that Jesus showed
when he ate and drank
with his friends.
May our eating and drinking
be a sign
of life
in your kingdom,
of forgiveness and peace.

        *—David Jenkins, b. 1941*


494    Father of lights, from whom cometh down every good and perfect gift: enable us to receive these fruits of thy bounty with humility and gratitude, and give us grace, that whether we eat or drink, or whatever we do, we may do all things to thy glory, and be accepted through our great Redeemer.

        *—William Jay, 1769–1853*

We thank you, Jesus Christ our Lord:
You've been our guest at this our board.
If you stay close, we'll fear no need:
You are the Bread of life indeed.*

> —*Germany, Evangelical Hymnal for*
> *the Rhineland and Westphalia, 1898*

*May be sung to the tune TALLIS' CANON.

495

Accept, Heavenly Father, our humble thanks for this and for all thy blessings, through Jesus Christ.

> —*William Jay, 1769–1853*

496

Honor and praise be unto thee, O Lord, Heavenly Father, for all thy mercies bestowed upon us, and for all the food we have now received of thy bountiful hand. Make us thankful for it, and give a blessing to it, that thereby our health and strength may be continued for the better performing of all holy duties, and our several callings, to thy glory and our comfort, through Jesus Christ our Lord.

> —*Stephen Egerton, ca. 1555–ca. 1621*

497

O Lord, thou hast given me a needful caution that when I have eaten and am full, I should not forget thee. Teach me gratitude in heart and life, and help me to do thy will, through Jesus Christ my Lord. Amen.

> —*Samuel Wright, 1683–1746*

498

God, that Elijah by the raven fed
    And nourished Daniel in the lion's den,
And filled thousands with five loaves of bread,
    And us hath satisfied, be praised. Amen.
        *—Thomas Sorocold, 1561–1617*

# Last Prayer

O glorious resurrection! God of Abraham and of all our fathers, in all $\underline{500}$
the centuries during which the believers have placed their hope in
Thee, none has ever been deceived. Therefore my hope also is in Thee.

—*Idelette Calvin, 1505–1549*

# INDEX OF FIRST WORDS

Father, Son, and Spirit Holy, we give you thanks and praise 104
Father, we would willingly ask thee for nothing 225
For all your kindly gifts, good Lord 335
Foxes have holes and birds have nests: but you, O Lord 61
Frame our hearts, good Lord, with such humble obedience 60

Give me grace, O sweet Jesus, to rest in thee 185
Give us, O God, the simplicity of children 330
Glory be to thee, O God the Father 228
Glory to God in the highest, on earth peace 118
God almighty, grant that the remembrance of the sufferings 45
God and Father of our Lord Jesus Christ, while with gratitude 86
God, be merciful to me a sinner 95
God of all mercy, we confess before you 141
God of all people, not only the achievements of the great 227
God of glory, because you disturb our expectations 260
God of life and glory, you have given us a share 61
God of mercy and of grace, you know the secrets of our hearts 39
God of mercy, behold what a poor . . . creature I am 229
God of the spirits of all flesh 289
God, that Elijah by the raven fed 338
Good and generous God, help us not to long for things 332
Good Father, pardon my sins past 202
Good God, whatever is set on the table for our refreshment 334
Gracious and compassionate God, we know you do not
    will that any should suffer 322
Gracious God, O let me behold thy adorable perfections 34
Gracious Lord, under whose protection we rest 133
Grant, Almighty God, that as thou art pleased to try 49
Grant, Almighty God, that as thou hast once given us 65
Grant, Almighty God, that since thou so kindly invitest us 111
Grant, Almighty God, that we may learn, whether in want 19
Grant, Almighty God, whatever revolutions happen 168
Grant, my Jesus, that like thee, I may soon get from the cross 110
Grant, O Lord, that like as Christ our Lord was raised 279
Grant us, Heavenly Father, so to come to know Thee 151
Grant us, O Lord, to know that which is worth knowing 92
Grant, we beseech thee, dear Father, that we, being fully persuaded 137
Great Bunji God, you sent your Son Jesus 74
Great God, incomprehensible, unknown by sense 94
Great God, since it is by the wonderful aid of your goodness 99

_Index of First Words_

*Index of First Words*

# Biographical Index

This section contains biographical descriptions of individuals, as well as descriptions of some books and churches. Since the focus of this book is principally on the prayers, a limited amount of information is provided here, and churches obviously in the Reformed family, as reflected in the words Congregational, Presbyterian, or Reformed in their names, are not described. The Church of Scotland, and the Churches of Bern/Berne, Geneva, Neuchâtel, and Zurich, which are all in Switzerland, are historic Reformed churches and are not provided entries.

### Joseph Alleine, 1634–1668
English Presbyterian Puritan minister and writer. Ejected from the Church of England in 1662. After this he suffered greatly for his ministry.

### Richard Alleine, 1611–1681
English Presbyterian Puritan minister and devotional writer.

### Rubem A. Alves, b. 1933
Brazilian theologian, a minister of the United Presbyterian Church of Brazil. Professor of philosophy, University of Campinas. Psychoanalyst.

### Epaminondas M. do Amaral, 1893–1961
A pastor of the Independent Presbyterian Church of Brazil; former secretary of the Brazilian Evangelical Council.

### Jonathan Amos, d. 1706
A Wampanoag Native American Congregational deacon and preacher to Native Americans at Chappaquiddick, his birthplace. His family prayed together morning and evening, and at mealtime observed grace.

### Anonymous
An eighteenth-century nonconformist Englishwoman (most likely, Presbyterian).

### Anonymous, d. 1690
A young French Reformed woman from a noble family.

### Anonymous, fl. 1830
A Polynesian man who was a member of a Congregational church; a friend of missionary John Williams.

### Susanna Anthony, 1726–1791
Born to an American Quaker family, but joined the Congregational church just before her sixteenth birthday. Of delicate constitution and troubled by much illness, she never married, but supported herself by needlework. She considered prayer to be her highest service of God and neighbor.

### Associate Synod
A Scottish Presbyterian Secession church.

### Abigail Abbot Bailey, 1746–1815
New Hampshire Congregational laywoman. She was married to a landowner and bore seventeen children, naming the last one "Patience." Her husband was violent and unfaithful. They were divorced in 1793.

### John Baillie, 1886–1960
Church of Scotland minister. Professor of divinity at the University of Edinburgh; principal of New College. His *A Diary of Private Prayer* is a modern devotional classic.

### William Barclay, 1907–1978
Church of Scotland minister. New Testament professor at the University of Glasgow. Popular Bible interpreter.

### Karl Barth, 1886–1968
Swiss Reformed minister and influential theologian who taught in Germany, later, in Switzerland. One of the founders of the Confessing Church, he was banished from Germany for his opposition to Hitler's Nazi regime.

### Margaret Baxter (née Charlton) 1636–1681
English Puritan who married Richard Baxter a month after he was ejected from the Church of England. With her own funds and on her own initiative, she built several chapels, so that her husband as well as other ejected Puritans had a place to preach. She also set up a school for poor children and supported Richard's work in many ways. He wrote that she had a keen intellect and was better at resolving cases of conscience than most ministers. When she was attacked for "busying her head" too much with churches, Richard defended her, reminding her opponents that women helped the apostle Paul in ministry. He concluded: "I am not ashamed to have been much ruled by her prudent love in many things."

### Richard Baxter, 1615–1691
Influential English Reformed pastor who began his working life as headmaster of a school in Dudley. Minister in Kidderminster from 1641 to 1660. He championed moderation in church matters and worked to secure cooperation among ministers of varying persuasion in pastoral work. Among his many books are the devotional classic *The Saints' Everlasting Rest* (1650) and a memoir of his wife Margaret (Charlton) Baxter (1681).

### Lewis Bayly, ca. 1565–1631
Welsh bishop of outspoken Puritan views. His *Practice of Piety* was a bestseller among Puritans and was translated into many languages.

### Thomas Becon, ca. 1512–1567
English preacher; the most widely read popular religious author of the Reformation era in England. His modern biographer detects "incipient Puritanism" in his devotional books. He suffered imprisonment and exile for his beliefs.

### Henry Ward Beecher, 1813–1887

American preacher and writer. Ordained a Presbyterian minister—he served two Indiana Presbyterian churches, then, Plymouth Congregational Church, New York, where he remained for forty years. An abolitionist, he urged President Lincoln to issue the Emancipation Proclamation.

### Benjamin Bennet, 1674–1726

English Presbyterian minister and devotional author. He spent whole days in intercessory prayer and fasting.

### Eugène Bersier, 1831–1889

Swiss Reformed pastor in Paris. A leader of liturgical reform.

### Joanna Bethune (née Graham) 1770–1860

Born in Canada, she was the founder of the Orphan Asylum Society and a pioneer in American Christian education. A member of the Associate Reformed Church. Daughter of Isabella Graham.

### Robert Bolton, 1572–1631

English Puritan minister and writer; lecturer in logic, moral, and natural philosophy. Beloved as a pastor, many people, including people from abroad, turned to him for spiritual counsel.

### Lawrence W. Bottoms, 1908–1994

A minister of the Presbyterian Church (U.S.A.) born in Selma, Alabama. Among many distinguished posts, he was the only African American Moderator of the General Assembly of the Presbyterian Church in the U.S.

### Samuel Bourn, 1689–1754

English Presbyterian-Unitarian minister and writer.

### Michel Bouttier, b. 1921

A Reformed Church of France pastor, now retired. He served as professor of New Testament at the Protestant seminary in Montpellier, France.

### John Bradford, 1510–1555

English Protestant martyr. A personal friend of the Reformer Martin Bucer, he also translated some works of German Reformers. In 1553, he was arrested and imprisoned, and later burnt at Smithfield.

### Katharine Brettargh (née Bruen), 1579–1601

English Puritan. She and her husband, William, were said to have suffered persecution for their religious beliefs.

### John Brinsley, fl. 1584–1630

English Puritan minister, educational theorist, and schoolmaster. Many of his students went on to a university education.

### Charles Brooks, 1795–1872

A lay reader in the Protestant Episcopal Church, he resigned to become pastor of the Third Congregational Church in Hingham, Massachusetts. Peace advocate, ornithologist.

## John Brown, 1722–1787

Associate Synod pastor at Haddington, Scotland. Before studying for the ministry, he worked successively as a shepherd, peddler, soldier (1745), and schoolmaster. He served as the Synod's theology professor and wrote some thirty books, ranging from church history to biographical accounts of devout men and women.

## Elizabeth Barrett Browning, 1806–1861

English poet. Although she did not attend church much, she classified herself as a Congregationalist. Well-read in theology, she also read seven chapters of the Bible daily.

## William Craig Brownlee, 1783–1860

Born, educated, and ordained in Scotland, he later served several Associate Reformed churches in the United States, then transferred to the Reformed Dutch Church. Pastor, [Marble] Collegiate Church, New York, 1826–1848.

## Frederick Buechner, b. 1926

A minister of the Presbyterian Church (U.S.A.); Pulitzer Prize-nominated author of fiction and nonfiction books. His works include *Peculiar Treasures: A Biblical Who's Who, Godric,* and *The Son of Laughter*.

## James Burns, 1875–1948

Born in Scotland, he was a minister of the Presbyterian Church of England which elected him Moderator of the General Assembly in 1937. He served a year as chaplain to the Presbyterian Church in Rome.

## Robert Burns, 1759–1796

The national poet of Scotland. He was baptized in the Ayr parish church [Church of Scotland] the day after his birth, and his body laid to rest in St. Michael's Kirkyard, Dumfries. He grew up in a religious home and knew Scripture well. In an age when Kirk sessions sent elders out on patrol to fine sabbath violaters, Burns attacked and satirized what he perceived as life-denying attitudes in the church. He worked for some time as a farmer and later as an excise (tax) official. For the latter post, he had to have his attendance at Communion in the Church of Scotland documented by a minister and witnesses.

## David J. Burrell, 1844–1926

Ordained a Presbyterian minister, he later transferred to the Reformed Church in America. Pastor, Marble Collegiate Church, New York, from 1891–1926. President of General Synod in 1920.

## John Cairns, 1818–1892

United Presbyterian Church pastor and leader (Scotland). Professor and principal of the United Presbyterian College, Edinburgh.

## Idelette Calvin (née de Bure), 1505–1549

A widow from Liège, Belgium. She married Jean Calvin in 1540. During their nine-year marriage, she sheltered Reformed refugees, visited the sick, and comforted those who were troubled and in sorrow.

## Jean Calvin, 1509–1564

French Reformed theologian and statesman whose writings, particularly the *Institutes of the Christian Religion* (1559), provide the theological foundation of the Reformed tradition. Pastor in exile in Strasbourg, then leader of the Reformation in Geneva.

## Hugh Cameron, 1855–1934

Church of Scotland minister.

## Catholic Apostolic Church

Nineteenth-century millenarian charismatic movement associated with Edward Irving, minister of a London Presbyterian congregation. Their *Liturgy* inspired liturgical renewal in the German Reformed Church, USA, and the Church of Scotland, and through them, other denominations.

## Thomas Chalmers, 1780–1847

Theologian, renowned preacher and social reformer. A minister of the Church of Scotland, he left that body in 1843, founding the Free Church of Scotland.

## In Soon Choi, b. 1934

Born in Korea, he is a naturalized American citizen. Pastor of the Korean Presbyterian Church of Metro Detroit. He has served as Moderator of the Synod of the Covenant and Moderator of the Detroit Presbytery.

## Church of South India

Formed in 1947 by four Anglican dioceses in southern India withdrawing from the Church of India, Burma, and Ceylon, and uniting with the Methodists and the South India Church, which itself was a union of Congregationalists, Dutch Reformed, Presbyterian churches, and the Malabar District of the Basel Mission. In 1958 and 1968, the churches of the Basel Mission (Calvinist and Lutheran) joined, and in 1975, the Anglican diocese of Nandyal joined the Church of South India.

## Church of the Electoral Palatinate

In the mid-sixteenth century, Frederick III, prince elector of this principality in west Germany, ended controversy between Lutheran and Reformed subjects by introducing the Palatine church order, which featured the Heidelberg Catechism as the standard of doctrine.

## Thomas Collins, fl. 1610

English Puritan poet.

## Melva Wilson Costen, b. 1933

An elder of the Presbyterian Church (U.S.A.), professor of worship and music at Interdenominational Theological Center, Atlanta, Georgia.

## John Cotton, 1584–1652

English Congregational Puritan minister who served in Boston, Lincolnshire (England), from 1612 to 1633, then moved to Massachusetts Bay Colony where he served a church in Boston, New England, as teacher. Grandfather of Cotton Mather.

## Helen M. Cowles, 1831–1851
American Congregational woman from Connecticut. Schoolteacher. The daughter of a minister, Henry Cowles, and his wife Alice (née Welch), she was "at a very early age, seriously impressed with gospel truth."

## Robert Crowley, ca. 1518–1588
English Puritan minister, printer, and poet. Printed some of the earliest Welsh books. Exiled in Frankfurt in 1544.

## Frances Cunningham (née Stewart Hawthorn), 1743–1811
A devout member of the Church of Scotland. Those close to her knew that she "cherished an habitual sense of the presence of God." In addition to her regular daily prayer, she set aside one day, most weeks, for fasting and prayer. She ministered to the poor and distressed with wisdom and tenderness.

## *Daily Offices* (1893)
A book for morning and evening prayer issued by the Church Service Society of the Church of Scotland.

## Horton M. Davies, contemporary
Born in Wales. A minister of the Congregational Union of England and Wales, later, of the United Church of Christ (U.S.A.). Distinguished scholar and author, he was professor of the history of Christianity at Princeton University from 1956 to 1984.

## Samuel Davies, 1723–1761
American Presbyterian minister-evangelist of Welsh ancestry who laid the foundation of Presbyterianism in Virginia. President of the College of New Jersey (now Princeton University) for a brief time until he contracted his fatal illness.

## Sarah Davy (née Roane), ca. 1638–ca. 1669
Englishwoman who began to know God as a child. She converted to the Congregational Church (probably from the Church of England). She kept a spiritual journal called "The Record of My Consolations and the Meditations of My Heart."

## Théodore de Bèze, 1519–1605
Born to a French Catholic family, he became Protestant after a severe illness. He succeeded Calvin as the head of the Church of Geneva, as well as the Calvinist movement in Europe. Professor at the Geneva Academy, poet.

## Daniel Defoe, 1660–1731
English Presbyterian, novelist (author of *Robinson Crusoe*), journalist, businessman, government spokesman, and secret agent.

## Jean de Gazel de Larambergue, ca. 1684–1749
French Reformed layman and a cavalry officer in the army of Louis XIV.

## John W. de Gruchy, b. 1939
Minister of the United Congregational Church of Southern Africa. Professor of Christian Studies, University of Cape Town.

## Purd E. Deitz, 1897–1987

American pastor, first, in the Reformed Church in the U.S., then, because of church unions, of the Evangelical and Reformed Church (ERC) and later, the United Church of Christ (UCC). Professor of theology at Eden Theological Seminary, 1938–1950. National church leader in both the ERC and UCC.

## Dianne E. Deming, b. 1956

A minister of the Presbyterian Church (U.S.A.). Youth Director, Mountaintop Presbyterian Church in Mountaintop, Pennsylvania, and writer.

## Arthur Dent, d. 1607

English Puritan minister and popular author.

## Edward Dering, ca. 1540–1576

English Puritan minister. A powerful preacher and gifted writer.

## Philip Doddridge, 1702–1751

English nonconformist minister at home in both the Congregational and Presbyterian traditions. Hymn writer. Principal and teacher at the Northampton Academy. Advocate of toleration, justice, and ecumenical cooperation.

## Charles Drelincourt, 1595–1669

French Reformed pastor in Paris and the most popular writer among French Protestants of his day. When alone he never heard the clock strike the hour without kneeling for prayer.

## Ruth C. Duck, b. 1947

American, United Church of Christ minister and hymn writer. Teaches worship at Garrett Evangelical Theological Seminary in Evanston, Illinois.

## Pierre Du Moulin, the Elder, 1568–1658

French Reformed pastor at Charenton for twenty-one years; church leader. His house was twice sacked by the majority population, and he barely escaped with his life. He later taught theology at the University of Sedan.

## Pierre Du Moulin, the Younger (a.k.a. Peter Du Moulin), 1601–1684

Ordained a minister of the Reformed Church of France, he became chaplain to King Charles II of England in 1660 and served on the staff of Canterbury Cathedral, apparently remaining a Reformed minister.

## Mary Duncan (née Lundie), 1814–1840

Church of Scotland laywoman and hymn writer.

## Philippe Duplessis-Mornay, 1549–1623

French Reformed statesman, soldier, and devotional writer.

## James O. Dykes, 1835–1912

Scots Presbyterian minister, theologian, and popular author. From 1888 to 1907, principal and professor of divinity in the Theological College of the Presbyterian Church of England.

## Jonathan Edwards, 1703–1758

Colonial American preacher and theologian. Pastor of the Congregational Church in Northampton, Massachusetts.

## Stephen Egerton, ca. 1555–ca. 1621

English Presbyterian Puritan minister. Author of a much-used catechism.

## *Euchologion*, 1896 (7th ed.)

A service book published by the Church Service Society of the Church of Scotland. An American edition was published by Presbyterian elder Benjamin B. Comegys.

## *Evangelical Hymnal for the Rhineland and Westphalia*, 1898

A hymnbook for the church in the Rhineland and Westphalia (Germany) which consisted of both Lutheran and Reformed congregations.

## *Evangelical Hymnal*, 1996

A hymnbook with prayers for these German churches: the Evangelical Church in the Rhineland (a union of Lutheran and Reformed congregations), the Evangelical Church of Westphalia (a union of Lutheran and Reformed confessions), and the Church of Lippe (a church with a Reformed majority and Lutheran minority).

## John Field, 1545–1587

English Puritan pastor, devoted to further reformation of the Church of England along Presbyterian lines.

## John Flavel, ca. 1630–1691

English Presbyterian Puritan minister. Ejected from the Church of England in 1662. Popular devotional writer.

## Free Church of Scotland

The Presbyterian Church formed in 1843 by nearly one-third of the ministers and members of the Church of Scotland withdrawing into a separate body. In 1900, it united with the United Presbyterian Church to form the United Free Church of Scotland.

## *Freedom's Lyre: or Psalms, Hymns and Sacred Songs for the Slave and His Friends* (1840)

Compiled by Presbyterian minister Edwin F. Hatfield at the request of the American Anti-Slavery Society.

## Liu Fung-sung, contemporary

Taiwanese Presbyterian writer, converted while in prison. He was jailed for his strong advocacy of democracy and freedom.

## Raimond Gaches, ca. 1615–1668

French Reformed pastor and celebrated preacher.

## Gaelic *Book of Common Order*

The *Book of Common Order* was the book for worship prepared by John Knox and used in the Church of Scotland until 1645. It was translated into Gaelic in 1567. Prayer 203 is apparently original to this translation.

### Garden of Spiritual Flowers, 1687 ed.
A much-used and representative English Puritan devotional manual, first published before 1609.

### Alan Gaunt, b. 1935
English Congregationalist, later United Reformed Church minister, hymn writer, and poet.

### Geneva Bible
English translation of the Bible first published in 1560 in Geneva. It was very popular among English Puritans.

### German Reformed Church in the USA
A church formally organized in 1747, composed largely of immigrants from the Rhineland, Germany, and German-speaking Switzerland areas. Later known as the Reformed Church in the United States, which in 1934 united with the Evangelical Synod of North America to form the Evangelical and Reformed Church; and in 1957, that body merged with the Congregational Christian Churches, forming the United Church of Christ.

### Boon Mark Gittisarn, fl. 1930–1960
A pastor of the Church of Christ in Thailand, later, of the Bible Presbyterian Church, also in Thailand.

### James I. Good, 1850–1924
A pastor of the German Reformed Church in the USA, later, of the Reformed Church in the United States. He taught at Ursinus College and Seminary, and in 1907 began teaching Reformed church history and liturgics at Central Theological Seminary in Dayton, Ohio. President of Foreign Missions, 1893–1924.

### Jeremiah H. Good, 1822–1888
A pastor of the German Reformed Church in the USA, later, of the Reformed Church in the United States. President and professor of dogmatics and practical theology at Heidelberg Seminary in Tiffin, Ohio. Uncle of James I. Good.

### William Gouge, 1578–1653
English Presbyterian Puritan pastor. He succeeded Stephen Egerton at a London church. Having inherited an estate, he provided funds for poor students to attend university.

### Simon Goulart, 1543–1628
French scholar and Church of Geneva pastor who succeeded Théodore de Bèze as head of the Company of Pastors. A prolific writer, his works included translations, works of religious instruction, and poetry. He also published music.

### Isabella Graham (née Marshall), 1742–1814
Born in Scotland where her pastor was John Witherspoon. Subsequently lived in America. Teacher and pioneer charitable worker. A member of the Associate Reformed Church.

## Ashbel Green, 1762–1848

American Presbyterian minister. Chaplain to Congress. President of the College of New Jersey (now Princeton University).

## Charlotte Green, d. ca. 1845

An orphan who died at age five or six. Charlotte, probably Armenian, was wandering the streets of Calcutta when she was brought to live in a Free Church of Scotland mission. In her brief life she learned English and her chief delight was to pray and read the Bible.

## Francis J. Grimké, 1850–1937

Born the son of a slave and her white owner, he was freed on his father's death (1852). Later arrested by his own white half-brother, and sold to a Confederate officer. After the Civil War, he graduated from Lincoln University at the head of his class, and also graduated from Princeton Theological Seminary. Pastor, Fifteenth Street Presbyterian Church in Washington, D.C. Social prophet and reformer; an early officer of the NAACP.

## Henry Grove, 1684–1738

English Presbyterian minister. A close friend of Elizabeth Singer Rowe and Isaac Watts. At the time of his death he was writing a biography of Elizabeth Singer Rowe.

## Haalilio, d. 1844

Native Hawaiian, Commissioner for the nation of Hawaii. Congregationalist.

## Jupiter Hammon, 1711–ca. 1806

African slave who worked as a clerk-bookkeeper for wealthy Long Island slave merchants his entire life. Part-time preacher and early leader among New England slaves. Early African writer and first published black preacher in America. A devout evangelical Christian shaped by the Quaker, Puritan, and Anglican traditions.

## Jedidah Hannit, ca. 1708–1725

A Congregational Wampanoag Native American from Martha's Vineyard. She delighted in reading her Bible. Shortly before her death she had a prophetic dream that a time of great distress would come upon the Indian peoples.

## Henry Harbaugh, 1817–1876

A pastor of the German Reformed Church in the USA, and theology professor at the Mercersburg Seminary in Pennsylvania. Author, poet, and editor.

## Howell Harris, 1714–1773

Welsh lay evangelist, one of the founders of Welsh Calvinistic Methodism.

## Edwin F. Hatfield, 1807–1883

American Presbyterian minister, Stated Clerk of the General Assembly. Advocate of Emancipation.

## Heidelberg Catechism and Prayers, 1752

An appendix to the first Reformed hymnbook printed in America, *Core of Old and New Spirit-filled Hymns* published in Germantown, Pennsylvania, by

Christoph Saur in 1752, and used in Reformed churches of Hessen, Hanau, the Palatinate (all in Germany), and Pennsylvania.

### Matthew Henry, 1662–1714
English Presbyterian minister, popular devotional writer and biblical commentator.

### Philip Henry, 1631–1696
English Presbyterian Puritan minister and diarist. For his nonconformity, he suffered seizure of all his household goods, imprisonment, and was silenced as a minister. Father of Matthew Henry and Sarah Savage.

### Oliver Heywood, 1630–1702
English Presbyterian Puritan minister, ejected from the Church of England in 1662. Each year he observed the anniversary of his baptism with a day of prayer.

### Samuel Hieron, ca. 1576–1617
English Puritan minister and eminent preacher.

### Home Prayers, 1879
A book of services for family worship published by members of the Church Service Society of the Church of Scotland.

### Hannah Housman (née Pearsall), ca. 1697–1735
English Congregational laywoman of deep piety.

### Peter Howat, ca. 1567–1645
Church of Scotland minister in Edinburgh. Suffered for his convictions.

### Alexander R. Howell, 1871–1943
Church of Scotland minister.

### Jane Parker Huber, b. 1926
Born in Tsinan, China. Elder of the Presbyterian Church (U.S.A.) and hymn writer.

### Huguenots
Another word for persecuted Reformed Church of France members, particularly in the sixteenth and seventeenth centuries. Many fled France, finding refuge in America, Canada, England, Holland, Switzerland, and elsewhere.

### John Hunter, 1848–1917
Born in Aberdeen, Scotland. Congregational pastor who served churches in York, Hull, Glasgow and the King's Weigh House, London.

### Petrus Immens, 1644–1720
Dutch Reformed minister at Middelburg (province of Zeeland). He also was the principal and chief teacher of a Latin school.

### William Jay, 1769–1853
English Congregational minister in Bath and popular devotional writer.

### David Jenkins, b. 1941
A minister of the United Reformed Church (United Kingdom) and writer.

### Elizabeth Joscelin (née Brooke), 1596–1622
English Puritan, educated in languages and history. While pregnant she had a premonition of her death. She wrote a book of guidance for her unborn child, and died nine days after giving birth to her daughter. She recommended Puritan Henry Smith's prayers for use in the morning and evening.

### Toyohiko Kagawa, 1888–1960
Japanese Presbyterian preacher (later, belonged to the Kyodan, the United Church of Christ in Japan). Evangelist and social reformer. He lived with the poor in great simplicity.

### Paul Kanoa, nineteenth century
Native Hawaiian and Congregational missionary to Micronesia.

### C. M. Kao, contemporary
Presbyterian Church in Taiwan minister and leader, now retired. He served as his denomination's General Secretary.

### Abigail Kenump, ca. 1694–1710
A Congregational Wampanoag Native American from Martha's Vineyard. During her long fatal illness, she was taken to church on horseback when she could not walk. She spent much time in prayer.

### John Knox, ca. 1514–1572
Ordained a Roman Catholic priest in 1536, he converted to Protestantism. In 1547, his convictions led to suffering nineteen months as a galley slave in France. He became recognized as the leader of the Reformation in Scotland, perceiving his vocation in life: "to blow my master's trumpet" through preaching the gospel.

### A. C. Kumah, contemporary
Presbyterian Church of Ghana pastor. Served at the Presbyterian Teacher's Training College in Akropong.

### Lazarus Lamilami, 1910–1977
First ordained Aboriginal minister of the Uniting Church in Australia.

### Amos Lawrence, 1786–1852
Boston (USA) businessman and philanthropist. A Congregationalist deacon.

### Robert Lee, 1804–1868
Church of Scotland minister. Professor of biblical criticism, University of Glasgow. Liturgical pioneer.

### William Leechman, 1706–1785
Church of Scotland minister. Principal, University of Glasgow. Moderator of the General Assembly in 1757.

### Dorothy Leigh (née Kempe), d. 1616
English Puritan. Her book *The Mother's Blessing* (1616) was very popular, being published in numerous editions over one hundred years.

### Robert Leighton, 1611–1684

Church of Scotland minister, university professor, and principal; writer and peacemaker. He reluctantly served as bishop, then briefly as acting archbishop in Glasgow in his desire to settle the dispute between Episcopalians and Presbyterians in Britain.

### William Liston, 1781–1864

Church of Scotland minister.

### Hui-chin Loh, contemporary

A member of the Presbyterian Church in Taiwan, she teaches Christian education and is the general editor of "Philosophies of Life," a series of textbooks for Christian high schools in Taiwan.

### I-to Loh, b. 1936

An ordained minister of the Presbyterian Church in Taiwan. President, Tainan Theological College and Seminary in Tainan, Taiwan.

### George Marion McClellan, 1860–1934

African American Congregational minister and educator, poet, and fiction writer.

### George MacLeod (Lord MacLeod of Fuinary), 1895–1991

Church of Scotland minister and pacifist leader. Founder and leader of the Iona Community, 1938–1967.

### Norman MacLeod, 1812–1872

Church of Scotland minister and close advisor to Queen Victoria. A church and social reformer, he championed the cause of working people and fostered a broad range of ministries among the poor.

### H. A. César Malan, 1787–1864

Swiss Calvinist minister of Italian-French origin; ordained by the Church of Geneva. He hoped to work for church reform but was deprived of his ministerial status. Pastor of a separatist congregation. One of the greatest writers of hymns in French.

### Marguerite of Navarre, 1492–1549

French Queen of Reformed Sympathies, poet, and major literary figure. Defender of the persecuted Reformed minority in France. Théodore de Bèze esteemed her as one of the most important figures of the Reformation.

### *Mariner's Divine Mate* (Boston, 1715)

A book of spiritual counsel for sailors by an anonymous, very likely, Puritan author known only by the initials "J. J."

### Augustin Marlorat, 1506–1562

French Augustinian monk (who retained his monastic name throughout life), later a Reformed pastor at Crassier, Vevey, and finally, Rouen. Theologian and author; a friend of Calvin. When the wars of religion broke out in France, he remained at Rouen to minister to his flock. When the town fell, he was executed.

**Cotton Mather, 1663–1728**
New England Congregational Puritan minister. A precocious child, he began
studies at Harvard at age eleven. Served the North Church of Boston, with his
father, Increase Mather, until his father's death in 1723. A prolific writer,
deeply religious, and learned man.

**Increase Mather, 1639–1723**
New England Puritan minister, ordained a teacher at the North Church,
Boston, where he remained for almost sixty years. A spiritual and intellectual
leader, he authored books on theology, natural science, and history, and served
as president of Harvard College.

**William May, 1706–1755**
English Presbyterian minister in London. In the year he was ordained, 1733,
his bride of twenty months died, then, his only child, and finally, his only
brother—all within four months. A student of Henry Grove.

**James Meikle, 1730–1799**
An elder in the General Associate Synod of Scotland (a Presbyterian church
body also known as the "Antiburgher Synod"). A surgeon, he cared for his
patients until the day before his death. Devotional writer.

**Caryl Micklem, b. 1925**
A minister of the United Reformed Church (United Kingdom); hymn writer
and musician.

**Colin F. Miller, 1911–1988**
Church of Scotland minister. Spent much of his ministry in Canada.

**Kornelius Miskotte, 1894–1976**
A pastor of the Netherlands Reformed Church and theologian. An active
member of the Resistance in Holland during Nazi occupation. He and his
family hid a young Jewish woman from the Nazis during World War II.

**John Morison, 1791–1859**
Born in Scotland, he was first an apprentice watchmaker, then entered the
ministry. Congregationalist pastor in London.

**Robert Murrey, fl. 1695–1735**
English Presbyterian minister.

**Reinhold Niebuhr, 1892–1971**
American theologian. A minister of the Evangelical and Reformed Church,
later, of the United Church of Christ (although Lutheran in orientation). He
taught at Union Theological Seminary in New York from 1928 to 1960.

**John Norden, 1548–1625**
English topographer, surveyor, and author of popular devotional books.
Apparently a Puritan, he remained in low profile to ensure government passes
necessary for surveying. From 1600 to 1614, while surveying crown woods, he
published no new prayer books. Several of his publishers were in trouble with
authorities: notably, Valentine Simmes (who helped typeset violent Puritan

attacks on episcopacy—the Marprelate Tracts) and Richard Bradock, who was ordered to turn over finished leaves of Norden's *Pensive Man's Practise*.

### Samson Occom, 1723–1792
Mohegan Native American, Presbyterian minister, and hymnbook compiler. He was converted through the ministry of George Whitefield and ordained by the Suffolk Presbytery on Long Island.

### Johannes Oecolampadius, 1482–1531
German Reformed minister and theologian. Principal Reformer of Basel, Switzerland.

### D. K. Ofosuapea, contemporary
A member of the Presbyterian Church of Ghana. YMCA leader in Takoradi.

### Stuart R. Oglesby, 1888–1977
American Presbyterian minister and author. Taught at Columbia Theological Seminary in Decatur, Georgia.

### Lydia Ohquanhut, 1710–1715
A Wampanoag Native American child of Congregational parents. She asked her father to teach her to pray as she was dying. He wrote down her prayers.

### Hughes Oliphant Old, contemporary
A minister of the Presbyterian Church (U.S.A.). Member, Center of Theological Inquiry in Princeton, New Jersey.

### William Orchard, 1877–1955
English Presbyterian minister who served the Congregational church, King's Weigh House from 1914 to 1932. Later he became a Roman Catholic priest. He began his working life at age fourteen as a railway clerk. One pair of his shoes were adorned with silver buckles that once belonged to John Wesley.

### Sarah Osborn (née Haggar), 1714–1796
Born in London, she came to America when she was eight years old. Her first husband died at sea soon after their first child was born. Since her second husband, Henry Osborn, failed in business and was infirm, she supported the family as a schoolteacher. A member of the Congregational church in Newport, Rhode Island, she held prayer meetings in the home several nights a week. They were attended by great numbers of both whites and blacks.

### Eusebius Paget, ca. 1542–1617
English Puritan minister who was persecuted for his beliefs. Educated at Oxford, he broke his arm there, and it was lame for the remainder of his life.

### Piambohu, seventeenth century
Algonquin Native American, Congregationalist, a ruling elder of the church at Natick, Massachusetts, founded by John Eliot ("Apostle of New England").

### *The Pilgrim Hymnal,* 1935 rev. ed.
A hymnbook for the Congregational Christian Churches in the United States.

### William F. Pitcairn, d. 1891
An angel (bishop) of the Catholic Apostolic Church in Edinburgh.

---

*Prayer Book for Families and other Private Persons*, ca. 1850
A pamphlet published by an anonymous Scottish Presbyterian.

**Elizabeth Payson Prentiss, 1818–1878**
American Presbyterian laywoman with strong ties to the Congregational church; author and hymn writer. A spiritual counselor to the troubled, she also ministered to those who were sick.

**John Preston, 1587–1628**
English Puritan minister and theologian. Dean, Queen's College, Cambridge. A close friend of John Cotton.

**William Prynne, 1600–1669**
English Presbyterian Puritan. Member of Parliament and writer. Twice confined to prison for extended periods because of his convictions.

**Martha Laurens Ramsay, 1759–1811**
American Congregational laywoman from Charleston, South Carolina. A learned, compassionate, and religious woman, who often prayed in her dreams. She led family worship when her physician/statesman husband David was away. Sometimes she read the New Testament to her sons in Greek, and to her daughters, in French.

**László Ravasz, 1882–1967**
Bishop and theologian of the Hungarian Reformed Church.

**H. Cordelia Ray, ca. 1849–1916**
African American poet and New York City teacher, from a Congregational ministerial family.

*Reformed Churchbook*, 1889 ed.
August Ebrard's 1847 collection of prayers from European Reformed churches. Gerhard Goebel edited the second edition of 1889.

**Joseph Renville, ca. 1779–1846**
Son of a French trader and a Dakota (Lakota) mother. Built and ran a trading house. Scripture translator and interpreter for missionaries. A member of the Presbyterian church organized at Lac qui Parle (Minnesota) in 1836, he was ordained a ruling elder in 1841.

**Jacobus Revius, 1586–1658**
Dutch Reformed pastor at Deventer from 1614 to 1642; theologian, translator, and poet.

**Mary Rich (née Boyle; Countess of Warwick), 1625–1678**
Anglo-Irish woman who spent her childhood in Ireland and became Puritan after a conversion experience. She prayed in her garden every morning, wrote a spiritual diary, and hosted ministers at her home. Among her charitable work, she provided food for the poor of the whole neighboring area. After 1662 she extended her charity to ejected Puritan ministers.

### André Rivet, ca. 1573–1651
A French Reformed minister, he taught theology at Leiden and Breda in the Netherlands.

### Francis Roberts, 1609–1675
Presbyterian Puritan minister and devotional writer. He conformed to the Church of England in 1660.

### Hugh Rose, ca. 1633–1686
Church of Scotland minister. A pious and learned man, he endured much illness.

### Francis Rous, 1579–1659
English Puritan layman. Provost of Eton College; member of Parliament between 1626 and 1656. He was Presbyterian, becoming Independent (Congregationalist) in 1649.

### Elizabeth Singer Rowe, 1674–1737
English poet and popular writer. A friend of Isaac Watts. She prayed at morning, noon, and night, entertained the poor in her home, and never neglected an opportunity to receive Holy Communion. She was very interested in the success of the gospel in the colony of Georgia. Born into a Presbyterian family, she was closely connected with the Rook Lane Meeting, a Congregational church with a Presbyterian pastor.

### Thomas Sampson, ca. 1517–1589
Puritan minister. Lived in exile in Strasbourg and Geneva. In 1561, appointed dean of Christ Church, Oxford. Later he was deprived of this post and placed in confinement for some time.

### Sarah Savage (née Henry), 1664–1752
English Presbyterian Puritan. Eldest daughter of Philip and Katherine Henry. Learned Hebrew when she was about seven years old so that she could read the psalms in that language.

### Robert H. Schuller, b. 1926
A minister of the Reformed Church in America. Founder and pastor of the Crystal Cathedral in Garden Grove, California.

### Scottish Psalter, 1595
The 1595 edition of the Church of Scotland *Book of Common Order* contains a metrical psalter with a prayer after each psalm. These are translated from the psalm prayers of Augustin Marlorat, and use distinctive Scottish language. Prayer 104 was reworked so much that it is basically a new prayer.

### J. Barrie Shepherd, b. 1935
Born in England, of Scots descent and education, he is a British citizen. A minister of the Presbyterian Church (U.S.A.), now retired, he served churches in Wooster, Ohio; Swarthmore, Pennsylvania; and New York City, as well as serving four colleges as campus pastor. Poet and writer.

### Hannah Sinclair, 1780–1818

An evangelical member of the Church of Scotland. She was educated at a London boarding school where she especially enjoyed astronomy. Her mother having died when she was an infant, her father remarried. Hannah taught her younger half-siblings. She regularly visited poor neighbors to read and explain Scripture to them.

### Elwyn A. Smith, b. 1919

A minister of the Presbyterian Church (U.S.A.), writer, and painter. Seminary and university professor. He served as dean of Dubuque Theological Seminary in Dubuque, Iowa.

### George Smith, 1803–1870

English Congregational minister. Secretary of the Congregational Union.

### Henry Smith, ca. 1560–1591

English Puritan minister. Esteemed as the "First Preacher in the Nation." His books of sermons were used by families in their household worship.

### Sarah Huntington Smith, 1802–1836

American Congregational missionary. She first worked among Mohegan Native Americans in Connecticut as a teacher, and to provide them a chapel. After marriage in 1833, she labored tirelessly at the American Mission in Beirut. She became fluent in Arabic to minister to the native women and established the first Protestant sabbath school for them.

### Thomas Sorocold, 1561–1617

English Puritan minister, popular preacher. His *Supplications of Saints* was a very popular prayer book.

### Michael Sparke, Senior, d. 1653

English Puritan. London bookseller at the Blue Bible from 1616 to 1653. A vigorous opponent of monopolies in Bible printing. He suffered for his convictions.

### John U. Stephens, 1901–1984

American Presbyterian pastor.

### Robert Louis Stevenson, 1850–1894

Scots essayist, poet, and novelist. His works include *A Child's Garden of Verses, Treasure Island,* and *The Strange Case of Dr. Jekyll and Mr. Hyde.* Born in Edinburgh and baptized a month later, he grew up in a traditional Church of Scotland family. The family nurse read him the Bible and religious literature. Ambivalent at best about Christianity in adulthood, during his last years he searched for spiritual integration. He wrote prayers for use in his household (in Samoa) and briefly taught a church school class. These ended after a student asked, "Who made God?"

### Joseph B. Stratton, 1815–1903

American Presbyterian minister in Natchez, Mississippi.

### Katherine Stubbes (née Emmes), ca. 1571–1590

English Puritan, married at age fifteen. She died some weeks after giving birth to a healthy son.

### A Swiss Reformed Psalter, 1558

Published in Geneva by Jean Crespin. Annotations, commentary by Calvin, and a prayer are provided for each psalm.

### Ze Tembe, fl. 1915

A Bulu Presbyterian man associated with the West African Mission directed by the Presbyterian Church in the USA in what is now Cameroon.

### Gerhard Tersteegen, 1697–1769

Raised in a pietistic German Reformed parish and intended for the ministry by his parents, the death of his father made university education impossible. After five years of depression and spiritual trial, he emerged as a spiritual counselor for many people and a deeply influential writer, though he no longer attended church. The historian W. R. Ward states that Tersteegen steered a middle course between traditional mysticism and the Reformed church.

### Hsu Tien-hsien, contemporary

A minister of the Presbyterian Church in Taiwan, he has also served as the denomination's moderator. Suffered over four years' imprisonment because of his advocacy of democratic reform.

### James M. Todd, 1912–1977

English Congregationalist, later, United Reformed Church, minister.

### Roger Tomes, b. 1928

British (Anglo-Welsh); a minister of the United Reformed Church, he has served pastorates in Yorkshire, London, and St. Albans, and taught Old Testament at Northern College, Manchester, England.

### Daniel Toussaint, 1541–1603

French minor nobleman. One of the pastors of the afflicted Reformed congregation in Orléans, France. Finally forced into exile, he became professor of theology at the University of Heidelberg (Germany) and rector of the same.

### Diane Karay Tripp, b. 1954

Baptized in the Reformed Church in America. A minister of the Presbyterian Church (U.S.A.) and a writer. Of Greek and Dutch ancestry, her earliest known Dutch forebears belonged to the Netherlands Reformed Church.

### Johann-Jakob Ulrick, 1683–1731

Church of Zurich minister and professor of ethics.

### United Church of Christ

The American church formed in 1957 by the merger of the Congregational Christian Churches and the Evangelical and Reformed Church (itself the result of the 1934 union of the Reformed Church in the United States

[German Reformed] and the Evangelical Synod of North America). The Calvin Synod of the UCC is a nongeographical conference of Hungarian Reformed churches.

### United Evangelical-Protestant Church of Baden (Germany)
A united church of Lutheran and Reformed congregations formed in 1821. Today known as the Evangelical Church in Baden.

### United Free Church of Scotland
The Presbyterian church formed in 1900 by the union of the United Presbyterian Church with the Free Church of Scotland.

### United Reformed Church
Founded in 1972 through the union of the Congregational Church in England and Wales with the Presbyterian Church of England. In 1980 some Church of Christ [Disciples] congregations joined the United Reformed Church.

### Uniting Church in Australia
Inaugurated June 22, 1977. Formed by union of Congregational, Methodist, and Presbyterian churches.

### Henry J. van Dyke, 1852–1933
American Presbyterian minister, university professor, diplomat, outdoorsman. A leading figure in the renewal of Presbyterian worship.

### Peter Martyr Vermigli (Pietro Martire Vermigli), 1499–1562
Italian, an Augustinian canon regular for over twenty years, then prior of St. Petrus-ad-aram in Naples. He became Protestant and fled Italy in 1542. A Reformer, he taught theology in Strasbourg and at Oxford, and later taught Hebrew in Zurich. Married Catherine Dammartin, a nun.

### Nathanael Vincent, ca. 1639–1697
English Puritan minister, ejected from the Church of England in 1662. He continued to preach, therefore suffering fines, imprisonment, and being dragged from the pulpit by soldiers.

### Thomas Waban, fl. 1646–1720
Algonquin Native American, Congregationalist, first convert of John Eliot. He was the justice of the peace in Natick (Massachusetts), town clerk, and Native American spokesman. *Waban* means "wind."

### Helen J. Waddell, 1889–1965
Medieval scholar and novelist. Irish Presbyterian, born in Tokyo to missionary parents.

### Robert Waldegrave, ca. 1554–1604
English Puritan printer and publisher. After suffering at the hands of church authorities, he and his family moved to Edinburgh where he was little harassed.

### Wampas, d. 1651
Algonquin Native American convert to Christianity through the ministry of Congregational pastor John Eliot. Schoolteacher. He died of smallpox.

### Charles E. Watson, 1869–1942

English minister. Converted to Congregationalism from the Church of England. Pastor, Rodborough Tabernacle, 1909–1942.

### John Watson (pen name: Ian Maclaren), 1850–1907

British. A minister first of the Free Church of Scotland, then of the Presbyterian Church of England.

### Lauchlan MacLean Watt, 1867–1957

Church of Scotland minister and writer. University lecturer at Aberdeen, Glasgow, Edinburgh, and St. Andrews. Created a Welsh bard.

### Isaac Watts, 1674–1748

English Congregational minister, hymn writer, and educational writer. He pioneered the transition from singing psalms to hymns. His work includes some of the finest and most loved hymns in the English language, including "Joy to the World!" and "When I Survey the Wondrous Cross."

### Watu wa Mgnu ("The People of God")

A religious group among the Gikuyu of Kenya which broke away from the Church of Scotland mission after a dispute that began in 1929. They hold all goods in common and claim direct communication with God.

### Neil Weatherhogg, b. 1939

A minister of the Presbyterian Church (U.S.A.). Pastor, First Presbyterian Church in Topeka, Kansas.

### James W. Weir, 1805–1878

American Presbyterian elder and banker. An early friend of the anti-slavery movement.

### Welsh Calvinistic Methodist Church

The religious body established in Wales through the work of Howell Harris and Daniel Rowlands. A founder member of the World Presbyterian Alliance, and a member of the World Alliance of Reformed Churches. Today known as the Presbyterian Church of Wales.

### Elisabeth West, fl. 1675–1707

A devout member of the Church of Scotland. She worked as a domestic servant.

### Phillis Wheatley, ca. 1753–1784

The first African woman poet in America. Kidnapped from her family and country, she was purchased as a slave in Boston Harbor in 1761 and freed in 1773. She mastered English in sixteen months. Her keen intellect brought her into the homes of distinguished Bostonians as a guest. First Black member of the Old South (Congregational) Church.

### George Whitefield, 1714–1770

A spellbinding preacher and leader of the Calvinistic wing of the evangelical revival in Great Britain and America. An itinerate evangelist of Anglican ordination, yet considered Reformed.

**Georg Willem (a.k.a. George Guillaume; Count), 1635–1709**
Dutch nobleman and Reformed layman, he was a baron. Through his
marriage to Anna van Ewsum in 1665, he became Lord of Nienoord; and in
1694 he was proclaimed a Count of the Holy Roman Empire. A wealthy
businessman, he also was a representative of the Ommelanden (part of the
Groningen province) in the States General.

**John Willison, 1680–1750**
A minister of the Church of Scotland and devotional author. Eminent
evangelical clergyman of his time.

**John Witherspoon, 1723–1794**
Evangelical Church of Scotland pastor, president of the College of New Jersey
(now Princeton University), only minister to sign the Declaration of
Independence. He presided at the first General Assembly (1789) of the
Presbyterian Church in the United States of America.

**J. C. Wit-Ribbers, b. 1933**
A member of the Netherlands Reformed Church living in Groningen, she
writes prayers, poems, and hymn texts for various church publications.

**Hezekiah Woodward, ca. 1590–1675**
English Congregational Puritan schoolmaster, later, a minister and writer.

**Samuel Wright, 1683–1746**
English Presbyterian minister.

**Thomas Wright, 1785–1855**
Writer and translator. He was a minister of the Church of Scotland until 1841
when he was deposed for "constructive heresy."

**Georg J. Zollikofer, 1730–1788**
Swiss minister of the Reformed congregation in Leipzig, Germany.

**Huldrych Zwingli, 1484–1531**
Swiss Roman Catholic priest who gradually adopted Reformed views.
Principal Reformer of Zurich, Switzerland. He served as "People's Preacher"
at the Old Minster, Zurich, from 1518 until his death on a battlefield.

# SOURCES OF THE PRAYERS

Many of the older titles listed below are short titles. Old-style capitalization, punctuation, and spelling have been retained. A year in brackets following a title indicates the first edition of a book or the year of the earliest known extant edition. Publishers are given for books appearing after 1874. The number or numbers concluding each entry correspond to prayer numbers as found in the body of the book.

Alleine, Joseph. *An Alarme to Unconverted Sinners*. London, 1672. (Prayers 10, 320, 326)

Alleine, Richard. *Vindiciae Pietatis: or, A Vindication of Godlinesse*. London, 1669. (Prayers 190, 211, 212, 322)

——.*Two Prayers: One for the Use of Familes [sic], the other for Childern [sic]*. n.p., [c. 1670]. (Prayer 485)

Alves, Rubem. *I Believe in the Resurrection of the Body*. Translated by L. M. McCoy. Philadelphia: Fortress Press, 1986. (Prayer 180)

Anthony, Susanna. *The Life and Character of Miss Susanna Anthony*. Edited by Samuel Hopkins. Hartford, CN, 1796. (Prayers 14, 59, 110, 167, 252)

Bailey, Abigail Abbot. *Religion and Domestic Violence in Early New England: The Memoirs of Abigail Abbot Bailey*. Religion in North America. Edited by Ann Taves, p. 184. Bloomington and Indianapolis: Indiana University Press, 1989. (Prayer 342)

Baillie, John. *A Diary of Private Prayer*. [1936] New York: Charles Scribner's Sons, 1949. (Prayer 191)

Barclay, William. *Epilogues and Prayers*. London: SCM Press, 1963. (Prayer 112)

Barth, Karl. *Prayer*. Edited by Don E. Saliers and translated by Sara F. Terrien. 2nd ed. Philadelphia: The Westminster Press, 1985. (Prayer 66)

Baxter, Richard. *The Poor Mans Family Book*. London, 1674. (Prayers 207, 213, 312, 474)

——. *A Breviate of the Life of Margaret . . . Baxter*. London, 1681. (Prayer 450)

——. *The Last Work of a Believer*. London, 1682. (Prayers 83, 96, 435)

Bayly, Lewis. *The Practise of Piety*. [3rd ed., 1613] 51st ed. London, 1714. (Prayers 87, 171, 294, 302, 353, 416, 432)

Becon, Thomas. *The Flower of Godly Prayers* (1560). In *Prayers and Other Pieces of Thomas Becon*, vol. [4]. Edited by John Ayre. Cambridge: Parker Society, 1844. (Prayers 91, 145, 158, 243)

Beecher, Henry Ward. *Prayers from Plymouth Pulpit.* 5th ed. New York, 1867. (Prayer 144)

Bennet, Benjamin. *The Christian Oratory.* 2nd ed. London, 1728. (Prayer 246)

Bersier, Eugène, ed. *Liturgie à l'usage des Églises Réformées.* Paris, 1874. (Prayer 161)

Bethune, Joanna. *Memoirs of Mrs. Joanna Bethune.* Edited by George W. Bethune. New York, 1863. (Prayers 77, 153)

Bevan, Frances, ed. *Hymns of Ter Steegen, Suso and Others.* First Series. New York: Loizeau Brothers, [1894]. (Prayer 147)

Bingham, Hiram. *A Residence of Twenty-One Years in the Sandwich Islands.* 3rd ed. Canadaigua, NY, 1855. (Prayers 130, 459)

Bolton, Robert. *Certaine Devout Prayers of Mr. Bolton.* London, 1638. (Prayer 254)

Bottoms, Lawrence W. Typescript with letter to the author. April 7, 1988. (Prayer 239)

Bourn, Samuel. *The Young Christian's Prayer-Book.* [1733] 3rd ed. Birmingham, [England], 1742. (Prayers 80, 487)

―――. *The Christian Family Prayer Book: or, Family Prayers, For Morning and Evening.* [1737] Recommendation by I. Watts. Birmingham, [England], 1747. (Prayer 8)

Bouttier, Michel. *Prayers for My Village.* Translated by Lamar Williamson. Nashville: Upper Room Books, 1994. (Prayers 55, 222, 415)

Bradford, John. "Meditations and Prayers." In *Writings of the Rev. John Bradford.* London [1827]. (Prayers 51, 68, 131, 265, 291)

Brinsley the Elder, John. *The Trve Watch and Rule of Life.* 8th ed. London, 1619. (Prayers 196, 457)

Brooks, Charles. *A Family Prayer Book.* New ed. Hingham, Mass., 1829. (Prayer 111)

Brown, John. *The Christian Journal; or, Common Incidents; spiritual Instructors.* Edinburgh, 1765. (Prayer 341)

Browning, Elizabeth Barrett. *Poems.* London: Smith, Elder and Co., 1888. (Prayer 280)

Brownlee, William Craig. *The Christian Youth's Book.* New York, 1844. (Prayer 164)

Buechner, Frederick. *The Hungering Dark.* San Francisco: Harper and Row, Publishers, 1969. (Prayer 127)

Burder, Samuel. *Memoirs of Eminently Pious Women.* New ed. from a London ed. in 3 vols. [vols. 1 and 2 edited by Thomas Gibbons; vol. 3 edited by

George Jerment]. Now complete in one vol. Philadelphia, 1834. (Prayers 3, 64, 100, 264)

Burnham, Richard. *Pious Memorials.* New ed. London, 1789. (Prayers 101, 119, 150, 200, 308, 311, 417)

Burns, James. *A Pulpit Manual Containing Forms of Prayers used in the Conduct of Public Worship.* London: James Clarke, [1914]. (Prayers 316, 368)

Burns, Robert. *The Complete Works of Robert Burns.* Edited by Alexander Smith. New York: A. L. Burt, Publisher [1890]. (Prayer 431)

Burrell, David James. *The Home Sanctuary.* New York: American Tract Society, 1911. (Prayer 268)

Calvin, Jean. *Commentaries on the Twelve Minor Prophets,* vol. 3. Translated by John Owen. Edinburgh, 1847. (Prayers 52, 78, 151)

—————. *Commentaries on the Book of the Prophet Jeremiah and the Lamentations,* vol. 2. Translated by John Owen. Edinburgh, 1851. (Prayer 4)

—————. *Commentaries on the Book of the Prophet Daniel,* vol. 2. Translated by Thomas Myers. Edinburgh, 1853. (Prayer 231)

—————. *Iohannis Calvini opera quae supersunt omnia,* vol. 6. In *Corpus Reformatorum.* [vol. 34]. Brunswick, 1867. (Prayers 358, 486)

Cameron, Hugh. *Prayers for Use in Public Worship.* Edinburgh: Alexander Brunton, 1921. (Prayer 168)

*Carmina Sanctorum: A Selection of Hymns and Songs of Praise.* Edited by Roswell Dwight Hitchcock, Zachary Eddy, and Lewis Ward Mudge. New York: A. S. Barnes, 1886. (Prayer 272)

Catholic Apostolic Church. *The Liturgy and other Divine Offices of the Church.* London: Chiswick Press, Co. [ca. 1899]. (Prayers 402, 455)

Chalmers, Thomas. *Sabbath Scripture Readings,* vol. 2 in *Posthumous Works,* vol. 5. Edited by William Hanna. Edinburgh, 1848. (Prayer 219)

Christian Reformed Church in North America. *Psalter Hymnal.* Grand Rapids, MI: CRC Publications, 1987. (Prayer 344)

Church of Bern. *Gëbatte bey dem offentlichen Gottesdienst der Kirche zu Bern.* Bern, 1761. (Prayer 349)

Church of Geneva, Church of Neufchatel. *The Liturgy used in the Churches of the Principality of Neufchatel . . . to which is added, The Forms of Prayer lately introduced into the Church of Geneva.* [Compiled by Jean-Frédéric Ostervald]. London, 1712. (Prayers 23, 43, 106, 146, 221, 382)

Church of Scotland. *The Book of Common Order Commonly called John Knox's Liturgy.* Translated into Gaelic 1567 by John Carswell. Edited by Thomas M'Lauchlan. Edinburgh, 1873. (Prayer 203)

—————. *The Scottish Hymnal.* Edinburgh: William Blackwood and Sons, 1889. (Prayer 483)

————. Committee on Public Worship and Aids to Devotion. *Forms of Prayer for Use at Sea.* [Edinburgh: n. p.] [c. 1910]. (Prayer 303)

————. *Book of Common Order, 1928, For use in Services and Offices of the Church.* London: Oxford University Press [1928]. (Prayers 281, 383)

————. *Book of Common Order of the Church of Scotland.* London: Oxford University Press, 1940. (Prayers 305, 306, 442)

————. Committee on Public Worship and Aids to Devotion. *Prayers for the Christian Year,* 2nd ed., rev. and enl. London: Oxford University Press, 1952. (Prayer 398)

————. Committee on Public Worship and Aids to Devotion. *Prayers for Sunday Services: Companion Volume to The Book of Common Order* (1979). Edinburgh: Saint Andrew Press, 1980. (Prayers 400, 404)

————. *Book of Common Order of the Church of Scotland.* Edinburgh: Saint Andrew Press, 1994. (Prayers 36, 73, 142, 318, 357, 376)

Church of South India. *The Book of Common Worship.* London: Oxford University Press, 1963. (Prayer 370)

Church of the Electoral Palatinate. *Chur-Pfaelzische Kirchen-Ordnung.* Heidelberg, 1684. (Prayers 15, 120, 379, 380, 390)

Church of the Servant. Worship Committee. Grand Rapids, Michigan. "Pentecost Liturgy." 1984. Photocopy. (Prayer 393)

Church of Zurich. *Liturgia Tigurina: Or, the Book of Common Prayers . . . usually practiced . . . in all the Churches and Chappels of the City and Canton of Zurick in Switzerland.* Translated by John C. Werndly. London, 1693. (Prayers 249, 258, 340)

Church Service Society, Members of. *Home Prayers.* Edinburgh: William Blackwood and Sons, 1879. (Prayers 13, 105, 290)

Church Service Society. *Book of Common Order. Daily Offices for Morning and Evening Prayer throughout the Week.* Edinburgh: William Blackwood and Sons, 1893. (Prayers 49, 58)

————. *Euchologion: A Book of Common Order.* 7th ed. Edinburgh: William Blackwood and Sons, 1896. (Prayer 195)

————. *The Book of Common Order of the Church of Scotland. Commonly known as John Knox's Liturgy.* Edited by G. W. Sprott. Edinburgh: William Blackwood and Sons, 1901. (Prayer 177)

Clarke, Samuel. *A Collection of the Lives of Ten Eminent Divines.* London, [1661–] 1662. (Prayer 188)

Collins, Thomas. *The Penitent Publican.* London, 1610. (Prayer 132)

Congregational Christian Churches. *Pilgrim Hymnal.* rev. ed. Boston: Pilgrim Press, 1935. (Prayer 121)

Costen, Melva W. "The Prayer Tradition of Black Americans." *Reformed Liturgy & Music* 15 (1981): 83–93. (Prayer 251)

Cowles, Helen M. *Grace Victorious: or, The Memoir of Helen M. Cowles.* Edited by [Henry Cowles]. Oberlin, OH, 1856. (Prayer 468)

Cross, Christopher, comp. and ed. *A Minute of Prayer: Prayers of All Faiths, for Every Purpose and Every Occasion.* New York: Pocket Books, 1954. (Prayer 444)

Crowley, Robert. *A brief discourse against the outwarde apparell.* London, 1566. (Prayer 37)

Cumberland Presbyterian Church and Presbyterian Church (U.S.A.). Office of Worship. *The Funeral: A Service of Witness to the Resurrection. The Worship of God.* Supplemental Liturgical Resource 4. Philadelphia: Westminster Press, 1986. (Prayer 424)

Davies, Samuel. *Miscellaneous Poems, Chiefly on Divine Subjects.* Williamsburg, VA, 1751. (Prayer 93)

Davy, Sarah. *Heaven Realiz'd, or The Holy Pleasure of daily intimate Communion with God.* London, 1670. (Prayers 184, 240, 329)

de Bèze, Théodore. *Maister Bezaes hovshold Prayers.* [Translated by John Barnes]. London, 1603. (Prayers 172, 179, 446)

———. *Chréstiennes Méditations.* Edited by Mario Richter. Textes Littéraires Français. Geneva: Librairie Droz, 1964. (Prayers 45, 114)

de Félice, Paul. *Les Protestants d'autrefois. Vie intérieure des églises.* 2nd ed. Paris: Librairie Fischbacher, 1897. (Prayer 492)

Defoe, Daniel. *The Meditations of Daniel Defoe.* Edited by George Harris Healey. Cummington, MA: The Cummington Press, 1946. (Prayers 19, 24)

de Gruchy, John, ed. *Cry Justice! Prayers, meditations and readings from South Africa.* London: Collins, 1986. (Prayer 115)

Deming, Dianne E. *A Time with Our Children: Stories for Use in Worship.* New York: Pilgrim Press, 1991. (Prayer 481)

Dent, Arthur. *The Plaine-Mans Path-Way to Heaven . . . & three praiers necessary to bee used in private families.* 25th ed. London, 1640. (Prayer 201)

Dering, Edward. *Godlye priuate Praiers for householders in their Families.* London, 1574. (Prayers 70, 187, 333)

Doddridge, Philip. *The Family Expositor.* [1739–1756] 5 vols. [Pr. from vol. 1] London, 1810. (Prayer 472)

———. *The Rise and Progress of Religion in the Soul.* [1745] Philadelphia, n.d. (Prayers 234, 266)

Drelincourt, Charles. *De l'honnevr qui doit estre rendv à la saincte et bien-hevrevse Vierge Marie. Avec une meditation sur l'incarnation et la naissance de nostre Seigneur & Sauueur Iesus-Christ.* [1634] Charenton, 1638. (Prayers 365, 367, 374, 392)

———. *The Christian's Defence Against the Fears of Death.* [1651] Translated by Marius D'Assigny. New ed. London, 1814. (Prayers 69, 314, 423, 433)

Duck, Ruth C., ed. *Flames of the Spirit: Resources for Worship.* New York: Pilgrim Press, 1985. (Prayer 449)

Duff, Alexander. *More Fruits from India; or, the Outcast safe in Christ. The Life and Happy Death of Charlotte Green.* Philadelphia, 1848. (Prayer 473)

Du Moulin, the Elder, Pierre. *The Christian Combate, or, A Treatise of Affliction.* [1622] Translated by John Bulteel. London, 1623. (Prayer 448)

———. *The Right Way to Heauen: Prayers and Meditations of the Faithful Soule.* Translated by [Richard Baily]. London, 1630. (Prayers 12, 192)

Du Moulin, the Elder, Pierre, Charles Drelincourt, and Raimond Gaches. *Recueil de préparations et prières pour la S. Cène.* Middelburg, 1665 (reprinted). (Prayers 352, 355)

Du Moulin, the Younger, Pierre. *A Week of Soliloquies and Prayers.* London, 1657. (Prayers 155, 174, 351)

Duplessis-Mornay, Philippe. *Discovrs et Meditations Chrestiennes.* Saumur, [1610–1611]. (Prayer 269)

Dykes, James Oswald. *Daily Prayers for a Household for a Month.* London: James Nisbet, 1881. (Prayer 484)

Ebrard, August, and Gerhard Goebel. *Reformirtes Kirchenbuch.* 2nd ed. Haale [an-der-Saale]: Max Niemeyer, 1889. (Prayer 377)

Edwards, Jonathan. *The Life of the Late Reverend, Learned and Pious Mr. Jonathan Edwards.* Edited by [Samuel Hopkins]. Boston, 1765. (Prayer 440)

Egerton, Stephen. *A Brief Methode of Catechizing.* [5th, 1597]. 22nd ed. London, 1615. (Prayer 497)

Evangelical Church in the Rhineland, Evangelical Church of Westphalia, Church of Lippe. *Evangelisches Gesangbuch.* Gütersloh: Gütersloher Verlagshaus; Bielefeld: Luther-Verlag GmbH; Neukirchener Verlag des Erziehungsvereins GmbH, 1996. (Prayer 317)

Evangelical Reformed Churches in German-speaking Switzerland. Liturgy Conference. *Liturgie.* Vol. 1. *Sonntagsgottesdienst.* Bern, 1972. (Prayers 54, 71, 163, 270, 286)

———. *Liturgie.* Vol. 2. *Festtagsgottesdienst.* Bern, 1974. (Prayer 362)

Evangelical Reformed Congregations in Lippe. *Gesangbuch für die kirchliche und häusliche Andacht.* 4th ed. Detmold: Meyersche Hofbuchhandlung (Max Staerke), 1925. (Prayer 182)

*Evangelisches Gesangbuch für Rheinland und Westfalen.* Dortmund: W. Crüwell, 1898. (Prayer 495)

Flavel, John. *Husbandry Spiritualiz'd and Navigation Spiritualiz'd,* in *The Whole Works of the Reverend Mr. John Flavel.* 2 vols. London, 1701. (Prayers 18, 218, 284)

Fleming, Daniel, ed. *The World at One in Prayer.* New York: Harper and Brothers, 1942. (Prayers 237, 289)

Free Church of Scotland. Public Worship Association. *A New Directory for the Public Worship of God.* 2nd ed. Edinburgh: Macniven and Wallace, 1898. (Prayer 225)

*Garden of Spiritual Flowers.* [1609] Planted by Richard Rogers, William Perkins, Richard Greenham, [Matthew Mead], and George Webb. London, 1687. (Prayer 16)

Gaunt, Alan. *Prayers for the Christian Year.* Section D (Easter 1–Pentecost 21). Leeds, England: John Paul The Preacher's Press, 1982. (Prayer 138)

Geneva Bible. *The Holy Bible, That is, The Holy Scriptvres Contained in The Old and New Testament.* Edinburgh, 1610. (Prayer 335)

German Reformed Church in the United States of America. *A Liturgy, or, Order of Christian Worship.* Philadelphia, 1857. (Prayers 32, 260, 395)

Goddard, Josiah. *A New and Beautiful Collection of Select Hymns and Spiritual Songs.* Conway, MA, 1798. (Prayer 295)

Good, James I. *Aid to the Heidelberg Catechism.* Cleveland, OH: Central Publishing House, 1904. (Prayer 479)

Good, Jeremiah H. *Prayer Book and Aids to Private Devotions.* Tiffin, OH: E. R. Good, 1894. (Prayer 491)

Gouge, William. *A Short Catechisme.* 3rd ed. London, 1621. (Prayer 338)

———. *Of Domesticall Duties.* 2nd ed. London, 1626. (Prayers 405, 411, 412)

Goulart, Simon. *The Wise Vieillard, or Old Man.* Translated by [T. Williamson?]. London, 1621. (Prayer 430)

Graham, Isabella. *The Power of Faith: Exemplified in the Life and Writings of the Late Mrs. Isabella Graham.* Edited by [Joanna Bethune and Divie Bethune]. London, 1816. (Prayers 253, 477)

Green, Ashbel. "A Prayer" published with William Rogers, *An Oration, Delivered July 4, 1789 at The Presbyterian Church, in Arch Street, Philadelphia.* Philadelphia, 1789. (Prayer 299)

Grimké, Francis J. *Stray Thoughts and Meditations,* vol. 3 in *The Works of Francis J. Grimké,* edited by Carter G. Woodson. Washington, D.C.: Associated Publishers, 1942. (Prayer 343)

Grove, Henry. *A Discourse Concerning the Nature and Design of the Lord's*

*Supper . . . To which are added . . . Devotional Exercises . . . .* 3rd ed. Dublin, 1738. (Prayer 348)

Guillaume, George (Willem, Georg). *Entretiens Solitaires d'une Ame Dévote avec son Dieu.* [1693?] 1st Pt. 4th ed. Amsterdam, 1745. (Prayers 7, 241, 250)

Harbaugh, Henry. *The Golden Censer.* Philadelphia, 1860. (Prayers 261, 354, 388, 389, 394)

Harris, Howell. *The Last Message, and Dying Testimony of Howell Harris, Esqr.; Late of Trevecka in Wales.* Trevecka, 1774. (Prayer 17)

Hatfield, Edwin F., comp. *Freedom's Lyre: or, Psalms, Hymns and Sacred Songs for the Slave and His Friends.* New York, 1840. (Prayer 79)

Henry, Matthew. *An Account of the Life and Death of Mr. Philip Henry.* [1698] 4th ed. [Shrewsbury], 1765. (Prayer 469)

———. *A Method for Prayer* [1710]. Philadelphia, 1831. (Prayers 60, 98, 128, 226, 309)

Heywood, Oliver. *The Rev. Oliver Heywood, B.A. 1630–1702; His Autobiography, Diaries, Anecdote and Event Books.* Edited by H. Horsfall Turner. 4 vols. Brighouse and Bingley: 1882–1885. [Pr. from vol. 1] (Prayer 248)

Hieron, Samuel. *A Helpe Vnto Devotion.* 14th ed. London, 1634. (Prayer 336)

Hornus, Jean-Michel, ed. "La Prière du Soir et Confession des péchés calviniste d'un officier de dragons de Louis XIV." *Bulletin de la Société de l'Histoire du Protestantisme Français.* 126 (1980): 229–239. (Prayers 135, 176)

Housman, Hannah Pearsall. *The Power and Pleasure of the Divine Life: Exemplify'd in the late Mrs. [Hannah Pearsall] Housman of Kidderminster, Worcestershire* [1744]. Edited by Richard Pearsall. 2nd ed. Boston, 1755. (Prayer 476)

Howat, Peter. "A Form of Service." In George W. Sprott, ed., *Scottish Liturgies of the Reign of James VI. The Book of Common Prayer.* Edinburgh, 1871. (Prayers 94, 156, 337)

Howell, A. R. *Church Prayers for War-Time For Use in Presbyterian and Other Churches.* London: Oxford University Press, 1940. (Prayer 443)

Huber, Jane Parker. "Prayer of Intercession" for the Communion Service of the 1985 General Assembly of the Presbyterian Church (U.S.A.) [Indianapolis, Indiana]. Typescript with letter to the author. March 21, 1988. (Prayer 324)

Hunter, John. *Devotional Services for Public Worship.* [1886] 6th ed. Glasgow: James Maclehose and Sons, 1895. (Prayers 170, 216, 385, 478)

Huxtable, John, John Marsh, Romilly Micklem, and James Todd, comps. *A Book of Public Worship Compiled for the Use of Congregationalists.* 2nd ed. London: Oxford University Press, 1949. (Prayer 445)

Immens, Petrus. *The Pious Communicant Encouraged.* Translated by John Bassett [from a 1758 printing in Amsterdam]. 2 vols. New York, 1801–1802. [Pr. from vol. 1] (Prayer 255)

Jay, William. *Prayers for the Use of Families; or, The Domestic Minister's Assistant.* [1820] Philadelphia, 1834. (Prayers 494, 496)

Joscelin, Elizabeth. *The Mothers Legacie.* London, 1624. (Prayers 62, 113)

Kagawa, Toyohiko. *Meditations.* Translated by Jiro Takenaka. New York: Harper and Brothers Publishers, 1950. (Prayer 453)

Kenyatta, Jomo. *Facing Mount Kenya: The Tribal Life of the Gikuyu.* London: Secker and Warburg, 1938. (Prayer 20)

*Kern Alter und neuer, in 700. bestehender Geistreicher Lieder.* [Germantown, Penn.], 1752. (Prayer 271)

Lawrence, Amos. *Extracts from the Diary and Correspondence of the Late Amos Lawrence.* Edited by William R. Lawrence. Boston, 1855. (Prayer 11)

Lee, Robert. *Prayers for Family Worship.* Edinburgh, 1861. (Prayer 90)

———. *The Order of Public Worship.* Edinburgh, [1865]. (Prayer 307)

Leechman, William. *The Nature, Reasonableness, and Advantages of Prayer.* Glasgow, 1743. (Prayers 224, 310)

Leigh, Dorothy. *The Mothers Blessing.* London, 1616. (Prayer 126)

Leighton, Robert. *The Genuine Works of Robt. Leighton.* New ed. 4 vols. London, 1812. [Prs. from vol. 2] (Prayers 238, 323)

Liston, William. *The Service of God's House, or Forms for the Guidance of Ministers and Heads of Families.* 2nd ed. Glasglow, 1866. (Prayer 125)

Loh, Hui-chin, and I-to Loh. Typescript with letter to the author. May 4, 1990. (Prayer 9)

M'Crie, Charles Creig. *The Public Worship of Presbyterian Scotland.* Edinburgh: William Blackwood and Sons, 1892. (Prayer 104)

MacKenzie, Jean Kenyon. *An African Trail.* West Medford, MA: Central Committee on the United Study of Foreign Missions, 1917. (Prayers 108, 183)

Maclaren, Ian [John Watson]. *Beside the Bonnie Brier Bush.* New York: Dodd, Mead and Co., 1895. (Prayer 273ab)

MacLean Watt, Lauchlan. *Prayers for Public Worship* (*Service Book, Glasgow Cathedral*). London: H. R. Allenson, [1924]. (Prayer 375)

MacLeod, George F. *The Whole Earth Shall Cry Glory.* Glasgow: Wild Goose Publications, 1985. (Prayer 215)

MacLeod [The Younger], Norman. *The Home Preacher, or Church in the House.* Glasgow, [1868–1869]. (Prayers 205, 409)

Malan, César. *Chants de Sion*. Paris, 1841. (Prayer 157)

Marguerite of Navarre. *Les Marguerites de la Marguerite des Princesses*. 1547 ed. Edited by Felix Frank. Paris, 1873. (Prayers 63, 103, 301, 313)

―――. *The Mirror of the Sinful Soul*. 1544 trans. by Princess (afterwards Queen) Elizabeth. Edited by Percy W. Ames. Royal Society of Literature in the United Kingdom. Facs. ed. London: Asher, 1897. (Prayer 223)

*Mariner's Divine Mate: Or, Spiritual Navigation Improved*, by [J. J.]. Boston, 1715. (Prayer 325)

Martyr Vermigli, Peter. *Preces Sacrae ex Psalmis Davidis*. [1564] Zurich, 1566. (Prayers 88, 95)

Mather, Cotton. *The Negro Christianized*. Boston, 1706. (Prayer 149)

―――. *Diary of Cotton Mather*. Edited by [Worthington Chauncey Ford]. Vol. 1. *Massachusetts Historical Society Collections*, vol. 7. 7th series. Boston, 1911. (Prayer 41)

Mather, Increase. "Autobiography of Increase Mather." Edited by M. G. Hall. *Proceedings of the American Antiquarian Society*. n.s. 71 (1961): 271–360. (Prayer 198)

May, William. *The Family Prayer Book*. 4th ed. Abridged by [S. Palmer]. London, 1815. (Prayer 129)

Mayhew, Experience. *Indian Converts: or, Some Account Of the Lives and Dying Speeches, of a Considerable Number of the Christianized Indians of Marthas Vineyard in New-England*. London, 1727. (Prayers 169, 158, 161, 167)

Meikle, Jame. *Solitude Sweetened*. [1803] New ed. Edinburgh, 1843. (Prayer 470)

Merivale, Samuel. *Daily Devotions for the Closet*. 3rd ed. Edited by [J. Hogg]. London, 1796. (Prayers 29, 44, 99)

Micklem, Caryl, ed. *Contemporary Prayers for Church and School*. London: SCM Press, 1975. (Prayer 220)

Miller, Colin F. *Prayers for Parish Worship*. London: Oxford University Press, 1948. (Prayers 175, 371, 372, 373)

Morison, John. *The Book of Family Devotions for the Morning and Evening of Every Day in the Year*. Glasgow, 1861. (Prayer 319)

Murrey, Robert. *Closet Devotions*. Preface by Matthew Henry. London, 1713. (Prayer 202)

Netherlands Reformed Church, Walloon Synod. *Les Pseaumes de David . . . Dévotions Particulières pour se préparer à la Sainte Céne*. New ed. The Hague, 1730. (Prayer 347)

Netherlands Reformed Church. *Dienstboek voor de Nederlandse Hervormde Kerk*. Draft. The Hague: Boekencentrum, N.V., 1955. (Prayers 275, 361, 396, 410, 456, 490)

Netherlands Reformed Church, Reformed Churches in the Netherlands. Service Book Commission of the Cooperative Working Party on Worship. *Liturgie in Dagen van Rouw.* Proeven voor de Eredienst, no. 1. Leidschendam, 1987. (Prayers 425, 428)

Niebuhr, Reinhold. *Justice and Mercy.* Edited by Ursula M. Niebuhr. New York: Harper and Row Publishers, 1974. (Prayer 109)

Norden, John. *A pensiue mans practice.* London, 1584. (Prayer 406)

———. *An eye to Heauen in Earth, A Necessarie Watch for the time of Death.* London, 1619. (Prayer 434)

———. *A Poore Mans Rest . . . true Consolation in all Kinds and Times of Affliction.* 8th time augmented and much reformed by the author. London, 1620. (Prayer 210)

———. *The Imitation of David . . . Meditations and Prayers out of the 27. Psalme.* London, 1624. (Prayer 297)

———. *A Progress of Piety.* [1591 and 1596 eds.] Reprint. Parker Society, Vol. 30. Cambridge, 1847. (Prayers 186, 282, 451)

Oecolampadius, Johannes. *Das Testament Jhesu Christi.* Zwickau [Germany], 1523. (Prayers 40, 232, 384)

Oglesby, Stuart R. *Prayers for All Occasions.* Atlanta: John Knox Press, 1940. (Prayer 482)

Old, Hughes Oliphant. *Leading in Prayer: A Workbook for Worship.* Grand Rapids, MI: William B. Eerdmans Publishing Co., 1995. (Prayer 283)

O'Neale, Sondra A. *Jupiter Hammon and the Biblical Beginnings of African-American Literature.* ATLA Monograph Series, No. 28. Metuchen, N.J.: American Theological Library Association and Scarecrow Press, 1993. (Prayer 247)

Orchard, William, ed. *The Order of Divine Service for Public Worship.* 2nd ed. London: Oxford University Press, 1926. (Prayer 401)

Osborn, Sarah. *Memoirs of the Life of Mrs. Sarah Osborn.* Edited by Samuel Hopkins. Worcester, MA, 1799. (Prayers 26, 65, 117, 140, 165, 173, 193, 214, 230, 244, 363, 465)

Paget, Eusebius. *Short Questions and answeares.* [1579] London, 1614. (Prayer 334)

Pawelzik, Fritz, ed. *I Sing Your Praise All the Day Long: Young Africans at Prayer.* New York: Friendship Press, 1967. (Prayers 159, 199)

Pitcairn, William F. *Prayers for the Use Specially of such Families as are in Trades, or in Oppressive Toil, or in Sickness or in Poverty.* 3rd ed. Edinburgh, [ca. 1873]. (Prayer 61)

*Prayer-Book for Families and other Private Persons.* Glasgow, [1850?]. (Prayer 85)

Presbyterian Church in Canada. General Assembly. *The Book of Family Devotion*. Toronto: Oxford University Press, 1919. (Prayers 30, 407, 438)

Presbyterian Church in the U.S.A. *The Book of Common Worship*. Philadelphia: Presbyterian Board of Publication and Sabbath-School Work, 1906. (Prayer 488)

Presbyterian Church of Ghana. *Liturgy and Service Book*. Vol. 2. Accra, Ghana: Presbyterian Book Depot, 1966. (Prayers 300, 387)

Presbyterian Church (U.S.A.). *The Presbyterian Hymnal: Hymns, Psalms, and Spiritual Songs*. Louisville: Westminster/John Knox Press, 1990. (Prayer 1)

Presbyterian Church (U.S.A.). Cumberland Presbyterian Church. Theology and Worship Ministry Unit. *Book of Common Worship*. Louisville: Westminster/John Knox Press, 1993. (Prayers 331, 421)

Presbyterian Church (U.S.A.). Stewardship Education, Congregational Ministries Division. *Stewardship 1996*. Part One. Louisville, 1996. (Prayer 42)

Preston, John. *The Onely Love of the Chiefest of Ten Thousand: or An Heavenly Treatise of the Divine Love of Christ*. London, 1640. (Prayers 56, 107)

Prynne, William. *Movnt Orgveil: or Divine and Profitable Meditations*. London, 1641. (Prayer 475)

*Le Psavltier, qui est le Livre des Pseavmes de David . . . extraites des Commentaires de M. Iean Caluin, Auec Oraisons en la fin de chacun Pseaume*. [Geneva], 1558. (Prayer 257)

*Les Pseavmes de David. mis en rime Francoise par Clement Marot, & Theodore de Beze. Auec . . . vne Oraison a la fin d'vn chacun Pseaume, par M. Augustin Marlorat*. [1567] Geneva, 1577. (Prayers 53, 133, 227, 259, 287, 454)

Ramsay, Martha Laurens. *Memoirs of the Life of Martha Laurens Ramsay*. Edited by David Ramsay. Charleston, SC, 1812. (Prayers 242, 328)

Ray, H. Cordelia. *Poems*. New York: Grafton Press, 1910. Facs. reprint In Joan R. Sherman, ed. *Collected Black Women's Poetry*, Vol. 3. The Schomburg Library of Nineteenth-Century Black Women Writers. New York: Oxford University Press, 1988. (Prayer 386)

Reformed Church in America. *The Liturgy of the Reformed Church in America together with the Psalter*. New York: Board of Publication and Bible-School Work, 1915. (Prayer 441)

————. Commission on Worship. *Worship the Lord*. Edited by James R. Esther and Donald J. Bruggink. New York: Reformed Church in America. Grand Rapids, MI: William B. Eerdmans Publishing Co., 1987. (Prayers 418, 420)

Reformed Church in the United States. *An Order of Worship for the Reformed Church*. 5th ed. Philadelphia, 1866. (Prayer 399)

Reformed Church of France. *Liturgie des Églises Réformées de France*. Paris: Berger-Levrault et Cie, 1897. (Prayer 391)

————. *Liturgie*. Paris: Éditions Berger-Levrault, 1963. (Prayers 82, 84, 102, 427)

Reformed Church of the Canton of Berne. *Liturgie Pour Les Paroisses De Langue Française*. Vol. 1 *Le Culte*. [Berne], 1955. (Prayers 47, 97, 141, 197, 288, 378, 397)

Rich, Mary. *Occasional Meditations Upon Sundry Subjects*. Edited by Anthony Walker. London, 1678. (Prayers 22, 162)

Roberts, Francis. *A Communicant Instructed: or, Practical Directions For Worthy Receiuing of the Lords-Supper*. [1651] 3rd ed. London, 1659. (Prayer 359)

Robinson, William H. *Phillis Wheatley and Her Writings*. Critical Studies on Black Life and Culture, no. 12. New York: Garland Publishing, 1984. (Prayer 124)

Rose, Hugh. *Meditations on Several Interesting Subjects*. Edinburgh, 1762. (Prayer 267)

Rous, Francis. *The Mystical Marriage*. London, 1656. (Prayer 296)

Rowe, Elizabeth Singer. *The Miscellaneous Works in Prose and Verse of Mrs. Elizabeth Rowe*. Edited by Theophilus Rowe. 2 vols. London, 1739. (Prayer 35)

————. *Devout Exercises of the Heart*. [1737] Edited by Isaac Watts. Alcester, 1814. (Prayers 76, 81, 178, 208)

Sampson, Thomas. *Prayers and Meditations Apostolike*. Cambridge, 1593. (Prayer 148)

Schuller, Robert H. *Positive Prayers for Power-Filled Living*. New York: Hawthorn Books, 1976. (Prayer 426)

Sergio, Lisa, ed. *Prayers of Women*. New York: Harper and Row, 1965. (Prayer 500)

Shepherd, J. Barrie. *Diary of Daily Prayer*. Minneapolis: Augsburg Publishing House, 1975. (Prayer 285)

Sherman, Joan R., ed. *African-American Poetry of the Nineteenth Century: An Anthology*. Urbana: University of Illinois Press, 1992. (Prayer 38)

Smith, Elwyn A. *A Spiritual Exercise for the Grieving*. Philadelphia: Fortress Press, 1984. (Prayer 429)

————. *A Spiritual Exercise for New Parents*. Philadelphia: Fortress Press, 1986. (Prayer 408)

Smith, George. *The Domestic Prayer Book, or, a Course of Morning and Evening Prayers, for One Month*. London, 1844. (Prayers 33, 39, 330, 462)

Smith, Henry. *The Soules Comfort Containing Godly Prayers and Meditations for the Comfort of the Afflicted*. London, 1609. (Prayers 256, 277)

———. *Six Sermons . . . Two Zealous Prayers.* London, 1614. (Prayers 229, 298)

———. *The Works of Henry Smith,* 2 vols. Edinburgh, 1866–1867. [Pr. from vol. 2] (Prayers 123, 189, 263)

Smith, Sarah Huntington. *Memoir of Mrs. Sarah L. Huntington Smith.* [1839], 3rd ed. Edited by Edward W. Hooker. New York, 1845. (Prayer 437)

Song, Choan-Seng, ed. and trans. *Testimonies of Faith: Letters and Poems from Prison in Taiwan.* Studies from the World Alliance of Reformed Churches, no. 5. [Switzerland] [1984]. (Prayers 118, 122, 154, 480)

Sorocold, Thomas. *Supplications of Saints. A Book of Prayers and Prayses.* [3rd, 1612] 25th ed. London, 1639. (Prayers 2, 74, 116, 217, 235, 276, 304, 381, 489, 499)

Sparke, Michael, comp. *Crvmbs of Comfort and Godly Prayer.* [6th ed. 1627]. 42nd ed. [London], [1722?]. (Prayers 181, 356)

———. *Crumms of Comfort. The Second Part.* London, 1652. (Prayers 27, 206)

Stephens, John Underwood. *Prayers of the Christian Life for Private and Public Worship.* New York: Oxford University Press, 1952. (Prayers 6, 28, 134, 233, 413)

Stevenson, Robert Louis. *Prayers Written at Vailima.* New York: Charles Scribner's Sons, 1904. (Prayer 21)

Stoudt, John Joseph, trans. and ed. *Private Devotions for Home and Church.* Philadelphia: Christian Education Press, 1956. (Prayer 274)

Stratton, Joseph B. *Prayers for the Use of Families.* Richmond, VA: Presbyterian Committee of Publication, 1888. (Prayers 31, 34)

Stubbes, Philip. *A Christal Glasse for Christian Women . . . the godly life and Christian death of Mistresse Katherine Stubs.* London, 1592. (Prayer 436)

Ten Harmsel, Henrietta, trans. *Jacobus Revius: Dutch Metaphysical Poet— Selected Poems.* Detroit: Wayne State University Press, 1968. (Prayer 366)

Todd, James M. *Prayers and Services for Christian Festivals.* 2nd ed. London: Independent Press, 1959. (Prayers 72, 403)

Toussaint, Daniel. *The Exercise of the faithfull soule.* Translated by Fernando Filding. London, 1583. (Prayer 86)

United Church of Christ. Board for Homeland Ministries. *Services of the Church: 8 The Collects for the Christian Year.* Philadelphia: United Church Press, 1969. (Prayer 360)

———. Office for Church Life and Leadership. *Book of Worship.* New York: United Church of Christ, 1986. (Prayer 194)

United Evangelical-Protestant Church of Baden. *Kirchenbuch.* Draft. Karlsruhe, 1930. (Prayer 185)

United Free Church of Scotland. Church Worship Association. *Anthology of Prayers for Public Worship*. Edinburgh: Macniven and Wallace, 1907. (Prayers 46, 152)

United Reformed Church in the United Kingdom. *The Word and the World*, The Prayer Handbook for 1986. Edited by Edmund Banyard. [London: United Reformed Church], [1986]. (Prayer 493)

Uniting Church in Australia. Assembly Commission on Liturgy. *Uniting in Worship: Leader's Book*. Melbourne: Uniting Church Press, 1988. (Prayers 5, 48, 204, 321, 345, 422)

———. Assembly Commission on Liturgy. *Uniting in Worship: People's Book*. Melbourne: Uniting Church Press, 1988. (Prayer 92)

Van Dyke, Henry. *The Spirit of Christmas*. New York: Charles Scribner's Sons, 1905. (Prayer 369)

Vanuatu, Luganville. Talua Ministry Training Centre. Presbyterian Church of Vanuatu. Typescript with letter to the author from Varisipiti Livo, May 8, 1990. (Prayers 137, 278)

Vincent, Nathanael. *The Spirit of Prayer . . . Unto which is added, A Direction for the Attaining the Gift of Prayer, That Family-Duty may not be Omitted, nor Secret-Duty Discouraged, through Inability of Utterance and Expression*. London, 1674. (Prayer 339)

Waddell, Helen. Manuscript photocopy with letter to the author from Mollie Martin, March 31, 1989. (Prayers 143, 245)

Waldegrave, Robert? *A Castle for the Soule: Containing many godly prayers*. London, 1578. (Prayers 25, 262)

Watson, Charles E. *The Rodborough Bede Book*. [Privately printed, 1930]. Reprint: London: Independent Press, 1943. (Prayers 139, 209)

Watts, Isaac. *Guide to Prayer* [1715] and *Prayers, Composed for the Use and Imitation of Children* [1728]. In *The Works of the Late and Reverend Isaac Watts*, vol. 3. Edited by Dr. Jennings and P. Doddridge. London, 1753. (Prayers 89, 236, 315, 419, 452)

Weatherhogg, Neil. *Hope, Healing and Hospitals: Christian Reflections on Illness and Health for Use by Hospital Patients and Others Facing Illness*. [n.p., privately printed, 1978]. (Prayer 414)

Weir, James Wallace. *The Closet Companion: A Manual of Prayer*. Philadelphia, 1854. (Prayer 460)

———. *Home Worship*. Philadelphia: Presbyterian Board of Publication, 1879. (Prayer 57)

West, Elisabeth. *Memoirs, or Spiritual Exercises of Elisabeth West*. Glasgow, 1766. (Prayer 67)

Whitefield, George. *The Christian's Companion: or, Sermons . . . to which are added, Several Prayers*. London, 1739. (Prayer 447)

Whitfield, Henry. *Strength out of Weakness: or a Glorious Manifestation of the Further Progress of the Gospel among the Indians in New England* [1652]. Sabin's Reprints. New York, 1865. (Prayer 464)

Williams, John. *A Narrative of Missionary Enterprises in the South Sea Islands.* New York, 1837. (Prayer 346)

Williams, John Bickerton. *The Henry Family Memorialized.* London, [1849]. (Prayer 471)

Willison, John. *Sacramental Meditations.* [1747] Newport, 1794. (Prayer 292)

———. *The Afflicted Man's Companion* [1737] New ed. Philadelphia, 1844. (Prayer 75)

Witherspoon, John. "A Practical Treatise on Regeneration," In *The Works of The Rev. John Witherspoon.* [4 vols.] Philadelphia, 1800. [Pr. from vol. 1] (Prayer 160)

Woodward, Hezekiah. *The Churches Thank-Offering to God.* London, 1642. (Prayers 136, 166, 439, 463, 466)

Wright, Samuel, ed. *Christian Directions Shewing How to Walk with God All the Day Long,* by Thomas Gouge, London, 1742. (Prayers 279, 498)

Wright, Thomas. *The Morning and Evening Sacrifice; or, Prayers for Private Persons and Families.* Edinburgh, 1823. (Prayer 327)

Zollikofer, Georg Joachim. *Devotional Exercises and Prayers.* [1785] Translated by William Tooke. London, 1815. (Prayer 50)

Zwingli, Huldrych. *A Short Pathwaye to the ryghte and true understanding of the holye and sacred Scriptures.* Translated by J. Vernon. Worcester, 1550. (Prayer 332)

———. "Action oder Bruch des Nachtmals." (1525) In *Codex Liturgicus,* vol. 3: *Ecclesiae Reformatae Atque Anglicanae.* Edited by Hermann Adalbert Daniel. Leipzig, 1851. (Prayer 293)

———. "Epichiresis" (1523) In Julius Smend, *Die Evangelischen Deutschen Messen bis zu Luthers Deutscher Messe.* Göttingen: Vandenhoeck und Ruprecht, 1896. (Prayer 350)

# Permission Acknowledgments

Grateful acknowledgment is made to the following authors and copyright holders for permission to reproduce the prayers in this book.

**Prayer 1**
From "Many and Great, O God, Are Thy Things," in *The Presbyterian Hymnal* (1990), no. 271.

**Prayer 5**
From *Uniting in Worship: Leader's Book* (1988), p. 423. The Uniting Church in Australia, National Working Group on Worship. Used with permission.

**Prayer 6**
From *Prayers of the Christian Life for Private and Public Worship,* by John Underwood Stevens (1952), p. 8. Used by permission of Horace D. Stephens.

**Prayer 7**
Translated by David H. Tripp, Ph.D. Used with permission.

**Prayer 9**
Used by permission of the authors.

**Prayer 15**
Translated by David H. Tripp, Ph.D. Used with permission.

**Prayer 19**
From *Meditations of Daniel Defoe,* edited by George Harris Healey (1946), p. 10.

**Prayer 20**
Adapted from *Facing Mount Kenya: The Tribal Life of the Gikuyu,* by Jomo Kenyatta, London: Secker & Warburg (1938; reprint 1953), p. 278. Used and altered by permission of The Random House Archive & Library.

**Prayer 24**
From *Meditations of Daniel Defoe,* edited by George Harris Healey (1946), pp. 6–8.

**Prayer 25**
From *A Castle for the Soule,* possibly (1578) by Robert Waldegrave. From a copy owned by the Folger Shakespeare Library, Washington, D.C.

**Prayer 28**
From *Prayers of the Christian Life for Private and Public Worship,* by John Underwood Stephens (1952), p. 41. Used by permission of Horace D. Stephens.

**Prayer 30**
From *The Book of Family Devotion,* pp. 11–12. General Assembly of the Presbyterian Church in Canada, Oxford University Press, Toronto, 1919.

**Prayer 36**
From *Book of Common Order of the Church of Scotland,* pp. 495–496 (1994). Used by permission of the Church of Scotland, Office for Worship.

**Prayer 38**
From "Hydromel and Rue," by George Marion McClellan in *African-American Poetry of the Nineteenth Century,* edited by Joan R. Sherman (1992), p. 429.

**Prayer 40**
Translated by David H. Tripp, Ph.D. Used with permission.

**Prayer 42**
From *Stewardship 1996,* Part One (1996), p. 7, a resource prepared by the Stewardship Education Team, a ministry of the General Assembly Council, Presbyterian Church (U.S.A.). Used and amended by permission.

**Prayer 45**
From *Chréstiennes Méditations,* by Théodore de Bèze, edited by Mario Richter. Textes Littéraires Français (1964), p. 45. Used by permission of the publisher. Translated by David H. Tripp, Ph.D. Used with permission.

**Prayer 47**
From *Liturgie pour les Paroisses de Langue Française,* p. 98, vol. 1 (1955). Used and translated with the permission of the Evangelical-Reformed Churches of the Canton Bern-Jura. Translated by David H. Tripp. Used with permission.

**Prayer 48**
From *Uniting in Worship: Leader's Book* (1988), p. 641. The Uniting Church in Australia, National Working Group on Worship. Used with permission.

**Prayer 53**
Translated by David H. Tripp, Ph.D. Used with permission.

**Prayer 54**
From *Liturgie,* vol. 1: *Sonntagsgottesdienst* (1972), p. 202. Prayer by S. Läuchli. Used by permission of the Liturgy Commission of the Evangelical Reformed Churches in German-speaking Switzerland. Translated by David H. Tripp, Ph.D. Used with permission.

**Prayer 55**
From *Prayers for My Village,* p. 53. English translation © 1994 by Lamar Williamson. Used by permission of Upper Room Books, Editions et Librairies Oberlin, and the author.

**Prayer 63**
Translated by David H. Tripp, Ph.D. Used with permission.

**Prayer 66**
From *Prayer,* by Karl Barth, pp. 91–92. Translated by Sara F. Terrien and edited by Don E. Saliers. 2nd edition (1985). Prayer translated by Keith Crim. Used by permission of Westminster John Knox Press.

**Prayer 71**
From *Liturgie,* vol. 1: *Sonntagsgottesdienst* (1972), p. 232. Used by permission of the Liturgy Commission of the Evangelical Reformed Churches in German-speaking Switzerland. Translated by David H. Tripp, Ph.D. Used with permission.

**Prayer 72**

From James M. Todd, *Prayers and Services for Christian Festivals,* p. 37. 2nd ed. Independent Press 1959, London, now The United Reformed Church. Used by permission.

**Prayer 73**

From *Book of Common Order of the Church of Scotland* (1994), p. 74. Used by permission of the Church of Scotland, Office for Worship.

**Prayer 82**

From *Liturgie* (1963), pp. 21–22. Used by permission of the General Secretary and the Committee for Liturgy of the Reformed Church of France. Translated by David H. Tripp, Ph.D. Used with permission.

**Prayer 84**

From *Liturgie* (1963), p. 83. Used by permission of the General Secretary and the Committee for Liturgy of the Reformed Church of France. Translated by David H. Tripp, Ph.D. Used with permission.

**Prayer 88**

Translated by David H. Tripp, Ph.D. Used with permission.

**Prayer 92**

From *Uniting in Worship: People's Book* (1988), p. 233. The Uniting Church in Australia, National Working Group on Worship. Used with permission.

**Prayer 95**

Translated by David H. Tripp, Ph.D. Used with permission.

**Prayer 97**

From *Liturgie pour les Paroisses de Langue Française,* p. 96, vol. 1 (1955). Used and translated with the permission of the Evangelical-Reformed Churches of the Canton Bern-Jura. Translated by David H. Tripp, Ph.D. Used with permission.

**Prayer 102**

From *Liturgie* (1963), p. 21. Used by permission of the General Secretary and the Committee for Liturgy of the Reformed Church of France. Translated by David H. Tripp, Ph.D. Used with permission.

**Prayer 103**

Translated by David H. Tripp, Ph.D. Used with permission.

**Prayer 109**

From *Justice and Mercy,* by Reinhold Niebuhr, edited by Ursula M. Niebuhr (1974), p. 11. Courtesy of the Estate of Reinhold Niebuhr.

**Prayer 112**

From *Epilogues and Prayers*, by William Barclay, (1963) pp. 172–173. Used by permission of the publisher, SCM Press.

**Prayer 114**

From *Chréstiennes Méditations* by Théodore de Bèze, edited by Mario Richter. Textes Littéraires Français (1964), pp. 75–76. Used by permission of the publisher. Translated by David H. Tripp, Ph.D. Used with permission.

**Prayer 115**
From *Cry Justice! Prayers, meditations and readings from South Africa,* edited by John de Gruchy (1986), pp. 219–220. Used by permission of HarperCollins Publishers Ltd.

**Prayer 118**
From *Testimonies of Faith: Letters and Poems from Prison in Taiwan,* edited and translated by Choan-Seng Song (1984), p. 60. Used by permission of the World Alliance of Reformed Churches.

**Prayer 120**
Translated by David H. Tripp, Ph.D. Used with permission.

**Prayer 121**
From *The Pilgrim Hymnal* (1935 rev. ed.), p. 52. Reprinted with the permission of The Pilgrim Press.

**Prayer 122**
Excerpt from *Testimonies of Faith: Letters and Poems from Prison in Taiwan,* edited and translated by Choan-Seng Song (1984), p. 85. Used by permission of the World Alliance of Reformed Churches.

**Prayer 124**
Excerpt from "On the Death of the Rev. Dr. Sewell, 1769," in *Phillis Wheatley and Her Writings,* by William H. Robinson (1984), p. 20. Used with permission of Garland Publishing.

**Prayer 127**
Prayer as submitted from THE HUNGERING DARK by FREDERICK BUECHNER, p. 24. Copyright © 1969 by Frederick Buechner. Reprinted by permission of HarperCollins Publishers, Inc.

**Prayer 133**
Translated by David H. Tripp, Ph.D. Used with permission.

**Prayer 134**
From *Prayers of the Christian Life for Private and Public Worship,* by John Underwood Stephens (1952), p. 45. Used by permission of Horace D. Stephens.

**Prayer 135**
From *Bulletin de la Société de l'Histoire du Protestantisme Français,* CXXVI (126) (1980, pp. 229–239). Used by permission. Translated by David H. Tripp, Ph.D. Used with permission.

**Prayer 137**
From Presbyterians of the Republic of Vanuatu, Talua Ministry Training Centre, Luganville, Vanuatu. Typescript dated May 8, 1990. Permission sought.

**Prayer 138**
From *Prayers for the Christian Year.* Sect. D, by Alan Gaunt (1982). Copyright © 1982 Alan Gaunt, published by John Paul the Preacher's Press. Used with permission.

**Prayer 139**
From Charles E. Watson, *The Rodborough Bede Book,* Independent Press 1943, London, now The United Reformed Church. Used by permission.

**Prayer 141**
From *Liturgie pour les Paroisses de Langue Française,* vol. 1, p. 103 (1955). Used and translated with the permission of the Evangelical-Reformed Churches of the Canton Bern-Jura. Translated by David H. Tripp, Ph.D. Used with permission.

**Prayer 142**
From *Book of Common Order of the Church of Scotland* (1994), pp. 39–40. Used by permission of the Church of Scotland, Office for Worship.

**Prayer 143**
Adapted and abridged from a manuscript photocopy supplied by and used with the permission of Mollie M. Martin.

**Prayer 154**
From *Testimonies of Faith: Letters and Poems from Prison in Taiwan,* edited and translated by Choan-Seng Song (1984), p. 44. Used by permission of the World Alliance of Reformed Churches.

**Prayer 157**
Translated by David H. Tripp, Ph.D. Used by permission.

**Prayer 159**
"I Lie Down to Sleep," from *I Sing Your Praise All the Day Long: Young Africans at Prayer,* edited by Fritz Pawelzik, p. 62. Copyright © 1967 by Friendship Press, Inc. Used by permission.

**Prayer 161**
Translated by David H. Tripp, Ph.D. Used with permission.

**Prayer 163**
From *Liturgie,* vol. 1: *Sonntagsgottesdienst* (1972), p. 239. Used by permission of the Liturgy Commission of the Evangelical Reformed Churches in German-speaking Switzerland. Translated by David H. Tripp, Ph.D. Used with permission.

**Prayer 176**
From *Bulletin de la Société de l'Histoire du Protestantisme Français,* CXXVI (126) (1980, pp. 229–239). Used by permission. Translated by David H. Tripp, Ph.D. Used with permission.

**Prayer 182**
From *Gesangbuch für die kirchliche und häusliche Andacht* (1925), p. 616. Used by permission of A. Sutter Telefonbuchverlag GmbH. Translated by David H. Tripp, Ph.D. Used with permission.

**Prayer 185**
From *Kirchenbuch für die Vereinigte evangelisch-protestantische Landeskirche Badens* (1930), pp. 259–260. Used by permission of the Evangelical Church in Baden. Translated by David H. Tripp, Ph.D. Used with permission.

**Prayer 194**
From *Book of Worship,* by Office for Church Life and Leadership (1986), pp. 81–82. Used by permission of the United Church of Christ.

**Prayer 197**
From *Liturgie pour les Paroisses de Langue Française,* pp. 100–101, vol. 1 (1955). Used and translated with the permission of the Evangelical-Reformed Churches of the Canton Bern-Jura. Translated by David H. Tripp, Ph.D. Used with permission.

**Prayer 198**
From "The Autobiography of Increase Mather," edited by M. G. Hall, *Proceedings of the American Antiquarian Society* 71 (1961): 265. Used with permission.

**Prayer 199**
"My Family," from *I Sing Your Praise All the Day Long: Young Africans at Prayer,* edited by Fritz Pawelzik, p. 32. Copyright © 1967 by Friendship Press, Inc. Used by permission.

**Prayer 204**
From *Uniting in Worship: Leader's Book* (1988), p. 423. The Uniting Church in Australia, National Working Group on Worship. Used with permission.

**Prayer 209**
From Charles E. Watson, *The Rodborough Bede Book,* Independent Press 1943, London, now The United Reformed Church. Used by permission.

**Prayer 215**
From Rev. George F. MacLeod, *The Whole Earth Shall Cry Glory* (Copyright Wild Goose Publications, The Iona Community, Glasgow (1985), p. 54. Used by permission of the publisher.

**Prayer 220**
From *Contemporary Prayers for Church and School,* edited by Caryl Micklem (1975), pp. 50–51. Used by permission of the publisher, SCM Press.

**Prayer 222**
From *Prayers for My Village,* p. 86. English translation © 1994 by Lamar Williamson. Used by permission of Upper Room Books, Editions et Librairies Oberlin, and the author.

**Prayer 227**
Translated by David H. Tripp, Ph.D. Used with permission.

**Prayer 228**
Written by Diane Karay Tripp. All rights reserved.

**Prayer 232**
Translated by David H. Tripp, Ph.D. Used with permission.

**Prayer 233**
From *Prayers of the Christian Life for Private and Public Worship,* by John Underwood Stephens (1952), p. 147. Used by permission of Horace D. Stephens.

**Prayer 237**
Prayer as submitted from THE WORLD AT ONE IN PRAYER, EDITED by DANIEL J. FLEMING, p. 14. Copyright 1942 by Harper and Row, Publishers,

Inc. Copyright Renewed 1970. Reprinted by permission of HarperCollins Publishers, Inc.

**Prayer 239**
Blanket letter of permission from author dated June 7, 1989.

**Prayer 241**
Translated by David H. Tripp, Ph.D. Used with permission.

**Prayer 245**
Adapted and abridged from a manuscript photocopy supplied by and used with the permission of Mollie M. Martin.

**Prayer 247**
From *Jupiter Hammon and the Biblical Beginnings of African-American Literature,* by Sondra A. O'Neale, ATLA Monograph, no. 28 (1993).

**Prayer 250**
Translated by David H. Tripp, Ph.D. Used with permission.

**Prayer 251**
African American folk prayer as recollected by Melva Wilson Costen. From Melva W. Costen, "The Prayer Tradition of Black Americans," in *Reformed Liturgy and Music* 15 (1981): 83–93. Used with permission.

**Prayer 257**
Translated by David H. Tripp, Ph.D. Used with permission.

**Prayer 259**
Translated by David H. Tripp, Ph.D. Used with permission.

**Prayer 262**
From *A Castle for the Soule*, possibly by Robert Waldegrave (1578). From a copy owned by the Folger Shakespeare Library, Washington, D.C.

**Prayer 269**
Translated by David H. Tripp, Ph.D. Used with permission.

**Prayer 270**
From *Liturgie,* vol. 1: *Sonntagsgottesdienst* (1972), p. 239. Used by permission of the Liturgy Commission of the Evangelical Reformed Churches in German-speaking Switzerland. Translated by David H. Tripp, Ph.D. Used with permission.

**Prayer 271**
Translated by David H. Tripp, Ph.D. Used with permission.

**Prayer 273a**
Translated by David H. Tripp, Ph.D. Used with permission.

**Prayer 274**
From *Private Devotions for Home and Church,* translated and edited by John Joseph Stoudt (1956), p. 125. Used by permission of Nancy Stoudt.

**Prayer 275**
From *Dienstboek voor de Nederlandse Hervormde Kerk* (1955). Used by permission of Uitgeverij Boekencentrum. Translated by David H. Tripp, Ph.D. Used with permission.

**Prayer 278**
From Presbyterians of the Republic of Vanuatu, Talua Ministry Training Centre, Luganville, Vanuatu. Typescript dated May 8, 1990. Permission sought.

**Prayer 283**
From Hughes Oliphant Old, *Leading in Prayer: A Workbook for Worship*, p. 23. Copyright © 1995 Wm. B. Eerdmans Publishing Company, Grand Rapids, Michigan. Reprinted by permission of the publisher; all rights reserved.

**Prayer 285**
From *Diary of Daily Prayer* (1975), p. 45. Used by permission of the author.

**Prayer 286**
From *Liturgie,* vol. 1: *Sonntagsgottesdienst* (1972), p. 233. Used by permission of the Liturgy Commission of the Evangelical Reformed Churches in German-speaking Switzerland. Translated by David H. Tripp, Ph.D. Used with permission.

**Prayer 287**
Translated by David H. Tripp, Ph.D. Used with permission.

**Prayer 288**
From *Liturgie pour les Paroisses de Langue Française,* p. 77, vol. 1 (1955). Used and translated with the permission of the Evangelical-Reformed Churches of the Canton Bern-Jura. Translated by David H. Tripp, Ph.D. Used with permission.

**Prayer 289**
Prayer as submitted from THE WORLD AT ONE IN PRAYER, EDITED by DANIEL J. FLEMING, pp. 125–126. Copyright 1942 by Harper and Row, Publishers, Inc. Copyright Renewed 1970. Reprinted by permission of HarperCollins Publishers, Inc.

**Prayer 293**
Translated by David H. Tripp, Ph.D. Used with permission.

**Prayer 300**
Adapted from *Liturgy and Service Book,* Part Two (1966), p. 80. Copyright by the Presbyterian Church of Ghana. Used with the permission of the publisher, Presbyterian Book Depot. Ltd.

**Prayer 301**
Translated by David H. Tripp, Ph.D. Used with permission.

**Prayer 313**
Translated by David H. Tripp, Ph.D. Used with permission.

**Prayer 317**
From *Evangelisches Gesangbuch* (1996). Translated and used by permission of

the Hymnbook Society, Evangelical Church of Westphalia. Translated by
David H. Tripp, Ph.D. Used with permission.

**Prayer 318**
From *Book of Common Order of the Church of Scotland* (1994), pp. 449–450.
Used by permission of the Church of Scotland, Office for Worship.

**Prayer 321**
From *Uniting in Worship: Leader's Book* (1988), p. 613. The Uniting Church in
Australia, National Working Group on Worship. Used with permission.

**Prayer 324**
Used by permission of the author. Alt.

**Prayer 331**
From *Book of Common Worship* (1993), p. 520.

**Prayer 342**
From *Religion and Domestic Violence in Early New England,* edited by Ann
Taves (1989), p. 184. Bloomington and Indianapolis: Indiana University Press.
Used by permission.

**Prayer 343**
From *The Works of Francis J. Grimké,* edited by Carter G. Woodson, vol. III,
*Stray Thoughts and Meditations,* (1942), p. 496. Used by permission of the
Association for the Study of African Life and History, Inc. This prayer is the
property of The Association for The Study of African Life and History, Inc.

**Prayer 344**
From *Psalter Hymnal* (1987), p. 973. Used by permission of CRC
Publications.

**Prayer 345**
From *Uniting in Worship: Leader's Book* (1988), p. 597. The Uniting Church in
Australia, National Working Group on Worship. Used with permission.

**Prayer 347**
Translated by David H. Tripp, Ph.D. Used with permission.

**Prayer 349**
Translated by David H. Tripp, Ph.D. Used with permission.

**Prayer 350**
Translated by David H. Tripp, Ph.D. Used with permission.

**Prayer 352**
Translated by David H. Tripp, Ph.D. Used with permission.

**Prayer 355**
Translated by David H. Tripp, Ph.D. Used with permission.

**Prayer 357**
From *Book of Common Order of the Church of Scotland* (1994), pp. 193–194.
Used by permission of the Church of Scotland, Office for Worship.

**Prayer 358**
Translated by David H. Tripp, Ph.D. Used with permission.

**Prayer 360**
From *Services of the Church: 8 The Collects for the Christian Year* (1969).
Reprinted with the permission of The Pilgrim Press.

**Prayer 361**
From *Dienstboek voor de Nederlandse Hervormde Kerk* (1955). Used by
permission of Uitgeverij Boekencentrum. Translated by David H. Tripp, Ph.D.
Used with permission.

**Prayer 362**
From *Liturgie*, vol. 2: *Festtagsgottesdienst* (1974), p. 19. Used by permission
of the Liturgy Commission of the Evangelical Reformed Churches in German-
speaking Switzerland. (*Note:* This prayer is based on a 1598 Strassburg
prayer.) Translated by David H. Tripp, Ph.D. Used with permission.

**Prayer 364**
Written by Diane Karay Tripp. All rights reserved.

**Prayer 365**
Translated by David H. Tripp, Ph.D. Used with permission.

**Prayer 367**
Translated by David H. Tripp, Ph.D. Used with permission.

**Prayer 370**
From Church of South India, *Book of Common Worship* (1963), p. 25. Used by
permission of Oxford University Press.

**Prayer 374**
Translated by David H. Tripp, Ph.D. Used with permission.

**Prayer 375**
From *Prayers for Public Worship* (*Service Book, Glasgow Cathedral*), by
Lauchlan MacLean Watt [1924], pp. 156–157. Used with permission of
Glasgow Cathedral.

**Prayer 376**
From *Book of Common Order of the Church of Scotland* (1994), p. 435. Used by
permission of the Church of Scotland, Office for Worship.

**Prayer 377**
Translated by David H. Tripp, Ph.D. Used with permission.

**Prayer 378**
From *Liturgie pour les Paroisses de Langue Française,* p. 204, vol. 1 (1955).
Used and translated with the permission of the Evangelical-Reformed
Churches of the Canton Bern-Jura. Translated by David H. Tripp, Ph.D. Used
with permission.

**Prayer 379**
Translated by David H. Tripp, Ph.D. Used with permission.

**Prayer 380**
Translated by David H. Tripp, Ph.D. Used with permission.

**Prayer 384**
Translated by David H. Tripp, Ph.D. Used with permission.

**Prayer 386**
From *Poems* (1910), by H. Cordelia Ray, as reprinted in *Collected Black Women's Poetry,* edited by Joan R. Sherman, New York: Oxford University Press (1988), pp. 69–70.

**Prayer 387**
From *Liturgy and Service Book.* Part Two (1966), p. 150. Copyright by the Presbyterian Church of Ghana. Used with the permission of the publisher, Presbyterian Book Depot. Ltd.

**Prayer 390**
Translated by David H. Tripp, Ph.D. Used with permission.

**Prayer 391**
Translated by David H. Tripp, Ph.D. Used with permission.

**Prayer 393**
From Church of the Servant, Grand Rapids, Michigan. Used by permission.

**Prayer 396**
From *Dienstboek voor de Nederlandse Hervormde Kerk* (1955). Used by permission of Uitgeverij Boekencentrum. Translated by David H. Tripp, Ph.D. Used with permission.

**Prayer 397**
From *Liturgie pour les Paroisses de Langue Française*, p. 369, vol. 1 (1955). Used and translated with the permission of the Evangelical-Reformed Churches of the Canton Bern-Jura. Translated by David H. Tripp, Ph.D. Used with permission.

**Prayer 398**
From *Prayers for the Christian Year.* 2nd edition (1952), p. 49. Used by permission of Oxford University Press.

**Prayer 400**
From *Prayers for Sunday Services: Companion Volume to the Book of Common Order (1979).* (1980), p. 120. Used by permission of the Church of Scotland, Office for Worship.

**Prayer 401**
From *The Order of Divine Service for Public Worship,* [by William Orchard] 2nd edition (1926), p. 163. Used by permission of Oxford University Press.

**Prayer 403**
From James H. Todd, *Prayers and Services for Christian Festivals,* p. 69. 2nd

edition. Independent Press 1959, London, now The United Reformed Church. Used by permission.

**Prayer 404**
From *Prayers for Sunday Services: Companion Volume to the Book of Common Order (1979).* (1980), p. 118. Used by permission of the Church of Scotland, Office for Worship.

**Prayer 407**
From *The Book of Family Devotion,* p. 55. General Assembly of the Presbyterian Church in Canada, Oxford University Press, Toronto, 1919.

**Prayer 410**
From *Dienstboek voor de Nederlandse Hervormde Kerk* (1955). Used by permission of Uitgeverij Boekencentrum. Translated by David H. Tripp, Ph.D. Used with permission.

**Prayer 413**
From *Prayers of the Christian Life for Private and Public Worship,* by John Underwood Stephens (1952), p. 41. Used by permission of Horace D. Stephens.

**Prayer 414**
Adapted from *Hope, Healing and Hospitals: Christian Reflections on Illness and Health for Use by Hospital Patients and Others Facing Illness,* by Neil Weatherhogg (1978). Used with permission of the author.

**Prayer 415**
From *Prayers for My Village,* p. 78. English translation © 1994 by Lamar Williamson. Used by permission of Upper Room Books, Editions et Librairies Oberlin, and the author.

**Prayer 418**
From *Worship the Lord,* edited by James R. Esther and Donald J. Bruggink (1987), p. 39. Used by permission of the Reformed Church in America.

**Prayer 420**
From *Worship the Lord,* edited by James R. Esther and Donald J. Bruggink (1987), p. 39. Used by permission of the Reformed Church in America.

**Prayer 421**
From *Book of Common Worship* (1993), p. 1029.

**Prayer 422**
From *Uniting in Worship: Leader's Book* (1988). The Uniting Church in Australia, National Working Group on Worship. Used with permission.

**Prayer 424**
Reproduced from *THE FUNERAL: A Service of Witness to the Resurrection* (Supplemental Liturgical Resource 4), pp. 55–56. © 1986 The Westminster Press. Used by permission of Westminster John Knox Press.

**Prayer 425**
From *Liturgie in Dagen van Rouw* (1987), A4. Used by permission of the

author, J. C. Wit-Ribbers. All rights reserved. Translated by David H. Tripp, Ph.D. Used with permission.

### Prayer 426
"At the Death of a Parent," in *Positive Prayers for Power-Filled Living,* by Robert H. Schuller (1976), pp. 66–67. Used by permission of Crystal Cathedral Ministries. All rights reserved by Crystal Cathedral Ministries.

### Prayer 427
From *Liturgie* (1963), p. 338. Used by permission of the General Secretary and the Committee for Liturgy of the Reformed Church of France. Translated by David H. Tripp, Ph.D. Used with permission.

### Prayer 428
From *Liturgie in Dagen van Rouw* (1987), A3. Used by permission of the author, J. C. Wit-Ribbers. All rights reserved. Translated by David H. Tripp, Ph.D. Used with permission.

### Prayer 429
From *A Spiritual Exercise for the Grieving,* by Elwyn A. Smith (1984), p. 24. Used by permission of the author.

### Prayer 436
From *A Christal Glasse for Christian Women,* by Philip Stubbes (1590). From a copy owned by the Folger Shakespeare Library, Washington, D.C.

### Prayer 438
From *The Book of Family Devotion,* pp. 65–66. General Assembly of the Presbyterian Church in Canada, Oxford University Press, Toronto, 1919.

### Prayer 441
Adapted from *The Liturgy of the Reformed Church in America* (1915), p. 107. Used by permission of the Reformed Church in America.

### Prayer 443
From A. R. Howell, *Church Prayers for War-Time for Use in Presbyterian and other Churches* (1940), p. 74. Used by permission of Oxford University Press.

### Prayer 444
From *A Minute of Prayer,* edited by Christopher Cross (1954). Permission sought.

### Prayer 445
From *A Book of Public Worship Compiled for the Use of Congregationalists,* compiled by John Huxtable, John Marsh, Romilly Micklem, and James Todd, 2nd edition (1949), p. 110. Used by permission of Oxford University Press.

### Prayer 449
From *Flames of the Spirit: Resources for Worship,* edited by Ruth C. Duck (1985), p. 83. Reprinted with the permission of The Pilgrim Press.

**Prayer 453**
From *MEDITATIONS* by TOYOHIKO KAGAWA. Copyright 1950 by Harper & Brothers, renewed © 1978 by Sumimoto Kagawa. Used by permission of HarperCollins Publishers.

**Prayer 454**
Translated by David H. Tripp, Ph.D. Used with permission.

**Prayer 456**
From *Dienstboek voor de Nederlandse Hervormde Kerk* (1955). Used by permission of Uitgeverij Boekencentrum. Translated by David H. Tripp, Ph.D. Used with permission.

**Prayer 480**
Excerpt from *Testimonies of Faith: Letters and Poems from Prison in Taiwan,* edited and translated by Choan-Seng Song (1984), p. 39. Used by permission of the World Alliance of Reformed Churches.

**Prayer 481**
From *A Time with Our Children: Stories for Use in Worship,* by Dianne E. Deming (1991), p. 105. Reprinted with the permission of The Pilgrim Press.

**Prayer 482**
Reproduced from *Prayers for All Occasions,* by Stuart Oglesby (1940, 1967 imprint), p. 176. Used and adapted by permission of Westminster John Knox Press.

**Prayer 486**
Translated by David H. Tripp, Ph.D. Used with permission.

**Prayer 488**
From *The Book of Common Worship* (1906), p. 167.

**Prayer 490**
From *Dienstboek voor de Nederlandse Hervormde Kerk* (1955). Used by permission of Uitgeverij Boekencentrum. Translated by David H. Tripp, Ph.D. Used with permission.

**Prayer 492**
Translated by David H. Tripp, Ph.D. Used with permission.

**Prayer 493**
David Jenkins, 1986, from *The Word and the World,* The Prayer Handbook for 1986. Published by The United Reformed Church. Used by permission.

**Prayer 495**
Translated by David H. Tripp, Ph.D. Used with permission.

**Prayer 500**
From *Prayers of Women,* edited by Lisa Sergio (1965), p. 27. Used by permission of the Manuscripts Librarian, Special Collections Division, Joseph Mark Lauinger Library, Georgetown University.